Holmes Rolston, III

RELIGIOUS INQUIRY-
Participation and Detachment

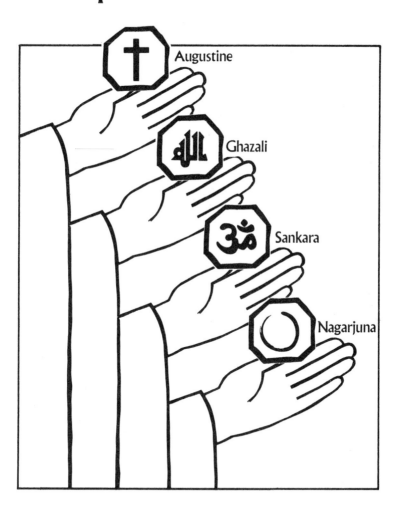

RELIGIOUS INQUIRY—
PARTICIPATION
AND
DETACHMENT

Holmes Rolston, III

Philosophical Library
New York, N.Y.

Library of Congress Cataloging in Publication Data

Rolston, Holmes, 1932-
   Religious inquiry—participation and detachment.

   Bibliography: p.
   1. Spirituality—Comparative studies.   2. Religion—
Philosophy—History.   3. Augustine, Saint, Bishop of
Hippo.   4. Ghazali   1058-1111.   5. Nāgārjuna, 2nd cent.
6. Śaṅkarācārya.   I. Title.
BL624.R64   1984   291.4   83-24602
ISBN 0-8022-2450-4

Contents

Preface

The spiritual adventure, says Augustine, "is a sort of journey or voyage to our native country." (CD 1-10)[1] Books are poor substitutes for journeys, but nevertheless religious pilgrims write about their trips, and these reflections help others. Enlightenment is a kind of voyaging across a sea, Nagarjuna contends, and teaching (*dharma*) is a raft (*yāna*) abandoned upon arrival, for traveling there is so much more than speaking about it. "This Atman cannot be attained by study of the Vedas, or by intelligence, or by much hearing of sacred books," Sankara repeatedly reminds us (*KaU* 1-2-23n), for the self in its immediate experience must plumb the divine Self, which lies so deeply within us, so far beyond verbal experience.

Using words as they do, books cannot capture the reality of religious experience, but they can help each of us discover personally the country of religious adventure. Because no one can travel this road entirely alone, even to attempt a solitary journey is unwise. "To travel the road of the world-to-come without guide or companion, when its mischances are so many, is wearisome and laborious," advises Ghazali. (Ih I, 1, 2)[2] To despise the diaries of

---

[1] The system of reference will be found in the bibliography.
[2] The translation is from Watt, *Muslim Intellectual*, p. 111.

other pilgrims, thus, is almost certainly to wander. Each of the four saints featured in this book has left a journal, a commentary, as a path to the performative nature of religious truth. Each is an intense personality embodying a faith. Each is a stout-hearted mind standing at the springs of a superior tradition. Though they are not prophet-seers, though they are not seminal originators of faiths, not saviors, they are companions and midwives of discipleship, delivering their messages so compellingly that each has set the mold for an entire stream of faith, touching it with the finger of genius and bequeathing a course millions have traveled after them. Taken together, these four saints walk the axial routes over which the human race has sought the divine.

Chosen not only for their piety (which includes their *participation*) but also for their capacity to think (which includes their *detachment*), these four offer us a chance to probe the depths of spirituality. Given their different visions, however, they would have been surprised, perhaps dismayed, to find themselves in dialogue here together. Their visions—God the Father of Jesus Christ, Allah, the Absolute, Emptiness—have long provided and still provide the dominant spiritual conflicts on our planet. As humans and as saints, as representatives of their different traditions, they nevertheless provide the mix we want of biographical detail, reflective piety, competing plurality, and most of all the unitive search. This study, then, is an essay in comparative spirituality focusing on Augustine, Ghazali, Sankara, and Nagarjuna.

Accompanying these giants on their spiritual journeys will be two others, both more modern. First the author—inevitably and intentionally—will be everywhere present, and the reader, I hope, will want to travel along. Indeed, the reader must participate in our colloquy. For like the accounts it studies, this study, too, is a searching-report. It has required the author and will require the reader to take a spiritually thoughtful journey. The reader must bring to this study, or find along the way, enough spirituality to make this inquiry of more than historical, or philosophical, or comparative religious interest. But come as the reader may, this book, like those of our four saints, must finally fall short of its goal of reaching the land of religious experience. In principle, logical control over logically unstable terrain is impossible. In practice, the book will doubtless fall short for more human reasons as well.

Our thesis here soon returns on itself, for one needs both *participation* and *detachment* to ask about it. Here religion is an especially demanding professional field. Life is felt to be on the shores of an ocean, out of which persons have somehow come, but which they can never fathom. To plunge into, to set sail on this ocean, and not to be lost but to find a vision and way across it, is an awesome pilgrimage that will have little point except to a kindred heart.

The naming of these six participants introduces certain disproportions and incongruences. How ancient they are! Must we seek the living Ultimate among the dead? Have the centuries passed for nothing? Do we not know more than they? To be sure, against our vastly expanded perspectives of time, history, nature, and culture, their worlds are small indeed, and much in our saints is hopelessly provincial. In particular they help us little in confronting the concepts of nature in physical and biological science or with interpreting the depths of historical change, of which we have since become aware. But they did know religious experience. Like love, courage, or beauty, religious faith too hangs with a curious looseness over the ages where it is manifested. Some kinds of knowledge accumulate across the centuries, but some kinds of spirituality punctuate the years.

Despite their local worlds, they broke beyond them. We must see their records of the mystic life under the cloud of their own climates. But if God has left a perennial witness, if God is known in the pure, devoted heart, their age matters little. So far as truth is linked to spirituality, wisdom becomes a function not merely of one's century but of one's character, and we can no longer rest any superiority with our modernity. Our sciences do not always leave us wiser about the values that lie deepest in the nature of things. Our saints in their combination of character and wisdom have made their several adventures classics for a thousand years and more. If we cannot find a plausible account of spiritual experience in their works, if an analysis of them does not clarify the elements of participation and detachment in religious inquiry, we cannot, probably, find it anywhere in our past cultural history.

But at this point we may be struck by an opposite mood. How great they are! To judge among such saints is a formidable task. Has the author, has the reader competence sufficient for the task? Nevertheless, if we are to take them seriously, we must try to regain their mixedly patristic, medieval, and timeless witness to reform it. We should and we must mine their ore, discarding dross. We must see for ourselves, and now. We can see further if we stand on giants' shoulders, and this is true even when our giants limp. In fact we have no alternative to such judgments about our predecessors, for every person's life is inescapably the making of some kind of journey, evaluating, accepting, rejecting, modifying, or ignoring those who have gone before.

A sketch of the route we will be traveling will get us off to a good start. The opening chapter introduces these four representatives of faith and examines the biographical nature of religious truth. Religious truth requires becoming righteous in order to become cognitively right. On this journey obedience is the road to truth; "being true" is required for "having truth." Religious truth is performative and personal; that is, in the first of the twin terms which title this book, it demands *participation*.

The second chapter fills in more specifically, although yet generally across all the traditions consulted, just what is the nature of this participation and how it contributes to gaining truth by examining four epistemic virtues: love, faith, purity, and humility. These participatory virtues direct the mind to truth by leading to a kind of *detachment*. This introduces what might at first be thought an opposite idea and the second main term which titles this book.

The third chapter, pressing the limits of religious language, argues from our four saints' convictions, however variantly developed, that religion embodies both a *perceptual* and a *conceptual* component. Religion is a way of seeing that gropes for words, rather as a map both depicts and falls short of the terrain it describes. Grasping religious truth requires active participation, a "being there" that personally backs the speech.

The fourth chapter treats subjectivity and objectivity, first analyzing the troubling, disabling subjectivity in those who seek to know, secondly analyzing the troubling, elusive objectivity of the

Ultimate that is sought as an object of knowledge. This leads beyond subjectivity and objectivity, finding that religious knowing is a kind of communicant or unitive tasting which intimately links the knower with, and even consumes the knower in, the known. *Participation*, thus, again leads to *detachment* as the self is given up in order to know what truly is.

Chapter five prepares the reader for a surprising turn, as the inquiry moves to interreligious understanding between those who are variously participant in and detached from the faiths they seek to judge. There we press concepts of *understanding* and of *undergoing* and we distinguish levels of understanding proportionately as an inquirer remains without faith, or comes into a domestic faith, or comes up against a foreign faith. Can one understand the *meaning* of religious experience, while yet maintaining that it has no *point*, rejecting as inappropriate that which he or she refuses to undergo?

Chapter six examines the acceptance and rejection of religious beliefs. Here the four saints, so long together, must be separated irreparably. Our logic of participation and detachment takes them past a divide where they part due to incommensurable meanings. *Nonunderstanding, counterstanding, misunderstanding*, and *reunderstanding* describe how understanding fails when we press an alien faith. An inquirer misses satisfactory meaning, because he or she can find no point, no referent in experience. Here, partly to demonstrate how one tradition misses meaning in another, and partly in the belief that no study of religion is quite genuine without a plunge into the question of ultimate truth, we shift from what has been largely a comparative study into a more apologetic posture. We show why those who adhere to the Augustinian theistic tradition do not and cannot ultimately adhere to traditions such as those in which Ghazali, Nagarjuna, and Sankara stand. But in doing this, we are driven to recognize an indeterminacy of meaning, and to grant that those of the other traditions will think that it is rather the Christian theist who misses understanding.

Chapter seven brings the results of this inquiry to bear on the learning of and learning about religion in the teacher-pupil and school context. Here we mark out four educational environments in which the study of religion can occur, moving from the outside in, beginning with the observer and ending with the communicant. With the shifting of these environments, the scope of inquiry shifts from inquiry about religion to religious inquiry. The conclusion of it all is the religious significance of any true education.

This is an essay in spirituality, which is to say that this is not primarily history or philosophy, and not even a typical study in comparative religion. These elements are all present only instrumentally to a further end and controlled by that end. We do here consult Ghazali, Augustine, Sankara, and Nagarjuna, and in that sense this work is anchored in the historical sources. Nevertheless this study will be misjudged if approached primarily as a historical work. There is no original linguistic or exegetical research in the ancient texts. This study must of necessity begin with what the historians have provided, documents and translations recording the spirituality of these distant men of faith. We depend upon the detailed work of those linguists who have already employed their skills so variously in the Latin, Arabic, Sanskrit, Tibetan, Greek, Pali, and Chinese languages. There is no one who can move across the terrain we wish to travel without the benefit of translators and we do so with gratitude. But our concern is not merely to range broadly over distant spiritual figures, but to bring these near for a present search. We want historical figures to stimulate a current inquiry.

Neither is this inquiry a philosophical analysis in traditional form. Its style of analysis may leave readers uneasy until they have realized that they cannot expect a linear analysis that moves to a calculated conclusion. The logic must be appropriate to the subject matter. This essay is not systematically inductive or deductive in computing from premises to conclusions; but, after the manner of the saints it studies, it reflects repeatedly over participation and detachment in religious experience, analyzing these so as to criticize, to clarify, and to enrich a vision, which in the end comes more by disclosure than by argumentation. In terms that will later be clearer, the logic here is as perceptual as it is conceptual. This is as much an invitation to a journey as an argument about routes.

Readers may sometimes regret that I utilize these aged doctors to express recent convictions, but they will also find that I argue that, in the end, no one can or ought to do otherwise. Graze where we will, we give our own milk. The position I advance here develops in the dialogue between these four saints, and it has, in the decade of the making of this book, steadily been revised by further research into the classical sources. Still it is a reconstruction, but that is what a productive religious scholarship ought to provide for present religious inquiry: help in reforming itself out of the classical materials. If I do not give a fair witness (a just one), I am ashamed of my work, but I can give none except comparatively through my local experience, as this by aspiration is enlarged through encountering these saints on their sacred trails. These demands are so great that we must be content with just a fair witness, only an approximate one.

I realized more worth in my own inheritance than I initially expected. But still, this came by loving and struggling with foreign memorial traditions, sometimes pleasant and sometimes baffling. The interaction with them helped me to uncover how constitutive of myself was the faith of a patristic predecessor. Across the whole study, I do not promise to succeed at every turn, but rather promise only that, even when I err, the issues are of such moment that any reader will be the wiser for having found these errors.

Religions are not monolithic, and, having chosen four representatives, we can forget that other voices might draw the differences we accent here into more overlap. Other interpreters might find more of the West in the East, and vice versa, more omnipresent and common mystical experience. Also, we should notice that the Far East has scarcely entered this study, for Nagarjuna (though he was preserved by the Chinese) is still an Indian, and the Chinese and Japanese reunderstandings of him are outside our scope. My analysis also expects others who are of closer kin elsewhere to be able to map their homelands better than I can. Meanwhile, there is enough here for us to take bearings on participation and detachment for at least an approximate compassing of the vast quadrants of world faith.

The initial research for the study was done during a year that I spent as Visiting Scholar at the Harvard University Center for the

Study of World Religions, and I am grateful for their support. I also thank Winston L. King, Henry McKennie Goodpasture, James W. Boyd, and Donald A. Crosby for critical readings of the manuscript.

Holmes Rolston, III
Colorado State University

Chapter 1. Correspondent Truthfulness

To launch an inquiry after truth is to find that proportionately as the knowledge sought is spiritual, the quest requires spiritual investment. All the higher faiths bind up wisdom with virtue, character, and being. We intend to specify that logic from Christian, Hindu, Buddhist, and Islamic witnesses, as we hear from four saints who classically embody this inner formation for information. On such a participatory journey truth is not the *correspondence* of *propositions* with what is the case, but of *persons* with the real. Believers do not merely, if at all, *have truth*, like scientists perhaps; but they must *be true*, as must lovers.

In India, Hindu and Buddhist illumination is ever on a way, a path, a career, a *mārga*, *dharma*, or *yāna*; it is a faring on the Great Way. The Christian follows one who is the Way; the Muslim prays, "Guide us in the straight path." (S 1.4*a*) Everywhere, truth-finding is a pilgrim's progress. During the processes of religious truth, "cognition (*jñāna*) is of the form of its object," (BhG 18-50) but this is not wrought by the scholar's words but by the saint's life. The self finds the divine Self, the soul images its God, the *bodhisattva*, or truth-being, enters *tathatā*, thusness.

By Jesus' bold claim, "I am the way, and the truth, and the life,"

1

the follower appreciates Jesus as the human-divine incarnation, a truth-being, who leads in sequel, if reduced in degree or kind, to the embodiment of that truth in his disciples. "If you continue in my word, you are truly my disciples and you will know the truth and the truth will make you free." (Jn. 14.6; 8.3lf) The word became flesh in the Savior, but it becomes flesh also, even if derivatively and rather differently so, in the saved.

The Buddhist *tathāgata* has himself gone (*gata*) to his "suchness" (*tathatā*) and entered "this dwelling of the Bodhisattvas who course in perfect wisdom, who dwell in it." (AP 264) The intimate coupling with the Ultimate which the Vedantan seeks, "That art thou," can only be understood by one who "identifies himself with the Universal Soul." (ChU 6-8-1) Knowledge is in union. On the Muslim "straight path," truth is in submission (*islām*). *Understanding* and *imperative* are both translations of one word for truth and law, *fiqh*; and rightness is the finding of one's sound nature. "Real revelation is an attribute of the essence of the heart and its inward part." (Ih I, 2, 38) By contrast, oppositely for all, error is the state of persons who are distanced and veiled from the real.

What we here call *correspondent truthfulness* alters for religious inquiry the otherwise more philosophical, Platonic account of knowledge as "justified true belief" by making the sense of "justified" biblical. Belief is justified as it *makes us just*. The Indian word for such truthfulness is *dharma, righteousness*, which at once also means *path, deed*, and *doctrine*. An Islamic expression for it is *jurisprudence, fiqh*, truth enshrined in the lawful life. Aphoristically put: To *be right* here one must *be righteous*. When F.H. Bradley sought the difference between religion and philosophy, he judged that as a cognitive enterprise, philosophy has matured over religion, but that the essence of religion is not simply cognitive. "Religion is rather the attempt to express the complete reality of goodness through every aspect of our being. And, so far as this goes, it is at once something more, and therefore something higher, than philosophy."[1] We advance beyond this if we recognize that

---

[1] F.H. Bradley, *Appearance and Reality*, 2nd ed. (Oxford: Clarendon Press, 1897, 1930), p. 401.

truth always comes as an address to us, never a bare philosophical expression. Understanding here comes as injunction is heard in the claim.

William James, asked once about spirituality, said that he could not define it, but could point to it. He pointed to Phillips Brooks. In this study we also find that "spirituality" resists a definition by which it can be delivered verbally to someone else. But we can point to it, and do so with Augustine, Sankara, Nagarjuna, and Ghazali. We next meet our four saints, sketching their careers, and then hear how these sages "so teach us to number our days that we may get a heart of wisdom." (Ps. 90.12)

I. Four Correspondents in Truth

1. Augustine: the Doctor of Grace

The recent trend to do theology as biography has no better classical instance than Augustine (354-430 A.D.). Augustine is the most influential of post-biblical Christians for his broad impact across multiple centuries of Christendom. His "faith in search of understanding" bequeathed a mood which has set the tone of most Christian piety since. In the perilous, upturned, faltering years of Rome, desperately seeking to make sense of himself, his age, and his world, he sought the eternal City of God. He discovered it and brought Athens within Jerusalem, blending faith and the intellect so thoroughly as to make him a transitional figure between the ancient world and the classical and modern West. This Augustinian faith underruns the medieval mind, and is again recovered by Luther and Calvin to energize the Reformation. It still persists today to temper critical faith as it becomes contemporary. Greece and Palestine run through this Roman, and, as much as any other person, he helps to found the West. Most readers of these pages owe him more than they realize.

Born in Mediterranean Africa, in his youth he rejected his Christian rearing, and sought a secular education in rhetoric, law, literature, and philosophy. For a decade he was a Manichean, but he became progressively disillusioned with the Manichean dualism of good and evil. Later, teaching rhetoric in Rome, he became disenchanted with the worth of his rhetorical profession. He denied the possibility of attaining absolute truth while yet clinging to the prowess of reason, and became more or less an Academic. Failing there, he shifted to Neoplatonism, and then, teaching at Milan, he came under the sway of Bishop Ambrose and moved closer to Christianity. His struggle was academic and personal. Troubled by his relationship to a mistress, though long faithful to her, he found he could understand only with moral reformation. In a famous garden vision, he was converted in mid-career by an experience in which divine grace brought conviction and chastity, the latter for him the final symbol of the submission of the ego. His faith, which had so come to focus, then launched a quest for understanding. For four decades as priest and bishop, he was pastor and defender of the intellectual faith, first locally at Hippo, his African see, and later ecumenically to the patristic church.

To the universal church Augustine became the doctor of grace and preacher of charity. Resulting from his search for the self, we have the autobiographical *Confessions*. Out of his search for permanence in the fluent Roman world, we have the *City of God*, theology as the recital of God's presence in history. Concluding his search for meaning in the natural world, we have repeated commentaries on Genesis, both as independent works and incorporated into the *Confessions* and the *City of God*. From his understanding of God, we have the *Trinity*. His struggle with error, personal and ecclesiastical, produced polemical and pedagogical tracts, some against the Manicheans, Donatists, and Pelagians, whose concepts of nature, sin, evil, grace, and, above all, faith were at odds with his experience. *The Teacher* and *Christian Education* take him into the field of education. Underrunning all is a continuing search of the Scriptures, exemplified in the *Narrations on the Psalms* or the *Lectures on the Gospel of John*. Augustine's full library, so massive as to be forbidding, left him the most impressive father of the church.

Not a line of this was written except as his pious intellect was true to his central vision: that the immutable God was graciously present in this mutable world, and could be known by the faithful, purified self. Augustine offers us a Christian witness which is consistent, insistent, and provocative. Profitably, if also with cost, we shall consult him on the trust and self-emptying requisite for understanding. Despite his antiquity, he is surprisingly abiding—perhaps most of all in his coupling of the faithful with the intellectual life. He is catholic of mind, protestant in temper, evangelical, ecumenical, and ever illustrative of the Christian thirst for righteous truth.

2. Sankara: The Advaitan Āchārya

For similar power in the Hindu East there is but one name typically given when we ask who stands astride the classical *dharma* as, post-scripturally, its most formative and exemplary Colossus. Sankara (788-820 A.D.) is without peer the Advaitan *āchārya*, teacher-saint. His impact sets the cast of the Indian mind, not only in Advaita Vedanta but in the challenging schools who must pass through him, even if they wish to move away from him. Like Augustine, Sankara does not originate a faith. He is rather a commentator on the *Vedas* and *Upanishads*. He too struggles to couple coherently the existential and the intellectual components in truth. For Sankara the *real* and the *true* are known only in personal union with them. "That subtle, ancient path stretching far away has touched me; I am realizing it myself," he avows from his scriptures, and continues, "Realization is that attainment which, as knowledge ripens, culminates in the ultimate results, as eating culminates in satisfaction." (BrU 4-4-8m)

Would that we had, as we do not, a *Confessions* from Sankara. His short-lived career is more legendary than we wish.[2] He was born in the Malabar coastal country of the Deccan Plateau, the son of Shiva-guru. His father died early, and his deepening attachment to his mother was shaken by his resolution at the age of nine to become an ascetic. First taught by Govinda, a disciple of Gaudapada, in a Himalayan hermitage, he later left to become a peripatetic about Benares. In his earliest writings, we find him already rejoicing before opponents that he is resolute in Vedanta. "This

---

[2] Old biographies by Madhava, by Anandagiri, and by Chidvilasa generally agree, though they embellish his life a great deal, and sometimes conflict. See Krishnaswami Aiyar, *Sri Sankaracharya: His Life and Times*.

itself is a blessing for me that you brand me as sworn to monism and faced by many who are wedded to plurality. Therefore I shall conquer all; and so I begin the discussion." (TaU 2-8-5)

He left to tour India, perhaps aided by a royal patron, and engaged opponents in debate far and wide, resulting in the notable conversion of Mandana and his wife Bharati. He practiced yoga astutely and established four monasteries which exist today, at Badari in the north, at Sringeri in the south, at Dwarka on the west coast, and at Puri on the east coast. By unanimous tradition, he broke his ascetic vows in order to return to his dying mother, first to comfort and then to cremate her, all despite the objections of his relatives and disciples. Soon himself in failing health, he passed on. The closing legend to embellish his spirituality is that no one saw him die, but, thirty-two years of age, he vanished at Kedarnath in the Himalayas. There pilgrims yet visit his shrine. Some believe that he was Shiva, Lord of the way of truth (*jñāna mārga*) come as avatar to earth.

Compensating for our lack of concrete historical data, Sankara's spirituality everywhere comes through his exegesis, always an *apologia pro vita sua* even when he is seemingly afield in argument. When he finds the Immutable One in the midst of the mutable world, he gives a fervent confession of rescue from the perishing Indian scene, given mediately in praise of Govinda, then immediately to his Absolute! "I offer my obeisance with my whole being to those sanctifying feet of my own teacher, through the light of whose illumined intellect was dispelled the darkness of delusion enveloping my own mind, who destroyed forever my fear of appearance and disappearance in this terrible sea of innumerable births." "After realizing that state that is inscrutable, profound, uniform, holy, and nondual, I bow down to that Brahman which, birthless, ever quiescent, and one, destroys the fear of those who take shelter in it." (GaK 4-100a) His written words are "vouched for by his heart's conviction" and "describe him who stands firm in the highest knowledge." (VS 4-1-15)

The great release which he himself enjoyed he preached to others in the form of his ten *Commentaries on the Upanishads: Īśā, Kena, Kaṭha, Taittirīya, Aitareya, Muṇḍaka, Māṇḍūkya* with *Gau-*

ḍapāda's Kārikā, Praśna, Chāndogya, and, at most length, the *Brihadāraṇyaka*. He provides us a systematic synopsis of traditional Vedanta in the celebrated *Commentary on the Vedānta Sūtras*, and with the *Commentary on the Bhagavad-Gīta* he completes his interpretation of the major Brahmanic spiritual materials. There is also a supplementary body of devotional tracts and hymns. Despite his medieval and exotic tones, through him has flowed an order of spiritual perception that remains a major world religious current. The Advaitan considers all Indian philosophy to be but a series of footnotes to this Hindu Plato.

3. Nagarjuna: the Patriarch of Mahayana
The most cryptic, both in person and in principles, of those we consult is Nagarjuna (2nd century A.D.). He was decisive in his impact on the unfolding of the Buddhist tradition, serving as the pivot, historically, between earlier Theravada Buddhism and its development into Mahayana Buddhism. This pivotal turning is around the baffling paradigm of "emptiness" (*śūnyatā*). He teaches the existential passage from erroneous theses, verbal claims, into enlightened "thesisless" or wordless truth. At a paradoxical extreme, he wants being and truth to fuse and go into quiet emptiness. What he recommends provides the world's most mixedly powerful and puzzling spiritual vision.

Like Augustine and Sankara again, this patriarch too denies founding his religion and he rather salutes the Buddha's launching of his faith. Still, many in the Madhyamika school, which he founded, reckon him to be the fulfillment of the prophecy by Gautama of a monk who will come to seal the faith. "In Vedalī, in the southern part, a Bhikshu most illustrious and distinguished will be born; his name is Nāgāhvaya, he is the destroyer of the one-sided views based on being and nonbeing. He will declare my Vehicle, the unsurpassed Mahāyāna, to the world; attaining the stage of Joy he will go to the Land of Bliss."[3]

Although we have a large Indian, Tibetan, and Chinese lore

---

[3] *Laṇkāvatāra Sūtra*; Sagāthakam, vss. 165f; translated by Inada prefacing the *Mūlamadhyamakakārikā*, p. 1. On the problematic passage, and Nagarjuna's career, see Walleser, "Life of Nāgārjuna."

which transforms him into an alchemist and wizard, as well as a *bodhisattva*, it is difficult to say when and where his life occurred. Some historical person behind these legends seems to be their only adequate basis, but Nagarjuna's actual life is virtually irretrievable from their excesses. Nagarjuna was born a brahmin in southern India. To avoid his predicted death his parents sent their seven-year-old son into seclusion. Eventually he came to a monastery in the mountains, Nalendra, where he gained a prodigious capacity in magic, and, more seriously, a thorough education not only in Brahmanism but in Theravada Buddhism. In ninety days he mastered the latter's canon, the *Tripiṭaka*. Afterward he collected and shaped the nascent scriptures of Mahayana.

Providing by his enchantments food and resources for the monks, he eventually became their high priest. He traveled abroad to debate and to found temples and schools, involving himself in extensive reformation and discipline of the Buddhist order. In later life, he befriended a king (whose identity is speculative), mysteriously communicating to the king such long life that the only surviving son despaired of ever gaining the crown. The heir apparent begged Nagarjuna to end his life and thereby to terminate also that of the king. Nagarjuna consented and was beheaded with a blade of kusha grass!

As with Socrates in the West, Nagarjuna's life is one of lasting impact, nevertheless lost for lack of assured historical detail. But despite what we must regard as the fancy of his disciples, his spirituality has survived not only embedded in his writings but in the Madhyamika inspiration that found his vision charismatic. A creative genius mixing dispassionate thirst for truth with ruthless skepticism toward dogma, he gained a silent wisdom (*śūnya-vāda*) which Buddhism has long shared. "I have spread over the perfect One," he writes of his work for the Buddha, "who is beyond our thoughts and any limitation, the flowers of his very attributes. Through the merit which I have begot may all living beings in this world participate in the extremely deep law of the sublime ascetic." To the resplendent deep and to the Buddha as its pathfinder he sings, "Homage unto Thee, the deep One.... I have praised the Well-gone (*Sugata*) who is neither gone nor come, and who is devoid of any going. Through the merit so acquired may this world go along the path of the Well-gone." (CS 1-25; 4-8ff)

Even in the *Fundamentals of the Middle Way (Mūla-mad-hyamaka-kārikās)*, which provides his most basic treatise, twenty-seven chapters of modest length, we are reading the veiled report of a spiritual quest. Two devotional hymns survive from what were once four in the *Catuḥ-stava*. There is an address to a king, the *Ratnāvalī*. Clear in major mood, these writings are often aphoristic and condensed. More discursive is a vast *Commentary on the Large Perfection of Wisdom Sūtra* (the *Mahā-Prajñā-Pāramitā-Śāstra*), for Nagarjuna too is a commentator on a faith he receives and reshapes. This *Sūtra* is the key early Mahayana scripture, "the great mother of the Buddhas and *bodhisattvas*." The commentary is only partially accessible in the West, nor is his authorship of it established; it has likely been gathered round his name. With reservations, we take it to belong, sometimes problematically, at least to Madhyamika, if not always to Nagarjuna himself. Mean-while, legendary though he is, we are dealing with an Indian Kant.

4. Ghazali: the Proof of Islam

If the whole of Islam should be lost, save only Ghazali, runs a Muslim tribute, then nothing should be lost, for he has said all. To Abū Ḥāmid Muḥammad al-Ghazālī (1058-1111 A.D.) we turn for the Muslim faith in its most influential post-Qur'anic form. Scholar and saint, he occupies single-handedly within Islam the positions of Augustine, Aquinas, and Luther in Christianity. After the early period of the first four companions of Muhammad, there is no other Muslim who so nearly gains a consensus of Muslims, both Sunni and Sufi, as to who was the greatest Muslim. Their admira-tion puts that judgment in its spiritual dimension by titling him "the Reviver of Islam" and in its intellectual dimension by declaring him to be "the Proof of Islam."

Born at the village of Tus in Persia, he was left in childhood without a father but was nevertheless well reared. Eventually he studied under al-Juwayni, an eminent theologian of that era. Appointed professor at the University in Baghdad by authority of the sultan, at thirty-three years of age he held one of the most distinguished academic positions in his medieval world. But he was deeply disquieted, for he recognized that his private progress had not matched his public success; and, worse, though intelligent and celebrated, his worldly stature was causing a spiritual atrophy. Four years later he fell into a psychosomatic illness, and lost his voice because he had lost his way. He had, in truth, nothing to say. Wounded and confused, he recovered only after he left Baghdad to become a wandering ascetic. He spent several solitary years at Damascus, then stayed for a time at Jerusalem, then performed the pilgrimage to Mecca. He returned home to Tus, maintaining retirement.

"I learnt with certainty," he confesses after this decade, "that it is above all the mystics who walk on the road of God; their life is the best life, their method the soundest method, their character the purest character; indeed, were the intellect of the intellectuals and the learning of the learned and the scholarship of the scholars, who are versed in the profundities of revealed truth, brought together in the attempt to improve the life and character of the mystics, they would find no way of doing so; for to the mystics all movement and all rest, whether external or internal, brings illumination from the light of the lamp of prophetic revelation; and behind the light of prophetic revelation there is no other light on the face of the earth from which illumination may be received." (D1 60) He wants truth from prophecy by way of the saintly life. By such a life the saint's capacity to think matures, for Ghazali nowhere disparages the intellect except as proposed in the stead of spirituality; and he amply grounds intellectual progress within, but only within, the sacred life. He blends Sunni and Sufi currents to become the type of the Muslim sage.

Newly motivated, he returned to teaching, first in a semimonastic community he founded at Tus, then in a college at Nishapur, and afterward, perhaps in failing health, again at home. He died in his early fifties, facing Mecca with the words, "Obediently I enter into the presence of the King."[4]

His spiritual quest is intimately recorded in *The Deliverance*

---

[4] Watt, *Muslim Intellectual*, p. 148.

from Error (al-Munqidh min aḍ-Ḍalāl), the equivalent of Augustine's *Confessions*. His encyclopedic masterwork is *The Revival of the Religious Sciences (Iḥyā' 'Ulūm al-Dīn)*, divided into four quarters and forty books. Only about half is in Western languages, though this fortunately includes the books (such as those on *Knowledge, Foundations of the Faith, Purity, Prayer, Ecstasy, Belief and Trust in God, Marvels of the Heart*, and, in part, *Love*) which best serve our interests here. His philosophical critique is *The Incoherence of the Philosophers (Tahāfut al-Falāsifah)*. Many smaller tracts help us, among them: *The Ninety-Nine Names of God, On the Divine Predicates, The Alchemy of Happiness*, and *The Niche for Lights*. Together these provide ample access to his outlook, though they are in the English world lamentably scattered for a Muslim witness so congenial to the West.

II. Performative Truth

We will now let these doctors begin to plunge us into an advancing insistence on obedience, as they report how religious truth is a living into truth, in the weaving of which obedience is the warp and knowledge the woof. We will call this a *performative truth*. In this kind of truth obedience must come not only *after*, but *along with*, and even *before* the coming of truth. But let us begin negatively, for something about failure in performance alerts us to trouble, from which we may take more positive bearings.

In the *Beginning of Guidance* Ghazali cautions the ambitious, would-be scholar-not-saint, "Be sure that, if in your quest for knowledge your aim is to gain something for yourself and to surpass your fellows, to attract men's attention to yourself and to amass this-worldly vanities, then you are on the way to bring your religion to nothing and to destroy yourself, to sell your eternal life for this present one; your bargain is dead loss, your trading without profit.... On the other hand, if in seeking knowledge your intention and purpose between God most high and yourself is to receive guidance and not merely to acquire information, then rejoice. The angels will spread out their wings for you when you walk, and the denizens of the sea will ask pardon from God for you when you run." (BG 86f) The *Book of Knowledge* opens by reflecting on Muhammad's warning, "The most severely punished of all men on the day of resurrection will be a learned man whom God has not blessed with his knowledge." (Ih I, 1, 1; cf. 154ff)

All this is bald, at once obvious yet troublesome. Ghazali is not cursing others, so much as remembering his experience and wondering. If those who would be smart without being pious are not prepared to reply to truth discovered, can we seriously trust their spiritual discretionary powers? Will not their judgment be colored by alternate aspirations, as their *will not* bends their *know that*? Their *no* reveals disqualifying insensitivity, for the *will to know* in alliance with a *will not be better* corrupts any power to know truth as it is joined to the good. Even for those religious "experts" who come somewhat less ambitiously, drawn by "knowledge for knowledge's sake," something worries us about their indifference to reformation. Do we want knowledge without guidance? Then the hidden agenda is—what are our deepest motives?

1. Consequent obedience

We really *know* only what we consequently *obey*. All our doctors link truth to what we term *consequent obedience*, though this but introduces us to the seriousness of their emphasis on performance, which will deepen in sections to follow. The *Dhammapada* summarizes the Buddhist path: "Cease to do evil; learn to do good, cleanse your own heart," (183 = 14,5) and remembering this Nagarjuna reminds the king that truth brings good done to others flowing from our self-reformation. "Truth in reality is not that which is merely devoid of falsehood, nor that which develops simply in a pure mind; truth is the absolute good done to others; its contrary is falsehood on account of its being harmful to others.... A man who has control over himself acquires deepness of mind; from deepness of mind he obtains dignity; from dignity luster is derived; from luster authority. Practice therefore control over yourself." (Rv 2-35ff,m) "Although a man may be learned in written works, yet if he does not apply what he knows, he resembles the blind man who even with a lamp in his hand cannot see the road." (PD 169m) In a treasured Buddhist idiom, "to course in wisdom" is for the lamp of *dharma* to light for us a way of doing and being so that our exemplary character confirms our authority in truth.

Sankara calls this outcome an "obedience" only with the stipulation, presently made carefully, that it is never of *works (karma)*, but is rather (like the literal Latin etymology of *oboedire, obaudio*) a *listening after* the word of truth. A suitable metaphor is that of fruit. "There is absolutely only one result of true knowledge," he retorts to the query whether one can know about Brahman indifferently. "The fruit of complete knowledge, viz., union with the universal Self, springs up at the moment when complete knowledge is attained." That is so, even though, owing to a discharge of *karma* impetus, release is delayed until death, like the flying arrow which must be spent. Still, "the passage, 'That art thou,' is referred to as something already accomplished," for no one can reach it except as one's *thou*, or inmost person, has already become *That*, the ultimate reality, thus "precluding the suspicion that true knowledge may be destitute of its result." (VS 3-3-32) We have no academic or neutral access here.

Those who, owing to its description as the path of knowledge (*jñāna mārga*), think Vedanta to be intellectual, not active, are right, only they have to remember that this kind of intellection is, like that of Augustine, on a plane which is life-orienting and entirely existential. "Righteousness, in its visible form as good conduct that is practiced, comes to be known as truth." (BrU 2-5-12m) Disease, Sankara reminds us, is not cured merely by studying medicine , but by taking it, and so with religion. (VC 42f)

Augustine found himself during a transient stage with truth seen but not yet followed. He had found the good pearl but not yet sold all to possess it. (Co 8-1f) But he really did not suppose even then that he had knowledge without obedience, for his early knowledge was already prodding his conscience. Augustine makes no pretense that we can ask of truth without its asking for us. "Knowledge summons works, and unless they respond, it departs," concludes Ghazali in a similar crisis. He found that until works come, the inquirer can go no further, and that failing them, there will be relapse. (Ih I, 1, 156) In a limited way, during moods of judgment, a theist might want to say that here inquiry had been successful, if unprofitable. One had learned some truth and failed to obey it; there is imperative without compliance. Perverse persons sometimes reject what they can fairly if not fully be said to know, for moral truth is thwarted by malice not less than by mistake. But Augustine adds that since there was no steadfastness, he then saw only in a glass, darkly. Halfway into truth, under its judgmental shadow, the sinner had the truth and the truth the sinner in discordant antithesis. Only by standing under its full rectifying light can saint and truth have each other in accordant synthesis, where "the peace of the rational soul is in the harmonious correspondence of conduct and conviction." (CG 19-13)

All this licenses a kind of pragmatism in religion. Only what works in, on, and out of the life of a claimant is what is really known, proportionately to levels of reformation, judgment, and aspiration. Until faith comes, Augustine holds, there is no understanding, for here with every "belief that" goes a "belief in." Where the latter is not present, the former may be doubted. No serious religion offers truth without its results in biography. The gospels begin long ago and far away, swiftly to build to a pressing "Who do you say that I am?" and its consequent "Follow me." Each *bodhisattva* at Vulture Peak, as Buddha begins discoursing in perfect wisdom, is deeply struck by the thought, "It is for me that the *tathāgata*, seated there, demonstrates *dharma*." (MPCl 525)

2. Concomitant obedience

After we start to believe, truth unquestionably places demands on us. But the chronology here is more probing, for submission *accompanies*, as much as *follows* our progress, and is not merely the ending result of conviction but the entering road to it. With this we reach *concomitant obedience*. Augustine advises those disciples who wish to understand Jesus' conjunction of the way and the truth: "If you seek the truth, keep the way, for the way is the same as the truth." Similarly, we remember how Jesus said, "If you love me, keep my commandments, and the Father will send the Spirit of truth." (GJ 13-4; Jn. 14.15f) Love first, obey next, and finally reach truth. How close this is to the nerve of *Islam, submission*, we can readily see in many Qur'anic promises and warnings:

"Those who strive for us, in our ways, We will guide them." (S 29.69) "Allah guides not the froward folk." (S 5.108p) The *traditions* of Muhammad repeatedly return to this point: "Whoever lives out what he knows will receive from God what he does not know." (Ay 69) "Avoid the prohibitions of God and fulfill his commandments and you will be wise." (Ih I, 1, 228) "No man will be learned unless he puts his knowledge into practice." (Ih I, 1, 154) "Seek no new knowledge unless you have put into practice what you already know." (Ih I, 1, 168) Those are the Qur'anic grounds for what Ghazali sets forth as an epistemic principle: "Whoever through his knowledge obeys God, his heart becomes illumined." (Ih I, 1, 64m) Theology for him is not one of the abstract disciplines; rather here, as in law or medicine, truth is learned in a never-ceasing practice.

The *Great Sūtra* repeatedly refers to "the gradual activity, training, and method of the Bodhisattva who courses in perfect wisdom." (MP 554) Consider here the elements of the noble eightfold path: right belief, aspiration, speech, action, livelihood, effort, mindfulness, concentration. These mingle truth and obedience (*vinaya*) under the classic threefold discipline of virtue (*śīla*), concentration of mind (*samādhi*), and wisdom (*prajñā*). In this discipline a contemplative regimen is coupled with a moral life. This sharpens our mental focus and through these "three doors to *dharma*" we reach truth beyond. (MPCv 141) The various ways these things interpenetrate is one of many meanings which Nagarjuna compacts into an aphorism: "The ultimate truth is not taught apart from practical behavior." (Ka 24-10m) The *Muṇḍaka Upanishad* cautions, "Let the truth of Brahman be taught only to those who obey his law." (*MuU* 3-2-10p) What underlies such an injunction is the conviction that only those who engage in the disciplinary practice can be successfully taught. Anything else is wasted effort.

Despite the occurrence sometimes of sudden conversions and flashes of insight, we also have to labor a long while over our convictions. Across this growth span the aspirant must be prepared to press obedience and knowledge as jointly incremental. Art, music, literature, and—intensely—religion require that we employ, enjoy, and embody what we know, and aspire to know, in order to confirm it. Those deeply laden creeds: "Jesus is the Son of God," "The Qur'an is the Word of God," "*Ātman* is Brahman," "*Nirvāṇa* is *saṃsāra*," are truths one must simultaneously *think about* and *travel into*. The structure of response conditions us for further stimulus. Even where enlightenment comes suddenly, there is always growth surrounding it, before it and after it. One matures in wisdom with maturing character, because, made tropic to truth, the conforming character fits us for the reception of knowledge. Discovery proceeds leap-frog, with alternate intellectual and existential jumps. When our deeds match our thoughts we gain a disclosure situation for further truth. "He who does the truth comes to the light." (Jn 3.21; Co 10-1)

3. Antecedent obedience

Now we have to invert the order with which we began. It was true, but superficial. We must with further progress contend that the discovery of ultimate truth is only made *after* the aspirant is true to hoped-for truth. This demands *antecedent obedience*. Jesus says to those who challenge his authority, "Whoever has the will to do the will of God shall know whether my teaching comes from him or is merely my own." (Jn. 7.17 NEB) From this Augustine derives his insistence on "the obedience of believing which makes understanding possible." " 'If you desire wisdom, keep the commandments, and God will give it to you.' (Ecclus. 1.26) Let no one, proceeding out of order, wish before he gains the humility of obedience to arrive at the height of wisdom. For he cannot reach it unless he has approached it in due order.... Thus we reach the wisdom of hidden things through obedience to the commandments, because obedience must be carefully kept that wisdom may be reached." (NP 118, 22-8)

Ghazali demands this same obedience before truth. "God says, 'Follow therefore before me and adopt the ways of the saints. Then I will pour knowledge into your hearts until they overflow.'" (Ih I, 1, 189m) "God made self-mortification the prerequisite for guidance when he said, 'And those who strive hard for us, in our way we will guide them, for God is assuredly with those who do righteous deeds.'" (Ih I, 1, 55m; S 29.69) Think what Augustine might of the truth in Islam, he would not dispute the order of obedience before truth, for, whatever our lights, it is only in and after our practice that our disclosures are forged. The psalmist invites us, "Hearken, O daughter, and see." Augustine adds a warning, "If you will not hearken, you will not see." (NP 44-25)

How does Sankara open his *Commentary on the Vedānta Sūtras?* Concerning "the inquiry into Brahman,...we maintain that the antecedent conditions are the discrimination of what is eternal and what is noneternal; the renunciation of all desire to enjoy the fruit of one's actions both here and hereafter; the acquirement of tranquility, self-restraint, and the other means; and the desire of final release." (VS 1-1-1m) These and the other "means of knowledge" prescribed in the *Commentary on the Brihadāraṇyaka Upanishad* are: "renunciation, calmness, self-control, withdrawal of the senses, fortitude, and concentration." (BrU 4-4-21ff) Often added is "faith." (PrU 1-10; VS 1-2-16)[5] These will require further fitting into our argument later on, but taken collectively they show us already how the inquiry into Brahman is only undertaken with what are called spiritual exercises (*upāsanas*) as "means" to discerning the eternal. These means are existential and disciplinary and go beyond argumentative propositional knowledge.

When Sariputra asks concerning the starting *bodhisattva*, "How then should he make endeavors in the perfection of wisdom?" Buddha answers at once with the six perfections. "He should perfect himself in the perfection of giving, of morality, of patience, of vigor, of meditation, and of wisdom."[6] (MP 45a) Nagarjuna fills a whole volume in commentary on how the first five lead to more and more of the sixth, interpreting them as a skill-in-means or a praxis (*upāya*). They form a tier upward toward the truth with

---

[5] Key root words with intershading meanings are *viveka*, "discrimination"; *vairāgya*, "repudiation," detachment from the karmic self; *śama*, "drawing away" into tranquility; *dama*, "restraining" of the sensory self; *uparati*, "giving up" of karmic duties and passions, hence dispassion; *titiksha*, "patience"; *samādhāna*, "concentration"; and *śraddhā*, "faith." See also BhG 2-21 & 64f, VC 37ff.

[6] The ascending *pāramitās* are: *dāna*, charity, *śīla*, virtue, *kṣānti*, forbearance, *vīrya*, effort, *dhyāna*, contemplation, *prajñā*, wisdom.

the last not to be had save from the steps below. (MPC1, vol. 2)
Here is Nagarjuna's order of knowing: "Whenever there is perfection in the law, the supreme happiness of salvation will appear later on, because those who have reached the perfect life in consequence of practice of the law will gradually attain to salvation (*prajñā* and enlightenment)." (Rv 1-3m) The Buddha says, "All the six perfections, in fact, are the good friends of a Bodhisattva, his Teacher, his path, his light, his shelter, his mother, his father, and they lead him to cognition, to understanding. I also, Subhuti, am a Tathāgata who has won full enlightenment, and my all-knowledge has come forth from the six perfections." (AP 236a)

Does it put the cart before the horse to ask obedience to truth for which one is yet still searching? Is that logically awry or even psychologically possible? Would it not be wiser, or safer, to use an order where we first discover intellectual certainty, then by decision put our confidence there and afterward live accordingly? That might seem so to the detached. But all our participants report how it is truer to the actualities of faith, and on reflection a nobler hermeneutic order, to find that out of a certain caliber of living there grows a veteran conviction concerning that divine reality in which we are investing life. So we live the good, righteous life, not only because we know it to be good and right, but in order that we may come to know how this corresponds to that sacred reality which ultimately is, is good, and is righteous. By following a sacred prescription for life, we find how in our lives we are sketching out a description of what the sacred reality is like. To put it aphoristically, here confirmation is by conformation. In this mood, Augustine explains Jesus' call, " 'Come to me, learn of me.' So it is, brothers. Believe the commandments of God, and do them, and he will give you the strength of understanding. You cannot presume to put the last first and to prefer wisdom over the commandments of God." (Sm 117-17) *Knowledge* always comes after *acknowledgment*.

4. Agentive obedience?

"Knowledge is not complementary to action." No theme is more frequent in Sankara, and he is never more adamant about it than in the *Commentary on the Gītā*. (BhG 2-10, 18-66) Injunction to works (*karma-kāṇḍa*) cannot mix with injunction to knowledge (*jñāna-kāṇḍa*). "The knowledge of Brahman refers to something which is not a thing to be done.... As soon as we comprehend Brahman, all our duties come to an end and all our work is over." (VS 1-1-4) This unequivocal renouncing of *karma* might seem, on first hearing it, to challenge the demand for obedience which we have been setting forth. But, on closer inspection, it rather deepens it. Here is the conviction, recurrent in faith, that knowledge is not by our works, not by what we call an *agentive obedience*. In the Augustinian evangelical covenant one is never saved by works, and so too with Sankara. One is never liberated by *karma*, for that is, *par excellence*, salvation by works, the stronghold of the self which must be given up as an illusion. For Augustine, any achieved righteousness of the law prevents our knowing God in his righteousness through grace. So it is with action and knowledge for Sankara. "For when knowledge arises, *karma* vanishes, since in the person in whom knowledge exists, *karma* cannot remain." (IsU 18)

That is analogous to the Christian destruction of law by grace, and, with variances, righteousness and spiritual action still remain present in both faiths, not as efficacious conditions on the basis of which knowledge and grace can come, but as the *sine qua non* without which they cannot adequately be received. No major faith really supposes that knowledge of the real is the fruit of our actions. If that seems otherwise in Mahayana's frequent talk of the *bodhisattva's* accumulation of merit, we onward find the whole concept of merit eroded away, the *bodhisattva* must have "no possessiveness about merit," else he will proceed no further toward wisdom. There can be "no taking refuge in the morality of an I-making." (cf. MP 173f, 365) *Emptiness* is put to work on our merit too, rather like Paul evicted the last of his pharisaical legalisms. Although Madhyamika specifies that charity and virtue are conditions of wisdom, it too repudiates *karma* and asks instead this correspondent truthfulness to *dharma*.

Yet these works which are proscribed if they are considered to be in *meritorious* self-release are still prescribed if considered as a *means* of knowledge. "Knowledge having once sprung up requires no help toward the accomplishment of its fruit, but it does stand in need of something else with a view to its own origination," remarks Sankara, "for there may be a difference of connection even when there is no difference of work," and "so the works enjoined...are not required by knowledge for bringing about its results, but with a view to its own origination." Sacrifice, gifts, penance, and fasting are means of knowledge, and "we conclude that they are, more especially, *means of the origination of knowledge*." (VS 3-4-26ff) Sankara is laboring with the larger principle that, regardless of what form virtues and devotion may take in any century, they do not operate so that we reach by them an *earned* divine truth, but rather they *condition* the person for an inflow of and a following after the sacred word.

This helps us to estimate the broader connection in religion between duty and knowledge, or action and contemplation. Religious inquiry is always kept close to law in Islam, to ethics in Christianity, to virtue in Buddhism; and even Sankara, whom we may sometimes fault for the neglect of the moral in his hurry to reach the spiritual, is careful to say that morality is a current through which we must sail in order to reach the spiritual regions beyond. (VS 2-1-14) Those who know nothing of duty may expect to know nothing of the divine. Yet "my duty" is never the highest trait in which we reflect God, for that is too legalistic, too *karmic*. We eventually explode duty, memorably in Augustine's, "Love, and do what you will," or in Sankara's "He who knows the truth does not think, 'I act,' nor does he long for the results of his own agency." (BhG 2-10m)

Though a route into theology, ethics with its sheer "ought" vanishes in the holy. Obligatory rituals drop out with a deepening sense of the sacred presence, rather like the way in which, when water is everywhere in flood, one has no need of local cisterns. (BhG 2-46) The heteronomous "Thou *must*" is replaced by the conjunctive "That *art* thou." In this mood, Augustine says that eternal wisdom is in contemplation, not in action. It is an outflow from us, not a levy upon us. But this is more, not less participatory. This dissolution of the agentive self introduces us to what will later become a larger theme, a kind of detachment into truth.

5. Renunciation and commitment

Religious inquiry is along an axis with reciprocal poles. Commitment to the eternal is by renunciation of the temporal, though for the moment we must leave open some crucial specifications of (and our own doubts about) the extent or nature of this renunciation. Augustine pictures Jesus calling, "Give me one who longs, give me one who hungers, give me one who is wandering in this wilderness and thirsting and panting for the fountain of his eternal home; give me such a one, and he will understand what I say. But if I speak to the cold and indifferent, he does not know what I am saying." (GJ 26-4)

Until we are sore in *saṃsāra*, according to the first of the noble Buddhist truths: that the world is unsatisfactory, no one will ask after the remaining three truths that point to *nirvāṇa*. For this reason Nagarjuna dwells at such length on the fleeting vanities around us. (MPC1 ch. 11, ch. 35) Sankara has already required a renunciation of the sensory world, and Ghazali's mood is similar. "When the Apostle of God recited the verse, 'And whom God shall please to guide, that man's breast shall be open to Islam,' he was asked...'Has that any signs?' To which he replied, 'Yes. The renunciation of this world of vanity and delusion, the repair to the hereafter, and the preparation for death before it arrives.'" (Ih I, 1, 205; S 6.125) "If you do not kill the fleshly soul with sincere struggle, you will not quicken your heart by the lights of knowledge." (Ay 62)

The quest—to state it starkly—must be renunciatory. That is a hard saying, but that there is some truth in it is difficult to deny. Most of us recognize that no hedonist can reach religious truth. "The good is one thing, the pleasant another; and he that wishes to live the life of the spirit must leave the sensual life far behind." (KaU 1-2-1; VC 81ff) "The carnal man does not perceive the things that are of the Spirit of God, for these are foolishness to him." (CG 14-4; 1 Cor. 2.14) But this is an extreme of the general principle that worldliness engages us in looking for happiness in the phenomena as such, and the result is that we are disorganized for deeper religious inquiry. No saint disagrees with this principle, though we here touch an issue which will be threaded through this entire book, and one where (we later judge) there is comparative agreement and final disagreement: whether and how far the world returns in the embrace of the Ultimate.

The texture of these various kinds and degrees of renunciation is as much felt as said. They slip between the world and the self in the world. What one renounces, Augustine tells us, is the love of Babylon, or self-love in Babylon, the secular city, for by that love errant souls became vain fools. The converse is the love of Jerusalem, the love of God in the holy city, a commonwealth built up as God's will is done on earth as it is in heaven. But this is not to despise the earth, so much as it is to know that Babylon is a doomed city in which we perish, except if, captive there, we long for the rebuilding of Jerusalem, an imperishable city in the midst of this perishable flux. We weep by the waters of Babylon, but we remember Zion. (NP 136)

Sankara's conditions, strictly understood, demand the life of the *sannyāsin*, the homeless ascetic. He insists on external renunciation of the world to match internal renunciation of the self, and never seriously allows us less for the highest knowledge. We give up "sons, wealth, and worlds." (BrU 4-4-22) Nagarjuna too promises wisdom only in the withdrawn, desireless, monastic "middle way." (MPCc 167) We will later have to do a good deal of puzzling over what he can mean by the coexistence of *saṃsāra* and *nirvāṇa*. Augustine was called to celibate poverty. But he reminds us that the Babylonian life according to the flesh is not having or enjoying a body in the world but forgetting the Spirit in the body and in the world. (CG 14, chs. 2-5) Revise these specific responses how we may, all higher faiths ask renunciation in some form. The world is rightly grasped, not by grasping at it in itself, but only by releasing it and reaching beyond, only *sub specie aeternitatis*. No one can simultaneously know, since no disciple can serve, the two masters God and mammon. Whoever takes as his god this world can never know any other beyond it, for his capacities to see through the world to its source are atrophied by his secular commitments.

This is what Buddha calls "the great resolve." "For it is not possible, O Subhuti," explains Buddha to a disciple, "that this discourse of Dharma could be learned by beings of inferior resolve, or by such as have a self in view. Nor can beings who have not taken up the pledge of Bodhisattvas either learn this discourse, take it up, bear it in mind, or study it." (SP 31a) "The Bodhisattva is so named for three reasons. He possesses the great resolve, his thought is unshakeable, and his effort knows no set back." (MPC1 242) Ever the pearl of great price, both in the *Sūtra* (AP 239) and in the *Gospel* (Mt. 13.45), truth is gained in proportion to discipline invested. Until we have become restless with the secular, until we resolutely will to have this sacred discernment, however ill defined the reality we seek, we do not have the minimum aptitude that makes inquiry possible. Not until the pull of the world becomes subdominant, replaced by this dominant quest for the eternal, can we gain an ear for the beat of a different drummer.

III. Personal Truth

The kinds of words used for reaching truth in religion join a cognitive and a personal scope, for example words such as *insight, discrimination, discernment*.[7] Truth is correctness of judgment. What is true is not "up to us," yet judgment depends on the person of the judge who must be "up to" what is true. This is the richest sense in which religion is a critical science, for the saint is a critic (*kritikos*, divider), one personally skilled in judgment. Augustine calls this *intellection*. For all our saints this is the noblest intellectual act, but just so it must be biographical, as our moral and spiritual capacities go into every estimate. Augustine's *wisdom* and Ghazali's *actual knowing*, concepts which we later examine further, have etymological roots in "tasting" (*sapientia, dhawq*).

Nagarjuna's "truth-being" (*bodhisattva*) by critical skill breaks through to reach intuitive wisdom, *prajñā*. From the root for *prajñā* we have also Sankara's realized knowledge, *jñāna*. The same root also appears through a surprising East-West etymological kinship in the English *knowledge* (Latin: *cognosco, (g)nosco*), originally

---

[7] Typical vocabulary in Ghazali includes *baṣīra, firāsa, fiqh, idrāk*; in Sankara: *vidyā, vijñā, viveka, sākṣin*; in Nagarjuna: *bodhi, upāya, vikalpa, kuśala*; in Augustine: *(dis)cerno, iudico, percipio, video*.

with its intimate and gnostic flavor, as well as with its cognitive meaning. Argument of this kind must be *ad hominem*, to the person. We next sketch broadly this "methodology" of a *self/real* connection, really a kind of expansion of the self, preparatory to a closer look, in chapter two, at the requisite virtues involved.

1. The quest for self-knowledge

With a word such as *insight* we have a hinge which joins the knowledge of the ultimate and the knowledge of oneself into one epistemic unit. The self must be known with enough insight, sight inward, that the sacred can flow through it. Either by such conduct we personally express the sacred truth, serving as a "conductor" for it, or else by our personal resistance we block the flowing into us and through us of such truth. We search out the sacred by searching into our person. "He who knows himself knows God," runs a *tradition* of Muhammad, enlarging upon the Qur'anic verse, "God stands between a man and his heart." (S 8.24a) "Only if a man knows his heart does he know himself," insists Ghazali in his *Book of the Marvels of the Heart,* "and if he knows himself, he knows his Lord; and if a man is ignorant of what is in that heart, he is ignorant of himself, and if he is ignorant of himself, he is ignorant of his Lord." (Ih III, 1, 56)

With some denominational modifications, that is an ecumenical consensus. "Like two birds of golden plumage, inseparable companions, the individual self and the immortal Self are perched on the branches of the self-same tree." (*MuU* 3-1-1p) "He is my very Self, dwelling within the lotus of my heart." (*ChU* 3-14-2p) Deeply within, past the superficial ego, when the *ātman* is found, that is Brahman.

As the Madhyamika saint sees through his egoistic self, there he finds absolute truth, the discovery of one's Buddha nature. Manjusri, a famed disciple, explains this in a puzzling set of contradictories which we are hardly yet prepared to understand, except as they point to a *self-Buddha-emptiness* linking. "One who wants, Sariputra, to seek for the Tathāgata, should seek for the self. For 'self' and 'Buddha' are synonymous. Just as the self does, absolutely, not exist and cannot be apprehended, just so the Buddha.

The Buddha is the same as speechless silence." (SP 105m) The emptied I is found to be nondual with Suchness, *tathatā*.

Similarly, how does one reach the evangelical true religion? "Descend into yourself; go into your secret chamber, your mind. If you are far from yourself, how can you draw near God? I do not travel far for my examples. In the mind was man made in the image of God. In his own similitude let us seek God." (GJ 23-10) "Unless therefore a person has passed the measure of his own soul, he will not see that the God who said, 'I am who I am,' is what he is." (NP 130-12) Augustine here mingles two tributaries, the biblical pure heart of understanding combining with the Socratic "Know thyself."

Centuries downstream from Augustine, Calvin begins his *Institutes* with the knowledge of God and of the self inseparably intertwined. More existentially, recalling the *Confessions*, Luther laments, "I did not learn my theology all at once, but had to search ever more deeply for it, where my temptations took me."[8] Kierkegaard insists, "In so far as a man does not know himself, nor understand that he can of himself do nothing, he does not really become aware, in any deeper sense, that God exists.... The self-knowledge which reveals one's own nothingness is the necessary condition for knowing God."[9] Like the tree, notes Augustine in a revealing parable, we reach up with our leafy crown further toward the sky only by putting roots down ever deeper into the soul. (Sm 117-17) In the *Soliloquies*, Reason asks, "What then do you wish to know?" Augustine replies: "All those things for which I have prayed." Reason further asks: "What are they, briefly?" Augustine: "I desire to know God and the soul." Reason: "Nothing more?" Augustine: "Absolutely nothing." (S1 1-7)

All humanistic thought requires appreciatory powers which learn to judge the reality and worth of what is without us by forming within a character which is appropriately receptive. This is still more intensely the spiritual method of gaining truth. Every

---

[8] M. Luther, *Tischreden* (Weimar: H. Böhlaus, 1912), I, #352.

[9] Søren Kierkegaard, *Edifying Discourses* (New York: Harpers, 1958), p. 170, 175.

path to Brahman, to God, to *tattva* (reality) is by way of the self put right. "The kingdom of God is within you." (Lk. 17.21)

2. The valuational quest

We can seem to be recommending an alarming interiorism, uncontrolled subjectivity, so before we stretch to the further pole, let us consider the *self/real* axis as one of values. "The fundamental axiom of religion, that which expresses the innermost tendency of all religions, is the axiom of the conservation of value."[10] But value perception can only be by those who are adequate to what they judge. Beauty, courage, justice, as these may exist outside us, cannot be appraised by persons who are devoid of these qualities within. We may rise to new values; we may recognize our ideal not yet real. But what we can reach in outside contact is proportional to what we have personally become and hope to become.

This sort of judgment is dispositional; that is, only to him that has—holiness, righteousness, purity—shall more be given by divine recognition and inflow. And, grimly, from him that has not, even what he has shall be taken away. The deepest truth, the highest good, things noble and resplendent? Except as these are of worth to the person, they can never be judged for their universal truth. Oppositely, what of things which are empty, illusory, unsatisfactory? So long as life is mistakenly invested there with thirst, pride, and ignorance, by a kind of fallacy of misplaced value we ruin all logic for sound truth. Come from the sun light may, but if there is no light *in me*, I cannot see the sun.

So we say that the discovery of value transcending us is necessarily *incumbent*; it is beheld as it is held. If the self does not come to hold these values, it cannot estimate nor even comprehend them in the eternal. Whatever ultimate values one has, actually or aspirationally, will inevitably be one's god. Hence there is a spiritual axis which thrusts through the self to the real. Anyone who says he knows, "God is love," and yet in fact hates his brother simply has to be a liar. (1 Jn. 4.20) Whether we are in error or in truth, our values are invariably the forms with which we feel for God. That does not

[10] Harald Höffding, *The Philosophy of Religion* (London: Macmillan, 1914), p. 209.

mean that we only find what we project, though doubtless we too often do so; but it does mean that we cannot be right unless we reflect rightness personally as well as propositionally. To be right about what is real, then, is to get an accordant value set. Thereby perhaps we can let the sacred values enter into us, to find them both presented to us and present within.

Regardless of whether love is Christian, Buddhist, or Islamic (*agapē, karuṇā, mahabba*), a private, particular confession, "Love is *my* ultimate value," serves as the necessary means by which to verify the universal, "Love is *the* ultimate value." Formal deduction, from the universal *the* to the particular *my*, though this remains the order of being, is replaced by experiential induction, from the particular *my* to *the* universal ultimate, as the order of knowing. Meaning which is not *mine* cannot be known to be *divine*. However brokenly I may presently embody the truth of my aspiration, it must be true for me, and becoming true in me, before it can be known to be true of and in God. Or, more cryptically, here we need not only to be *logical* but also to be *axiological*, since to know *the* pearl of great price it must be *my* pearl of great price.

Is all this logically or psychologically askew? We do concede that such a quest is circular. But this is the impasse to which we are put by participatory truth, and we find the circularity positive and reinforcing. Discovery is always of what *we* take to be of ultimate worth, and, beyond taking what flows or wells up within after self-chastening, we can do no other. But we do strive to take in, rather than to project, eternal meaning. If religion is ever true, it will be known to be true only as a person dwells on certain intuitions, undergoes moral and spiritual transformations, finds warmth and energy in life, and so finds these intuitions confirmed as knowledge. Thus, for Augustine, to *understand* is always to see the worth of the divine reality by *faith-full* appreciation, that is, by faith to be filled with the divine value.

The better to equip us for this valuational feeling after the sacred, these classical faiths propose the self-detaching virtues we will examine in chapter two. By these it makes the quest not so much circular as spirally incremental. Not linear, not calculatory, the process of religious inquiry is a holistic personal discerning by means of what we are calling *correspondent truthfulness*. This valuational interiorism accounts, in part, for the recurrent and sometimes troubling reach in religion for the supersensory level. Values never lie sheerly and simply there in raw data, objectively received. They must be forged in the pensive soul, found without as they are found within. With this we leave the open, public, sensory arena and are elevated to a more hidden and searching *self/real* axis. Here *ought* blends with *is* and existence with goodness.

3. The expansive quest

When it becomes pure, the self mirrors ultimate reality. Reflectively, we see through the self into the sacred. Though we will eventually grow concerned that their meanings here vary, still the saints we are now consulting concur, at least comparatively, that we expand out from the self to the sacred real. "We can recognize in ourselves an image of God,...which by nature is nearer to God than is any other created thing, and one that by reformation can be perfected into still closer resemblance." (CG 11-26) This way in which the human heart, when reflecting purely, points on to God is the chief of Ghazali's marvels of the heart. "The aim of moral discipline is to purify the heart from the rust of passion and resentment, till, like a clear mirror, it reflects the light of God." (Al 22; Ih III, 1, 105ff)

The mirror metaphor is finally too dualist and not expansive enough for Sankara or Nagarjuna; but they both use it, and then explode it. With increasing purity, we "catch a reflection of the blissful Ātman itself," and at length the mirroring self altogether expands into its Brahmanic object. (VC 64f) "Just as one sees oneself on the clean surface of a mirror, so knowledge arises for man on the exhaustion of sin." (TaU 1-4-3) Nagarjuna plays with a sort of ultimate emptiness of the perfect mirror, which disappears into its object. "Actually, the moon is high above us, but its reflection appears in the water. So the moon of true reality is in the sky of ultimate nature and highest being, but its reflection—false notions of 'my' and 'mine'—appears in the waters of the thoughts of the minds of men and gods." (MPC1 364) We must see into and through this self, that it catches but does not contain this reality. We err if we mistake image for reality and must expand beyond the reflective self to become nondual with the larger reality above. Like a mirror, the self must be empty to be reflective of *tattva*, reality in its *śūnyatā*. For each of these saints, the ultimately real is known as the self catches, admits, and empties out to the sacred light.

A favorite Islamic idiom is of "enlargement" into God. "Whenever God wills to guide a man, he enlarges his breast for submission." (S 6.125; D1 25) Developing this, we shall later hear a great deal of the Sufi "passing away into the unity of God," during which the Islamic self is opened out into, enlarged into the unitarian God. Paul enjoins the Corinthians to open up out of their private narrowness and to let God's greatness enlarge them. "Be you also enlarged." (2 Cor. 6.13) He is seeking, Augustine explains, our reception of that grace through which God's character can be known as we are put in communion with it. "Do not remain in yourself, transcend yourself too; put yourself in him who made you." (Sm 153-9) Alike in Ghazali and in Augustine, an outreaching trust (*tawakkul, fides*) bridges the human subject over to its divine object. The difficult movement which is so simply put in "That art thou" is precisely a vast dilation and amplifying of the self when the *ātman* flows into Brahman. We "become merged in the True," there is "reabsorption" into Brahman. We attain "the state of identity with all." (VS 2-1-9; BrU 4-3-20) "The nature of the Supreme Truth is beyond the ken of those who have not the requisite expansion of heart, who are not learned, who are outside the pale of Vedanta." (GaK 4-94)

Nor, in its own dialectical way, is the quest of Madhyamika any less expansive. With this we may begin to understand a cryptic routing which has already been hinted. One seeks the *tathāgata* by seeking the self; then finds, reversed, that the self in emptiness reflects the resplendent Void. So the doctrine of self-unreality (*anātman*) is complementary to that of world/ultimate unreality (*anitya*). Even the *ātman* and Brahman which the Hindus cherish are alike dissolved by these Buddhists into silent "suchness," into "emptiness." There, despite its negativity, *śūnyatā* contains a teasing vision of bound-up-ness. In a passage suspiciously absolutist for the undoubted writings of Nagarjuna, the *Śāstra* urges, "If the bodhisattva would...comprehend that all things blend into one essence in the great ocean, then, indeed has his cultivation of *prajñā-pāramitā* found fulfilment.... The indeterminate nature is the true nature of all things. Determinations and divisions are constructions of the imagination." (MPCv 259m) But even if we set aside such a positive oceanic essence and retreat with the austere Nagarjuna into a more reticent, silent nonduality, the *bodhisattva* still "enters emptiness" and is "born into nondual Suchness." "For the Suchness of the Tathāgata, and the Suchness of all *dharmas* (realities), they are both one single Suchness, not two, not divided." (AP 193)

Truth is had here by a sort of release and expansion into the divine reality. This general principle, joining with that of obedience, lies behind the specific virtues of chapter two, toward which we are now leading. Still later, after considering subjectivity and objectivity in chapter four, we will become concerned whether this unbridled dissolution of the self into God can be overdone. But at least for the present, we can rightly say that only the stretched self can reach and embrace the sacred. Perhaps we must say too that a significant stretching is demanded of the reader who asks what a stretched self can mean.

4. Conditioned disclosure

Religious truth is not of the scene everybody sees, but of something behind the scenes. "To believe in a God is to see that the facts of the world are not the end of the matter."[11] This overseeing prompts each of our teachers here to posit what we may call a noumenal beyond a phenomenal sight.

Sankara distinguishes "two kinds of vision, one eternal and invisible, and the other transitory and visible." (BrU 1-4-10) How is the *bodhisattva* enlightened? By a celebrated third eye, often featured on icons, the "perfectly pure Wisdom Eye" that sees beyond our two bodily eyes. (MP 77) The African saint preaches that "by the

[11] L. Wittgenstein, *Notebooks, 1914-1916* (New York: Harpers, 1961), July 8, 1916.

eye of the heart" we receive divine light, for "as surely as God gave us the sun to see with, he gave us eyes to see by its light, and so with the divine." (Sm 88-5f) "For faith has eyes of its own by which it sees, so to speak, that which it does not yet see." (Ep 120) We have a kind of "intellectual vision" beyond "corporeal vision." (LG, Bk 12) Ghazali continues, as though he had learned it from Augustine, "The heart possesses an organ of sight like the body, and outward things are seen with the outward eye, and inward realities with the eye of the mind. For the Apostle of God said, 'Every servant has two eyes in his heart,' and they are eyes by which he perceives the Invisible." (Ri 198) This metaphoric sight we will later subject to analysis. For the moment, let it only introduce us to a sort of *detective* quality in spiritual seeing.

Our spokesmen do all they can to make their faiths public, and the *Confessions*, the *Kārikās*, the *Deliverance*, the *Upanishadic Commentaries* offer ample evidence of that. But they nowhere allow that these truths can be known true out there in the forum, but only by an unveiling in the inner sanctum. This sense of Whitehead's famous dictum, "Religion is what the individual does with his own solitariness,"[12] was known centuries before in Ghazali's *Book of Solitude*. (Ih II, 6) No *critical* science is easily public. Rather, access to it is gained only by initiation into the community competent to judge. Religion is that sort of science, but it vests still more in the private person of the critic, more than does any other science.

To borrow a stark term from Ghazali, religion is ever an *esoteric science*. Ghazali says that he seeks "mysteries" (*asrār*), inner meanings. The titles of the opening books of the *Revivification* warn us of this: "*The Mysteries of...*" Sankara tells us that the root of *upanishad* is an inner, secretive "sitting near" by which private access is had to hidden truth. Religions argue in the marketplace, but they invite the common and the unregenerate to leave the marketplace and come into a sanctuary of holiness for further disclosure. Theology may be offered to the public, but God is not

---

[12] A.N. Whitehead, *Religion in the Making* (New York: New American Library, 1960), p. 16, 58.

at public reach. "Every religion which does not affirm that God is hidden, is not true."[13]

Though truth comes only to the expectant person, no amount of readiness will force its coming. Even the scientist who gropes for a theory still undiscovered finds that he is without a logic that will guarantee its discovery. Genius in art and music is laden with parallel testimony. But this is truer still in religion. When these faiths promise what we here term a *conditioned disclosure*, they never mean that wisdom comes by our competence and at our demand, but rather that the eternal will come, and only come, to those who seek it. Then our reaching out for it will very likely be redescribed as becoming receptive to a reaching in for us by the sacred. We ascend what Ghazali calls the *stages* (renunciation, poverty, patience, trust in God). But God must descend to give us the *states* (senses of nearness to God, of love, hope, tranquility, confidence). We must wait on God, says Augustine. Truth dawns upon us. This is less personalistic in India, but even there for one to suppose that spiritual performance is sufficient for knowledge would slip back into the error of *karma*. Truth only comes—here Ghazali's words will serve for all—by unveiling, by awakening, and by divination.

We conclude with two caveats. First, this conditioning is *necessary* but is not *sufficient* for truth. Any genuine disclosure implies that these conditions are met, however partially. But it by no means follows that those who have no sense of the sacred lack love, faith, purity, or righteousness—actually or aspirationally. We do not wish, or dare, to make judgments about performance; but if any one combines obedience, virtue, and value with less success than he or she wishes, or with a resulting agnosticism, such a person must find his or her own personal explanation of these sources of truth and value. We are often strong through powers that we do not wholly understand. All that is claimed here is that a moral spirituality is the only mode congenial for truth, and that an immoral secularity guarantees ignorance.

Nor, if these conditions are met, must any common conviction

---

[13] B. Pascal, *Pensées* (New York: Modern Library, 1941), #584.

follow. We have said little here to distinguish Islamic from Christian, Madhyamika from Vedantan spirituality. These have deliberately been surveyed formally, as partially empty categories into which each faith may yet fill diverse content. For the present we can conclude with this as an interfaith preface: We cannot give a prescription for right judgments, but we can be sure that no one avoids wrong ones until one's thinking rises from a life which progressively escapes from self-centeredness through a single-minded, obedient questing for the eternal.

Secondly, is this self-disposing self-fulfilling? To put it bluntly, brainwashed by these conditions of inquiry, that which we think we have found out is neither surprising nor trustworthy. We should be careful what we long for because we shall probably find it. Our loves, holds Augustine, determine our discoveries. The criticism comes to this: that the premises we gather do, after all, necessitate a conclusion. To meet these conditions is to know that religion is true, but in vicious circularity and in various specific forms according as various obediences are undertaken. "God" will be of like character to ourselves, and so we beg the question. But this is to be caught in an odd crossfire, for there is no reason to think that persons who draw nonreligious conclusions are any freer from ego-fulfilling dispositions, not at least until we have estimated their secular epistemic biases. That wish-fulfillment is our worst enemy is exactly what each of our sainted doctors teaches, and they propose what we next term epistemic virtues to dispel it.

That truth comes to those who are conditioned for it there can be little doubt, and the only real query is what sort of biographical sensitivity best facilitates it. If the Real exists and has anything to do with goodness, holiness, justice, or any of the recurrent spiritual virtues, then only those can know such a Real whose character is accordantly adjusted. That rightly, richly conditions; otherwise the critic is too slenderly equipped to judge. If there is in the self any disposition to go awry through pride, individuality, grasping, rationalizing, or any of those other deranging and anesthetizing vices which the religions have so often detected within us, then only a reconditioned self can succeed in religious inquiry. That no doubt is apologetics, but what is amiss about its logic?

Chapter 2. The Epistemic Virtues

We now unfold this correspondent truthfulness in terms of four epistemic virtues, which are, so to speak, the quarters of the circle of obedience. Make ample allowance, as we unfold these, that they are importantly equivocal, for their exact content needs further filling in. "Love of...," "faith in...," "purity from...," "humility in respect to..."—all these virtues we are about to describe take objects, and we will subsequently find that our saints here seriously diverge. But we first find how they converge in a common focus, how these virtues are epistemic because they are cathartic, cleansing. We shall call this catharsis at the conclusion of this chapter a kind of detachment in which virtue yields truth.

I. Love

1. Studential love

Love, holds Augustine, must precede and accompany all significant knowing. "The birth (of knowledge) in the mind is preceded by desire, through which by seeking and finding what we wish to know, an offspring, knowledge, is born." This desire which sustains inquiry is a sort of love. "Although it does not seem to be love,

34

yet that inquiry is something of the same kind." (Tr 9-12-18) "The insatiable desire to learn much," adds Nagarjuna somewhat surprisingly for Buddhist suspicions of desire, "is an indispensable condition of wisdom, and with its help one can practice the path with discernment." (MPCc 169m) Augustine moves deliberately in the ancient tradition of Socrates, philosophizing as he "loves wisdom" (CG 19-1), and that tradition has continued into modern times. Einstein insisted that, "There exists a passion for comprehension, just as there is a passion for music.... Without this passion, there would be neither mathematics nor natural science."[1] Such inquiry is not simply utilitarian, for our saints concur that it is contemplative, not active, in gnosis (*jñāna*), not from action (*karma*). It is at once intellectual and existential, as philosophy, science, and theology orient us to make our way through the world. We are enlarged, comforted, blessed; without such a sense of the worth of our undertaking, vanity will paralyze our study.

We engage in much unrewarded learning in the sense that such learning is not merely an instrument of reward. But there is not much learning of what we find intrinsically unrewarding, worthless. Spiritually, except in error, learning is not in order to be rewarded, any more than virtue is so. Each is its own reward, and neither is in self-interest; rather, when noble, both learning and virtue not only require but also redirect our love. We learn little randomly, more through curiosity; but *effective* knowing is an *affective* act, and no serious learning is casual. Without an appetite for it, none can be competent in art or French literature. There will be found energizing the zoologist, unless he is merely a hireling, a profound love of nature.

Everything that is or was, is worth knowing sufficiently to make legitimate the broad reaches of science and history. Yet every particular research that we undertake must develop in affection between the knower and the known, or, obliquely, as a corollary of some related undergirding affection to which scholarship contributes. Studies that we make of things we hate have their reciprocal loves, while indifference produces nothing. To be educated, Au-

---

[1] Albert Einstein, "On the Generalized Theory of Gravitation," *Scientific American*, 182, no. 4 (April 1950), 13-17, citation on p. 13.

gustine will later urge us, is "to fall deeply in love with understanding." This is what he calls "*studential love*," the love that inspires study. (Tr 10-1-3)

In spiritual inquiry this love must be intense in degree. "The Self is not to be known (simply) through study of the scriptures, nor through subtlety of the intellect, nor through much learning. But by one who longs for him is he known. Verily unto him does the Self reveal his true being." (*MuU* 3-2-3*p*) "A Bodhisattva should have a constant liking for Dharma, a delight in Dharma, fondness for Dharma, devotion to Dharma." (MP 125) "To enjoy the wisdom of God is nothing else but to cleave to it in love; no one has a penetrating grasp of anything unless he loves it." (FC 9-19) "He who knows God loves him inevitably, and as his knowledge of him strengthens, his love of him also strengthens, and love when it grows strong beyond bound is called passion." (Ih II, 8, 231m) Except for denominational accents, we can hardly tell which saint is speaking in such quotations from them. "If wisdom and truth is not desired with all the powers of the soul, it cannot possibly be found.... Through love we ask, through love we seek, through love we knock, through love truth is disclosed, and through love we abide in what has been disclosed." (CM 1-31) Everywhere there is this "great resolve," the same thing which we earlier called renunciation, but we can now redescribe it as devotion.

This love must also be right in its kind. To the Greek philosophical virtues—prudence, fortitude, temperance, and justice—Augustine says that we must add the biblical ones—faith, hope, and love—further to rectify our reason, for "without these three, no soul is sound enough to see and understand God." (Sl 1-12) At this point, he distinguishes two loves, scattered in all the religions of the world, the babbling love of self in Babylon, concupiscence, set against the sobering love of God in Jerusalem, charity. (LG 11-20) By Ghazali's parallel account in his *Book on Love and Yearning*, a person may at lesser levels love self, or others as they serve self. But in the highest form of love we love the other not merely for the happiness the other brings us; the thing itself *is* our happiness. (Ih IV, 6, 678) As he aphoristically puts it, we must seek God in heaven, not heaven in God. (NN 40f)

With equal fervor, Sankara warns the desiring aspirant that Brahman can be sought only in detachment, and Nagarjuna insists on our emptiness as we cherish *śūnyatā*. Inquiry cannot be loveless and in vain, but neither can it be vain, for self-love thwarts discovery. *My* interest may fund the sciences, although only in part and with some distortion. *Divine* interest is requisite for wisdom.[2] In this light we can understand Pascal's paraphrase of Augustine: "Human things must be known in order to be loved;...but divine things must be loved in order to be known."[3] Knowing before inquiry what it ultimately loves, *erōs* loves nothing penultimately until it knows whether this serves the final self-love. *Agapē* goes to its ultimate with self-abandon, in a passion that increases critical sensitivity just because of this selfless love of truth in and for its object.

2. Devotional love
Philosophical loves may be of things that neither reciprocate the love nor deeply implicate the being of the lover in any cosmic counterpart. They simply, methodically ask how the object is known, and this requires what we have called studential love. But religious inquiry also demands *devotional love*. It asks, relationally, what kind of subject is known. This elevates the student into a different sort of lover. "He that does not love does not know God, for God is love," remarks Augustine, and thus only those who respond in loving character can know this love cognitively. (Ep 138) By such a logic Paul makes love not only the means but also the end of Christian comprehension, when he prays "that you, being rooted and grounded in love, may have the power to comprehend...the love of Christ with all the fullness of God." Augustine adds, "What else, then, I ask, have we to do but first completely to love him whom we desire to know?" (Eph. 3.17f; CM 1-47)

---

[2] Respectively in Augustine, Nagarjuna, and Ghazali, the terms behind "my interest" are *cupiditas, tṛṣṇā,* behind "divine interest" are *caritas, karuṇā,* and *mahabba*.

---

[3] B. Pascal, "De l'esprit géométrique," in *Oeuvres Complètes* (Bruges: Éditions Gallimard, 1954), p. 592.

Recalling Paul's eulogy on love, philosophical love here "puffs up." Only devotional love "edifies." (GJ 27-5) In his abortive career, Ghazali failed to know because he failed to love God; he loved only to be a student of theology. "Whoever loves God succeeds, but whoever loves this world and persists in desires will not attain the science of revelation, though he might attain the other sciences." (Ih I, 1, 47m) "We sought knowledge for other purposes than the glory of God, but failed to grasp it," he sighs. "That knowledge has resisted our efforts to grasp it and consequently the truth was not revealed to us." (Ih I, 1, 128) At this level, logic alone cannot embrace the ultimate, only love can.

Neither Buddhism nor Hinduism is finally theistic, but both confer a mediate personification upon the ultimate in order to sustain inquiry. Nagarjuna and Sankara both write hymns, the piety of which often can embarrass those who suppose Vedanta's impersonal Absolute or Madhyamika's cold Void could never call forth worship. Brahman is Ishvara, the personal God; penultimately and relatively such a love of God is needed. Sankara endorses the invitation of Krishna to the devotee, "To love is to know me, my innermost nature, the truth that I am; through this knowledge he enters at once to my being.... Give me your whole heart, love and adore me, worship me always, and you shall find me. This is my promise." (BhG 18-55, 65p,m) "Devout meditations on the qualified Brahman," Sankara says, "may be conducive to the springing up of perfect knowledge." (VS 3-3-1) So he worships Shiva, and that passionately. (Hy 107ff)

Though only a few of Nagarjuna's hymns have survived, they are just as intense. In a set of four, the *Catuḥ-stava*, apparent prayers, he sings, "I shall praise my Master with devotion," and he invokes in ascending order the threefold Buddha essence, an early form of what later became the *trikāya*. Finally he lies prostrate before the silent Supreme Reality. (CS 4-2) In the *Great Sūtra*, the *Perfection of Wisdom* is repeatedly addressed as a maternal figure. She was devoutly portrayed in icons. (MP 283) There are also in the *Sūtra* ample references to worship (*pūjā*) of Gautama Buddha and the other Buddhas who can empower and quicken the saints in their search. When Sariputra asks, "Is it through the Buddha's might, sustaining power, and grace that the Bodhisattvas study this deep perfection of wisdom, and progressively train in Thusness?" the Lord replies, "So it is, Sariputra." (AP 159; MPCl 1933f)

We move too swiftly, too philosophically, if we dissociate this kind of religious devotion from a more depersonalized contemplation, keeping the latter while discarding the former. The aim of this devotion is to produce an epistemic love uniting the self and the real. The attributeless (*nirguṇa*) Brahman, en route to final knowledge, must be known as personified with divine attributes (*saguṇa*). Devotion to the Buddhas and *bodhisattvas* fits us for entrance into *śūnyatā*. The dry dialectic of the *Kārikās* or the cold logic of the *Commentary on the Vedānta Sūtras* must pass into a passionate worship of the sacred. Nor is this love personified merely instrumentally in order to stimulate us. Though they are not finally personal in the theistic sense, the Indian ultimates too are in some sense love-like, whether as oneness, nonduality, commiseration, compassion, or grace at the sacred center. For us as persons the real is necessarily treated, if still relatively and not absolutely treated, "as if" it were the subject of pious devotion.

The Occidental theist will dislike this "as if." It intimates that the sacred is not finally personal in the way we suppose; it seems to add pretense and untruth. But the Oriental must have such an "as if" to mark the relative truth to which the inexpressible absolute has been reduced. Meanwhile both West and East concur that not only on account of our character, but also on account of its own nature, the sacred cannot be known without devotional love. The level of this love must pass through, if also beyond, the highest love of which we are capable, personal love. If love is god, even though there is no God who is love, the intellectual and the devotional components in religious inquiry remain as joined as ever.

3. Charitable love

In our compassion toward neighboring lives we find the human analogue of the divine. By this sort of logic Augustine couples the two great commandments, finding again that no one can know God who hates a brother. "The love of God comes first in the order of enjoining, but the love of our neighbor first in the order of doing.... As you do not yet see God, you earn the seeing of him by loving your neighbor. By loving your neighbor you purge your eyes.... Love your neighbor, therefore, and look for the source of this love, and you may be able to see God." (GJ 17-8) Ghazali gives us a Sufi form of this: "Then know that becoming a Sufi has two characteristics: uprightness with Allah the Exalted, and quietness with mankind; and whoever is upright, and improves his character among the people, and treats them with forbearance, he is a Sufi." (Ay 68) "God has not given any of his servants knowledge without giving him tolerance, humility, good-nature, and kindliness as well." (Ih I, 1, 201m) This love begets knowledge because by purity of heart toward others we polish that mirror in the heart which reflects the divine.

Nagarjuna finds in the Madhyamika faith a similar focus: "The essence of this religion is compassion; it must be taken hold of with great energy." (Rv 4-99m) "In order to attain the supreme knowledge of a Buddha," begins Candrakirti, a disciple, in exposition of the *Kārikās*, "the first step to be taken is an initial vow of devoting oneself to the final deliverance of all living creatures, this vow harmonizing with a monistic view of the universe, and inspired by a feeling of great commiseration (*mahā-karuṇā*)." (Ca 83m) Though the monism suggested here by Candrakirti may be doubted in his master, Nagarjuna, the great commiseration is fully present in him, with its power to open us to the interrelatedness of all things. "How should a Bodhisattva behave and train, if he wants to go forth into the full enlightenment? The Bodhisattva should adopt the same attitude toward all beings, his mind should be even toward all; friendly, well disposed, helpful, free from aversion, avoiding harm and hurt, he should handle others as if they were his mother, father, son, or daughter." (AP 199a)

"Wherein, O Lord, must a Bodhisattva train to be trained in all-knowledge?" asks the *Sūtra* in a chapter on *Training*. The reply: "He is trained in the *dharmas* which make him into a savior, in the great friendliness, the great compassion, the great sympathetic joy, the great evenmindedness." (AP 249)[4] There is a puzzling skill-in-means demanded to blend emptiness with this compassion, since

---

[4] For compassion as requisite for *prajñā*, see MPCl, ch. 42.

the Void might seem to devalue things. Rather it revalues all in the nonduality of *śūnyatā*, the bosom from whence we come and go. Charity (*dāna*) insures that we correspond in truthfulness to the cosmic sympathy (*karuṇā*).

To a group of disciples who approach Prajapati seeking the sort of conduct which fits us for the disclosure of Brahman, he replies: "Be compassionate. Be charitable. Learn self-control." Even self-control here involves a moral forbearing. As "aids that form part of all meditation," comments Sankara, "self-restraint, charity, and compassion have to be enjoined as steps to the understanding of Brahman." The *Upanishad* has just exhorted that to know Brahman is to become Brahman, but in conclusion we are warned by a voice from heaven that no one knows Brahman except as he comes in disciplined and compassionate love and mercy. (BrU 5-1-1ff) We may fairly complain against Sankara that across vast stretches of the *Commentaries on the Vedānta Sūtras* and *the Upanishads* we receive no further instruction in this moral charity. It is difficult to say whether Sankara has presupposed or neglected this. If the latter is the trouble, perhaps it is due to his perspective on the world-illusion (*māyā*), which results in a devaluing of human relations. But there is much charity in the *Gītā* and Sankara's *Commentary* on it. Who, for instance, is the person most led by a "tendency toward the divine? He is charitable, can control his passions, harms no one, is compassionate toward all; not greedy, gentle and modest, he can forgive and endure." (BhG 16-1f,*p*,a)

"Good is the nonharming of living beings." (MP 41) *Ahiṃsā*, reverence for life, is the Eastern way of ordering the second biblical commandment as a preparation for the first. By a love of neighbors which softens the spirit, melts the ego, and mitigates pride, this reshapes the self so as to sensitize it to the divine. Following the emotional action required by such a widening sense of kinship, we are ready to proceed to intellectual contemplation of the untruth of the separating I, to realize the truth of nonduality or divine love. Ignorance follows passion; wisdom follows compassion, and so we are transformed to hear truth by a redirected passion. Love is foremost among the Augustinian epistemic virtues. When we recall the Pauline eulogy, "Love seeks not its own," this is enormously detaching and epistemically liberating. So love, whether studential, devotional, or compassionate, unites us with that which we wish to know.

II. Faith

"We believed that we might understand, for if we first wished to understand and then to believe, we should not be able to understand or to believe." (GJ 27-9) In his "*Crede ut intelligas*," Augustine takes a biblical motif and develops it to shape a lasting Christian doctrine. But the Latin phrase has its translation into Arabic and Sanskrit. Though Nagarjuna is otherwise quite remote from Augustine, in this he broadly concurs: "The concise enunciation of the method of realizing that enlightenment is summarized in faith (*śraddhā*) and wisdom (*prajñā*).... Of the two virtues wisdom is the foremost; faith, however, comes first." (Rv 1-4f,m) However much they may differ as to other means and ends, they both use one chronology: first faith and secondly wisdom. This order we will next examine.

1. Systemic faith

To inherit any truth we must believe that a heritage is of sufficient worth to justify attention. None of us gains a world view privately and from scratch; rather, as do our geniuses, we borrow it in the vastest part. To know is to find things out for oneself, choosing from among possibilities that are initially only promising truths. Learning is pushing on where we first hope. Some of these prospective beliefs will fall aside as unwarranted, casualties of critical discrimination; others we will interiorize. Still others remain mediately held. We believe what we do not yet know. As with the unloving person in the previous section, here the nonbeliever, demotivated, will know nothing, since the skeptic cannot tolerate the requisite span of epistemic faith. A faith which is learning steers judiciously between credulity and skepticism.

Our discretionary powers do not first yield knowledge directly but they rather focus faith. We seek the most credible legacy and, believing in some system of truth, invest in what we term a *sys-*

temic faith. By this we mean that we see whether we can justify a system of faith which surrounds us in a culture. But in order to do this we have to trust enough to make an exploratory investment in this, rather than some other, competing system of faith. Nor is this only a temporary affair affecting beginners; always on its growing edge understanding will be entrance into expected truth, which is not yet ours by immediate undergoing. This believing does not cease where, independently, we advance beyond, alter, or unfold a heritage, for on that frontier too we believe more than we know, and a faith serves as a paradigm to project our route. "The wholesomeness of faith is that it makes us seek that we may find, ask that it may be given us, and knock that it may be opened to us." (PJ 40)

Augustine often ponders how faith makes possible the sharing of knowledge. Truth is the tissue of language and kernel of culture. Faithfully to tell the truth is a moral process and to receive mediated truth is a fiduciary one. Memory or hard evidence will recall but a fraction of the past. All the rest is known by witnesses whom we critically adjudicate. No scientist has verified a thousandth part of what he knows; each one depends on truth-telling in colleagues and predecessors. This is so basic that it rises to our awareness only where malevolent or misguided persons distort history for political causes or suppress and falsify their research. When witnesses disagree, we often do not and cannot look into the matter directly, but must decide whom to trust, since our life and talents are too limited to do otherwise. The faithless are undone. (Ep 102 & 107; CM 4-2f; Co 6-5)

We come *in good faith*, as well as circumspectly. Positively, without the expectation that there is truth in religion, no truth will likely be found there; negatively, without caution error will not be detected. Any who believe that religion is only a web of gullible rationalizations will by such a belief probably arrive at unsympathetic understandings of it, because their secular faiths and confident rationalisms make religious inquiry pointless. Even a studied neutrality blocks anything more than a superficial introduction. We must come sympathetically, but to come in sympathy is already to come with a measure of faith. Before confirmation, this must rise to trust enough for us to make a costly investment in the truth-enshrining system. The *Gītā* says, "A man full of faith attains wisdom," and so Ishvara calls, "Those without faith in this, my knowledge shall fail to find me." (BhG 4-39 and 9-3*p*) Augustine insists, "No one can become able to find God unless he first believes that he will eventually find him." (FW 2-6) Nagarjuna agrees, for "by having faith in the Great Vehicle and by following the precepts enjoined in it one attains to the supreme ilumination." (Rv 4-98)

Christianity has the heaviest historical stake in faith, believing that God has acted in Israel and in Jesus of Nazareth. Augustine is quite aware of the need for an evaluation of witnesses, though his account of this is more literalistic than we can any longer employ since the rise of biblical criticism. Still, the question of biblical history is one of whom to trust. The scriptural history is, Augustine notes carefully, never directly or immediately "understood," that is, experientially verified by "intellection." It can always and only critically be "believed"; we invariably know by trusting others that Jesus died on the cross. We might first think that history for Augustine would be the domain of fact, not belief. But, to the contrary, Augustine teaches that history is always believed. "There are three kinds of objects of belief. One is those that are always believed and never understood. Such is all history, extending through the course of temporal events. Secondly, there are those things which are understood as soon as they are believed. Such is all human reasoning in the field of numbers or in any of the related (analytic) disciplines. Third are those things that are first believed and later on understood; such are those divine things that cannot be understood except by the clean of heart, achieved by obeying the commandments which have to do with living well." (DQ 48)

We might first think that religion is the domain of belief, not fact, but its inner core stretches through this believing others on into immediate personal understanding. What can be "intellected" is that Jesus cleanses me from sin. Such *wisdom* gives warrant for trusting the reported knowledge which produces this effect, but never such factual knowledge that the historical component ceases to be believed. Jesus' *historical* incarnation and atonement remain permanently to be believed, even following our passage into their *existential* understanding.

But an epistemic faith operates within any tradition whose form is historical, whether their content is or not, and at this point all our faiths are included. Verbal testimony (*śabda*) is among the means of knowledge (*pramāṇas*) in Indian thought generally. Sankara and Nagarjuna are commentators on scriptures, their very choice of a literary vehicle advertising that they propose entrance into a traditional faith. A faithful "hearing" is the first of three Vedantan stages on which, in our next chapter, we will find that the later ones are built. "Faith in this our religion," says the *Sūtra*, "means the believing in perfect wisdom, the trusting confidence, the resoluteness, the deliberation, the weighing up, the testing." (MP 101) Nagarjuna comments at great length on five learning faculties—faith, vigor, mindfulness, concentration, and wisdom—and this splendidly puts Buddhist faith in search of understanding. (MPCl 1195ff) Beside them, the Augustinian virtues—fortitude, justice, temperance, faith, hope, and love—are not so different. "I take refuge in the Buddha, the *Dharma*, the *Samgha*." (cf. SL 14) Augustine would translate this into the Christ, the Creeds, the Church. He would mean much else, but he would not really be altering this methodical entrance into truth by casting oneself into what we call a systemic faith. Or, what if someone were to refrain from either the Buddhist or the Christian plunge into faith? Must that not be on account of some other truth system in which refuge is taken, reached partially by insight, and yet also there too by faith which urges it as more promising?

"My mind tends to be impatient in my desire to apprehend truth not only by faith but also by understanding." (Ac 3-43) Augustine's haste can be found still more intensely in Ghazali and explains Ghazali's impatience with what he nevertheless finds necessary: traditional faith (īmān). Such a faith is introductory, borrowed belief (*taqlīd*), which later ought to increase to trusting (*tawakkul*). Augustine's *fides* has the scope of both Ghazali's beginning belief and his matured trusting (*tawakkul*). Ghazali finds traditional faith finally insufficient although initially inevitable. He wrestles with this in his creed for catechumens, the *Jerusalem Tract* in Book II of the *Ihyā'*. Īmān is a necessary doorway, a creedal acceptance which leads to the Islamic perceptual experience ('*ilm* and *ma-'rifa*). This is what Muhammad meant by a strange remark, "Belief is like unto a nude who should be clothed with piety," namely that belief should "increase" or "actively operate" so. (Ih 1, 2, 127 & 118) Ghazali is intolerant of stagnant *īmān*, traditional faith, but at the same time he knows no Islam without a passage through such faith. He expresses these sentiments in his commentaries and in his *Revival of the Religious Sciences*. There his plan is to begin with expectant belief and later to replace it by working conviction, direct experience.

2. Ontic faith

Understanding is not possible except by way of a borrowed creed, but it cannot rest there. At first we believe in a traditional teaching, when we do not yet fully understand. But when, later, we successfully understand or "see" with that faith, and thus no longer merely "believe" in it, this matured seeing remains "believing," but now of a further kind and at another level. Understanding is not possible so long as we remain with the merely or simply seen, the empirical, the sensible. Beyond this we must "see" intelligible patterns behind the scenes. Mature faith is the capacity to detect the hidden sacred reality with such a conviction that we can derive life there. That too is to believe where we do not see, to discern what is remote from physical vision. But this is no longer to enter borrowed belief. By means of entrance *into a religion* we move to entrance *into the reality* to which religion gives access.

Faith is first in Christianity, then in Christ; *islām*, submission, is yesterday to Islam, today to Allah; and, though problematically, belief is once in Brahmanism, then in Brahman; earliest in Buddhism, later in the Buddha-essence, in Suchness. Or, with more reticence, faith is in revered Wisdom and Truth (*Prajñā, Dharma*), for these concepts too shift their focus from mere reference to a traditional faith to a realized divine way, from a historical system to a union with the ultimate. Faith bridges the believer with the numinous, and we leave the earlier faith in a religious system, which we have called systemic faith, and come to faith in an ultimate, ontological reality, which we term *ontic faith*.

To reach understanding is, for Augustine, to find that the faith from which we had hoped to graduate is rather transformed.

Borrowed belief indeed terminates in accomplished faith, but such an ending commences another level of trusting, a confiding (*fides, fiducia*), in the present, invisible God. Faith is elevated from a historically objective Christianity to an existentially experienced subject, the Eternal God. "Temporal faith" matures into "eternal faith." (Tr 14-1-3f) "On occasion faith is invested even in falsehoods, for we sometimes speak like this, 'I put faith in him, and he deceived me.' Such faith, if indeed it is even called faith, disappears from the heart when truth is found and expels it. But faith in things that are true passes, as we wish it to, into the things themselves. Yet we must not say that faith perishes, when those things which were believed are (intellectually) seen. For is it not indeed still to be called faith, when faith, according to the definition in the *Letter to the Hebrews*, is the evidence of things not seen?" (Tr 13-1-3)

After we are instructed in the birth at Bethlehem and the crucifixion at Jerusalem, and with this remaining always believed, the saint later finds Christ evidenced within. He undergoes sacramental forgiveness and thus comes to *understand* incarnation and atonement. Faith lets the grace of God flow in; it is that personal investment by which God can be undergone. "Unless he is loved by faith, it will not be possible for the heart to be cleansed so that it may be ready and apt to see him. Where are those three things of which the building up in the mind is the strategy of the whole biblical edifice, namely, faith, hope, and love, unless in a mind believing what it does not yet see, and hoping and loving what it believes?" (Tr 8-4-6) "Faith therefore empowers us for the knowledge and love of God." (Tr 8-9-13) Here anticipation oscillates with experience. Fulfillment and promise alike involve a faithful seeing of the eternal. The saint walks not by vision but ever by faith, though such a pilgrim faith can also be redescribed as a maturing intellection of the invisible God. Paul says that "the righteous shall live by faith" (Rom. 1.17), and, though Jesus did not need redemption, even the Son of God exemplified this faith. Faith introduces understanding, but this is not the end of faith. An initial creedal belief later shifts to interiorized trust and this subsequently underrides and sustains all understanding.

"He who has so much as a grain of faith shall be kept from the fires of hell." This *tradition* from Muhammad reveals a chief marvel of the heart, the power of faith to effect saving union with God. (Ih III, 1, 148) To this Ghazali devotes a crucial book of his *Revival: The Book of Faith in One God (tawḥīd) and of Trusting in God (tawakkul)*. (Ih IV, 5) Like the Augustinian *fides*, here we find Ghazali insisting on the capacity to live receptively to God's transcendent power, so intensely as to be flooded with the divine omnipresence. Through trusting one enters the unity of God, and initial belief (*īmān*) leads to the actual experience that Ghazali so much cherishes and which we later will examine. Trusting (*tawakkul*) is always requisite for Sufi learning. It never ceases but rather is steadily intensified in the saint, for it yields that expansive, islamic contact with God necessary for truth.

"Faith is a great factor in the realization of Brahman." (BrU 2-1-int) "In one who is possessed of well-ascertained knowledge, there arises first faith." It is the "head" of the body of the wise man, and from among various faiths, only "enlightened faith" approaches Brahman in selfless union. (TaU 2-4; BhG, ch 16f) At the theistic level, this can be readily understood as trusting, on account of the epistemic union this effects with the Lord Ishvara. At monistic levels, faith becomes more nonspecific, but it deepens rather than disappears, for faith is still the capacity to give oneself over into the Ultimate, which is the primary Advaitan thrust otherwise described as renunciation, love, concentration, or sensory withdrawal. The coupling of That to thou, *vidyā*, seeing, like the Augustinian understanding, does not eliminate faith but rather transforms it into a perceptive, confident living in a reality that one cannot see.

The *bodhisattva* too must have "unbroken faith in the Buddha, Dharma, and Samgha." (MP 232) The foolish are ignorant because "they have no faith in the true dharma." Still, we get the further advice that "a Bodhisattva does not settle down in any dharma." (AP 87f) Everywhere we are urged to faith and yet also we are warned against clinging to doctrines and entities, and we may thus worry whether the *bodhisattva* actually trusts in anything. "It is not from taking refuge in views on the Buddha, Dharma, or Samgha that there is a vision of the Buddha, Dharma, or Samgha." (SP 75)

Madhyamika allows no views. Although we are asked a provisional trust, we are forbidden to put final trust *in religion*. But this is in extreme form among the Buddhists what we have already met in Augustine and Ghazali as impatience with any borrowed faith. To take refuge in mediated views is to miss the immediate vision. Emptying out the former to reach the latter, Nagarjuna falls into a silent emptiness. Does he then forbid any trust *in reality*? Perhaps. But however mystifying *śūnyatā* is, we must consider its operation. There is an orienting and funding of life from this Wisdom and Suchness, *prajñā* and *tattva*. Perhaps this is nonpropositional, but it is still a fiduciary taking refuge, a claim that without trusting the real cannot be known. If we are to see the invisible, this requires a nonclinging plunge into *śūnyatā, wisdom going beyond.*

Which of the variously recommended faiths we ought to begin to trust we cannot here say. We are saying only that, if any is true, this cannot be learned except by trusting in it. Faith, this receptiveness to a transcendent reality, is the channel by which the sacred is presented to us and empowers us. That may irritate persons inclined to be skeptical about religion, but how could truth come otherwise? If religion is everywhere false, we will know it to be so by counterexperiences, perhaps of the secular adequacy of worldly things, or of the indifference or absurdity in reality. But then perhaps our competing faiths, or perhaps our losses of faith, have prevented any spiritual unions? We forever understand pursuant to experiences, sensory and nonsensory, which follow from that in which we do and do not put our trust.

Some persons judge, uncritically, that in the sciences, unlike religion, one knows by paying no heed to borrowed tradition. But notice that in our geniuses the inner truths of a saint's affirmation are those tested in experience, albeit of the invisible, while gifted scientists, though they verify much within the confines of their specialties, subscribe to their broadest tenets largely on the authority of others. Meanwhile, saints too walk by faith, not sight; and scientists sometimes see and oftenest believe their deepest convictions. If God is ever known, only the pious can know him.

III. Purity

"Do you really want to reach him with your mind? Then purify your mind, purify your heart! Make clean that eye through which such reality can be reached. Make clean the eye of the heart, for 'Blessed are the pure in heart for they shall see God.'" (Sm 117-15) So Augustine preaches. Ghazali enjoins, "Purity of heart is a net for truth." (Ih II, 8, 272) The same theme continues when we move eastward. "Nothing but the sharp sword of knowledge can cut through this bondage. It is forged by discrimination and made keen by purity of heart, through divine grace." "Purify the heart until you know that 'I am Brahman.'" (VC 60, 70) "If the mirror is clear or the water limpid, we can see there our reflection, but if the mirror is dirty or the water disturbed, we see nothing; similarly those souls with pure thoughts see the Buddha; those with impure thoughts cannot see him." (MPCl 546)

Both moral and spiritual strands are interwoven here, and we next separate them. This helps us to see that, though sometimes denominational and equivocal, this purity is an ecumenical and univocal demand upon those who seek religious truth.

1. Moral purity

Once Buddha and his disciples Sariputra and Subhuti pondered the connection between wisdom and purity. "Sariputra: 'Deep, O Lord, is the perfection of wisdom!' The Lord: 'From purity.' Sariputra: 'A source of illumination is the perfection of wisdom.' The Lord: 'From purity.'" The litany continues for a dozen similar exchanges and then reaches a conclusion: "Subhuti: 'A Bodhisattva who understands it thus, he has perfect wisdom.' The Lord: 'Because of his absolute purity.'" (AP 142f) Nagarjuna accordingly develops at length how the six developing virtues—charity, morality, patience, energy, meditation, and wisdom—are all cathartic, emptying, beginning with the moral and passing to the spiritual. (MPCl, vol. 2) Elsewhere, he puts it this way: "Refraining from killing living beings, from theft and adultery, control over one's own words so as to avoid any false or slandering or cruel or futile speech; complete abstaining from covetousness, hatred, and wrong views denying the existence of karma; these ten virtues constitute the tenfold pure conduct. The actions opposed to these constitute the tenfold impure conduct. Not drinking intoxicating liquors, lawful livelihood, hurting nobody, kindness in giving, reverence toward those deserving reverence, and universal sympathy, this is in short the law." (Rv 1-8ff) "It is thus that a Bodhisattva, who courses in perfect wisdom, comes near to the knowledge of all modes. To the extent that he comes near it, he obtains the perfect purity of body, thought and marks, he produces no thought accompanied by greed, hate, or delusion, or by conceit, cupidity, or bad views." (MP 103) The Madhyamika saint finds that ethical purity is necessary for understanding. But this is just as true in our other saints, despite variant routes to the sacred.

The Christian *locus classicus* is Jesus' beatitude that only the pure in heart see God. (Mt. 5.8) Except for Isaiah's words about faith in order to understanding, no other biblical words come as often to Augustine's mind. The beatitude gathers Paul's trilogy of faith, hope, and love into one word, purity. "In order for us to see this truth, a great and perfect purity of heart is necessary, and this comes only by faith." (NP 109-12) "Expressed simply, this is the faith which is handed over in the creed to young Christians, to which they are to be faithful, so that, believing, they may subject themselves to God, and being so subject may live righteous lives, and living righteously may cleanse their hearts, and with a pure heart may understand what they believe." (FC 10-25) Augustine notices elsewhere, "Many who are not pure know many true things" (Rt 1-4-2), but this is not spiritually, not at the level of understanding.

Augustine and Ghazali both find that humans inescapably image God in their capacities for rationality and purposiveness. But humans also can image God in their holiness and goodness, and that image, erased in sin, must be recovered. Here we cannot know what we are not like, although the likeness may be in aspiration mixed with attainment. Only "those who hunger and thirst after righteousness will be satisfied" by knowing righteousness in God. (Mt. 5.6) "Without holiness no one shall see the Lord." (Heb. 12.14; Sm 53) If God is the locus of moral excellence, then whoever has no taste of or for such virtue can hardly discover this in God. The rash Augustine said, "Show me first that God exists, and then I will do my duty." But, maturing, he saw the connection between a bad will and spiritual blindness. Paul's better order puts striving for moral purity first, and afterward an increasing sense of God's presence and grace. "Finally, brethren, whatever is true, honorable, just, pure, lovely, gracious, if there is any excellence, anything worthy of praise, think about these things. What you have heard and seen in me, do, and the God of peace will be with you." (Phil. 4.8f,a) Living so, we discover and confirm the presence of God. In moral righteousness we find ourselves further along toward God intellectually than we may first suppose. Recalling a theme from chapter one, it is in being *made just* that we *justify* this true belief. We justify it as it justifies us, and so we are back to our earlier aphorism that to *be right* we need to *be righteous*.

Ghazali specifies purity first among the duties of the religious inquirer in his *Book of Knowledge*: "The first duty of the student (of God) is to purify his soul from impure traits and blameworthy characteristics.... Thus the Prophet said, 'Religion has been built on cleanliness.' " No doubt, concedes Ghazali, while yet impure one may learn something about religion, but such persons have only its "words and terms," hollow propositions that yield no existential experience and therefore no verified contact with God. (Ih I, 1, 126f) The heart by its created nature (*fiṭra*) is a mirror that reflects God, but sin has dirtied it. Moral purification permits intuitions of the divine; it teaches us "how to remove from the surface of this mirror that filth which bars the knowing of God.... Thus to whatever extent the heart is cleansed and made to face the truth, to that same extent will it reflect his reality." (Ih I, 1, 48f,m) This is the principal *Alchemy of Happiness*. (Al 24f) It is a leading secret of the *Revival*, which is present in the *Book on Purification* (I, 3) and the *Book of the Marvels of the Heart* (III, 1, esp. 105ff), and music and poetry are put to this use in the *Book on Music* (II, 8).

In the purity that Sankara repeatedly demands, the moral component is often further in the background than we might wish. But it is not absent. "The pure world of Brahman is attainable by those only who are neither deceitful, nor wicked, nor false." (*PrU* 1-15p)

Karma, morality, if properly used, can cleanse us from selfishness, preparatory to knowing. (BhG, int.) Sankara is finally unwilling to specify morality in Brahman and even finds the kind of morality which is in the common life ultimately unreal. Though, frankly, this dismays us and we fault him for it, we may for the moment give it this favorable interpretation. In Augustine grace, not moral law, is the deepest character of God. So with Sankara nondual knowing (*jñāna*), not moral law (*karma*), is the heart of Brahman. Sheer morality has not enough epistemic power to take either doctor to his real, though the moral is kept and treasured in God more evidently than in Brahmanic nonduality. Meanwhile, "one who has not desisted from bad conduct, whose senses are not under control,...cannot attain this Self through knowledge." (*KaU* 1-2-24)

Buddhists also teach how by a moral "ought" the self first arches outward. The moral life has an enormously detaching thrust; it looses the self for reattachment to concrete values transcending the self, which may lead to a transcendent goodness from which everything partakes. *Mere* morality—*karma,* justification by works, *my* duty, self-righteousness—is always self-defeating, since it is not really self-detaching. But *pure* morality opens us up for universal intent. It enables us to rise over our jaundicing passions, to discern worth about which we cannot do as we like, worth which we cannot reduce to our desires. This drawing of the self off self-center is the purgative and therefore noetic power of compassionate love.

In the philosophical ethical context, we perhaps say that others have rights intrinsically, but in the religious context their value, from which rights derive, is laid more deeply. The self is grounded in an ultimate; it has value relatively and not absolutely. When we have cut through the sense of self-essence or individual self (*anāt-man, jīva*), we can then see everything as the Buddha essence and as Brahman. Our souls image God. Purity first stretches us to recognize something precious over against the self, and then leads on to our common funding in God, Brahman, or *śūnyatā.* In this way the coming of morality displaces us from egoism toward altruism, and thus prepares us for theism, monism, and nonduality.

2. Spiritual purity

This detachment produced by moral purity leads, at the next level, to spiritual purity. Augustine has left us no legacy more timeless than his insight that our loves affect our knowing, and therefore that misplaced love insures fallacious understanding, while the clear mind belongs to the pure heart. "Now any who suppose to know truth while still living iniquitously are in error. For it is iniquitous to love this world, to lust after these things, to labor in order to acquire them, to rejoice when they are abundant, and to fear lest they perish. Such a life cannot see the pure, unde-filed, and immutable truth, and cleave to it." (Ac 14) Self-love in the world is too passionate to perceive truth, while the purified life learns truth because of its equanimous disinterest.

But this biasing caused by impurity grows subtle and troubles the whole philosophical and apparently academic quest for God. Even Socrates, Augustine remembers, saw that there is a purity which is requisite for mental excellence. "He denied that minds defiled by earthly desires could reach behind these limits to the divine.... This could only be comprehended by a purified mind. He concluded that all diligence must be given to the purification of life by good morals so that the mind, freed from the depressing weight of desires, might elevate itself by its natural vigor to eternal things, and might, with purified intellect, contemplate that nature which is immaterial and immutable light." (CG 8-3; cf. *Phaedo* 65c-66e) Augustine says that we ought to add to this the purifying capacity of faith. "God does not permit any save the pure to know the true. Now the eyes of the soul are sound when it is pure from every bodily stain, when all desire of mortal things is purged away, for which task faith alone is equal to beginning. For this cannot be disclosed to a soul marred and diseased by sin, since unless sound it cannot see, nor will it apply itself to the labor of making itself sound unless it believes that, when sound, it will be able to see." (S1 1-12) If we strive for purity, this will erase our tendency to rational-ize and to suppress the truth in the service of a perverted will. So long as anyone is still bent so, such a person cannot be trusted to think clearly.

"The knowledge of Brahman arises in a man who has attained the requisite holiness through the purification of heart. For it is a matter of experience that, even though Brahman is spoken of, there is either noncomprehension or miscomprehension in the case of one who has not been purged of his sin. Therefore knowledge dawns on one whose mind has been purified by concentration, as mentioned in the Vedic verse, 'These things get revealed when spoken to that high-souled man who has supreme devotion towards the Effulgent One.'" (KeU 4-8a) We recently complained that Sankara does not make the moral component here explicit enough, and we may wish also to worry about an uncompromising renunciation of the temporal scene. Purification is not everywhere fully or precisely tantamount to renunciation of the world in the three others we are here consulting. But Sankara is in concert with Augustine that sin—worldliness, however this is understood— thwarts knowledge, while cleansing from sin permits the coming of truth. The intent of all religious exercises, rightly understood, is to cleanse us for union with the Absolute. "Works are the washing away of uncleanliness.... When the impurity has been removed, then knowledge begins to act." (VS 3-4-26)

This purity is likewise one of the notable meanings of emptiness. Buddha says in the *Great Sūtra*: "The Bodhisattvas who course in perfect wisdom, having stood in the six perfections, cleanse the roadway to the knowledge of all modes, on account of absolute emptiness." They "cleanse the roadway to the knowledge of all modes because by means of absolute emptiness they have grasped at nothing at all." (MP 82f) "To the extent that one does not take hold of things and does not settle down in them, to that extent one can conceive of the absence of I-making and mine-making. In that sense can one form the concept of the purification of beings." (AP 237) Charity, morality, patience, vigor, and concentration, when coupled with nonclinging to things, coupled with the emptiness of the world and the emptiness of the grasping self, produce this remarkably beneficial purity in emptiness, which brings us to the last of the six perfections, this wisdom of and in the ultimate emptiness. In ways both like and unlike the Augustinian who has been emptied of selfish worldliness, it is the pure in heart who see the Buddha too. The *bodhisattva* "purifies the Buddha-field, and reaches the knowledge of all modes." (MP 83)

Ghazali's witness underscores especially the agony of this psychological purgation which prepares us for logical truth. "Truth is better, its discovery difficult, its attainment hard, and its road rough, especially as it pertains to the knowledge of the qualities of the heart and to its purification from blameworthy traits. It is a continual source of torment to the spirit; he who pursues it is like the person who takes his medicine and bears its bitterness in the hope of being cured." (Ih I, 1, 208) "The wisdom which passes all understanding is only achieved through self-mortification, and watching, the active fulfillment of outward and inward duties, and bringing the heart in solitude before God's presence through pure reflection and sole devotion. That is the key of illumination and the fountainhead of revelation. The science of revelation, the secrets of practical religion, and the subtleties of the passing thoughts of the heart are seas too great to be sounded in depth and can be traversed by seekers only to the extent to which each of them has been given the power and ability to do good. They are the outcome of the workings of a pure heart and the gracious blessing of God on the high mind which aspires to him." (Ih I, 1, 189f,a)

In sum, the enlightened way is the purgative way. Whitehead writes in the school of Augustine, a conviction shared by the others, when he says that "Religion is force of belief cleansing the inward parts. For this reason the primary religious virtue is sincerity, a penetrating sincerity."[5] What we are here especially noticing is the cognitive power of this sincerity. "Let the truth of Brahman be taught only to those who obey his law, who are devoted to him, and who are pure in heart. To the impure let it never be taught." (*MuU* 3-2-10*p*) That sort of restriction has sometimes and unfortunately yielded a rather secretive exclusivism; but the original intuition must have been, rightly, that one does not cast pearls before swine, because, grimly, one cannot cast before swine what they know to be pearls, for swine do not and cannot recognize as pearls what they trample underfoot. "Thus the venerable Sanatkumara taught Narada, after he was pure in heart, how to pass from darkness into light." (*ChU* 7-26*p*,m) We may not be altogether happy with the

---

[5] A.N. Whitehead, *Religion in the Making* (New York: New American Library, 1960), p. 15.

sometimes escapist focus of this purity, whether Sufi, Sunyavadin, Vedantan, or Neoplatonic. But it remains true that so far as the ultimate is noble, it will have to be known in corresponding nobility.

Respecify purity how we may, only the "puritan" can know God. God is known in the flight of vices.

IV. Humility

"Prepare for yourself no other way of seizing and acquiring the truth than the one prepared by him who as God has seen our infirmity. But that way is, first: humility, second: humility, and third: humility. And I will continue to repeat this, however many times the question is asked. Not there are no other precepts which can be given, but unless humility precedes, accompanies, and follows our searching,...pride completely wrests from our hand any good work in which we might rejoice." (Ep 118-22) According to the reservation of Jesus in a beatitude, only the meek will inherit the earth, and, again, only those who become as children can gain the kingdom of God. This idea goes elsewhere by many names— *islām*, submission; *vairāgya*, detachment; *śūnyatā*, non-clinging emptiness—and all these words may not have one common denotation for all their connotations. But they steadily cluster around the notion that a sense of psychological, spiritual self-sufficiency results in a logical, epistemic insufficiency. *I* must decrease that *truth* may increase.

1. Humility and the self

The conceited make poor scholars in any field, for they know too much. Know-it-all ignorance thwarts inquiry and dogmatism has to be deflated before there can be any advance. "As long as a man continues to seek knowledge he remains learned; but the moment he thinks he has mastered all knowledge, he recedes into ignorance." (Ih I, I, 158) One trouble is that the arrogant seek the capture of their known, hardly a favorable mood in which to cultivate an objective, sensitive reception of truth about it. To attack anything studied, whether a trillium, an African tribe, or

God, is to profane and therefore to mistake it. Although we can sometimes carry out successful manipulations of things by this approach, the deeper integrities of things are never so understood. An inflated self-confidence misfits us for believing in and coming to know worth other than our own. All this we take at a pitch in the spiritual quest, where the self must be redistributed across a much vaster field. An overweening self-concern provides no mood in which we can faithfully come to know God; the encapsulated ego cannot enter the nondual Absolute; the grasping self cannot estimate the emptiness of *śūnyatā*. Rather, we need to be taken out of our conceits.

The Buddha cautions, "The conceited can find no ground to stand on in this demonstration of Dharma. For it is outside their sphere to enter into this enlightenment of a Buddha.... They march along under the sway of conceit, and they cannot understand the deep Dharma." (SP 29) To be taught this path, warns Nagarjuna, "one must discard all conceit and arrogance, and become respectful and docile. The rain of the Dharma is like the rain which falls from the sky; it does not stay on the summits of the mountains, but is bound to flow down to the more low-lying country. So, if a man exalts himself, the Dharma and spiritual virtues will remain outside him." (MPCc 169) The *Sūtra*, in the *Aṣṭasāhasrikā* version, devotes two chapters to the epistemic blockages of pride. (AP, ch. 21, 24) Pride is among the last of the ten fetters binding us to darkness, and its final bursting brings the *bodhisattva*, through nonclinging, to enlightenment. Otherwise, pride produces the most serious of the deadly sins, self-righteousness, and so "that pride, arrogance, hauteur, and conceit keeps him away from all-knowledge, from the supreme cognition of a Buddha." (AP 231) "He who regards himself does not perceive real truth." (PD 62) Signless or nonclinging absence of pride, wishless absence of passion, and emptiness are the three gates to *nirvāṇa*. (MPC1 1210ff)

The same theme is continued in Vedanta. "Hear the purport of the Vedic passage by giving up all conceit, for not through conceit can the meaning of the Vedas be mastered even in a hundred years by all the people who pose to be learned." (PrU 4-6) In the *Upanishads*, Svetaketu's learning is judged by his father to be wrong because it is too presuming, as was Gargya's by Ajatasatru; both are humbled in order that they may understand. (ChU 6-1-1ff; BrU 2-1-1ff) The *Gītā* on two occasions lists virtues that lead us to Brahman. In one list humility is first, in the other it is last; both locations show it to be indispensable. "Though striving to know Him by means of proper authorities such as the scriptures, men of unrefined self—whose mind has not been regenerated by austerity and subjugation of the senses, who have not abandoned their evil ways, whose pride has not been subdued—behold Him not." (BhG 15-11m; ch 16, 13) "The endeavor after knowledge," Sankara carefully reminds us, "is furthered by the special inward state of a child." (VS 3-4-50m)

In Madhyamika, our errors are rooted in grasping (*trṣṇā*). We *mis-take*, that is, *mis-perceive* because we *seize* the world and the real. The sensory subjugation that Sankara demands is so austere because it has to subdue the presuming self to refine out lust and tranquilize us for vision. In both these Indian *vidyās*, the mistake is dislocated centricity. Our senses of agency and own-being prevent nondual insight. In that sense, pride is our elemental samsaric disorder. Those who are inclined to say that error is voluntarist in the West but intellectualist in the East are not altogether wrong, but we need also to reckon with this Asian conviction that what most disfigures our knowledge is egoism. Pride exalts the self. It produces a proportionate separating of the self from the other, from the real-whole. Thus a self-incurring anesthetizes our sensitivity to the divine ground. However much we secure in the separate self, just this much we subtract from our knowledge of the sacred.

"No one shall enter the Garden in whose heart there is the weight of a grain of pride." This *tradition* from Muhammad sees that the slightest pride spoils *islām*, surrender. (Ih III, 9, B 290f) "Whoever has these two characteristics, heresy and pride, will never be blessed with any of this science (of revelation)." (Ih I, I, 46) If the scholar tries merely to know God at the end of an argument, rather than with his forehead bowed to the dust, such an intellectual has succumbed to pride. This vice causes such trouble that Ghazali writes a whole book about it, the *Incoherence of the Philosophers*. But it is no vice to be laid against philosophers except as it is more insistently laid against the theologians who by "persistence in pride" attempt knowledge without *islām* and so disastrously part scholarship from wisdom. Ghazali's grief about this separation is what motived his even larger, encyclopedic *Revival of the Religious Sciences.* (Ih I, I, 1) He finishes the quarter on deadly sins with books on *Avarice,* on *Hypocrisy,* on *Arrogance and Conceit,* and on *Self-Deceiving Pride.* (III, 7-10) These vices result in a consummate idolatry which wholly destroys knowledge. But Ghazali does not write about places he has not been, and we have already heard him agonizing over his own struggle with "self-mortification" as the key to illumination. "Knowledge is not attained except through humility and hearkening." (Ih I, 1, 130)

The tour we have just made through these experiences in India and Persia show that a biblical teaching is more widespread than Augustine knew. Pride is the original sin which mars our knowledge from Eden onward. Pride is the Babylonian sin, and by humility we enter Jerusalem. "Humility is the virtue especially cherished in the City of God. The one city proceeds in the love of God; the other in the love of self. 'Pride is the beginning of all sin.' (Ecclus. 10.13) What is pride but an appetite for inordinate self-exaltation? The soul abandons the source to which it should keep near and becomes an end in itself." (CG 14-13a) "Who can with perfectly serene and pure mind contemplate this whole divine essence?... Who can do this except one who, confessing his sins, has leveled to the ground all the vain swellings of pride and prostrated himself in meekness and humility to receive God as his teacher?" (Ep 232-5)

Those persons who want God for knowledge, but not for worship, do not really desire to find him. Their truest desire is almost invariably to use him in self-interest. "What then? Will you be able to lift up your wounded heart to God? Must it not first be healed so that you can see? Do you not show your pride when you say, 'First let me see and then I will believe'?" (NP 139-21) Though superficially it seems rational, Augustine finds that this attitude of witholding commitment until after one clearly sees the truth is a form of rationalizing.

Unwilling to venture purity, love, faith, and humility, these prudent intellectuals outwardly search heaven and earth but all the while they are out of inward touch with truth. The *"proud* philosophers" will invariably by their pride miss incarnation and atonement. " 'You have hidden these things from the wise and have revealed them to little ones.' So, those who labor and are burdened may come to him and he will refresh them. For he is meek and humble of heart, guides the meek in judgment, and teaches them his way. But those who are puffed up and elated by some supposedly sublimer learning do not hear him as he says, 'Learn of me, for I am meek and lowly of heart.' " (Co 7-14)

The prudent cannot take the kingdom of heaven by strength of argument, by logical violence, for argument in the *proud* sense will deservedly fail. In this light we can understand the notorious way the theistic proofs and disproofs have of collapsing and remaining inconclusive. Those who are "pushy" and forward in religious inquiry cannot argumentatively run up to God, nor can they run God out; but the receptive may go further, and the "proofs" that earlier failed will now, in the *meek* sense, cohere, rising to make intellectual sense out of religious experience.

This is Pascal's point in claiming, "The God of Abraham, of Isaac, and of Jacob (is) not the God of the philosophers and scholars."[6] In the East and West alike, epistemology mixes here with psychology, and pride prevents the sort of experience that makes sense of religion. Although we still have to wonder—which we leave unresolved—that meekness guarantees no single denominational result, we also have to ponder how, ecumenically, the saints all say that pride guarantees no trustworthy results at all. Pride is always the invisible sin, as humility is an invisible virtue. The one runs close to our subconscious; the other cannot be willed without being destroyed. We conclude that we cannot trust any logic that conceives its truths in conceit. The vain seek in vain.

2. Humility and the sacred

In the two of our saints who are otherwise most disparate, Augustine and Nagarjuna, this humility belongs not only to the self

[6] B. Pascal, "Mémorial," in *Oeuvres Complètes* (Bruges: Éditions Gallimard, 1954), p. 554.

but also to the sacred. Here *human humility* is more than the channel of knowing. The *divine humility* is what is to be known, the content which flows in this only suitable channel. Sankara doubtfully approaches this thought, nor is it congenial to Ghazali; but it is explicit in Augustine and implicit in Nagarjuna. Though Islam accepts Jesus as a prophet, it finds offensive the Christian idea that God could will that he die on a cross. The followers of Allah cannot understand how Christ's humbling (*kenōsis*) can reflect his Father's deepest character. Vedanta is troubled to understand how in Brahman, Absolute Greatness, there could be any genuine *śūnyatā*, emptiness. But for Augustine *agapē* in the saint and for Nagarjuna *karuṇā* in the *bodhisattva* reflect the divine because they are divine, the Great Commiseration.

Let us take this at some length in a memorable Augustinian sermon: "Now what does he tell the weak? How does he say they will be able to recover the sight they once had, so as to reach even partly the vision of the Word through which all things were made? 'Come to me, all you that labor and are burdened, and I will refresh you. Take my yoke upon you, and learn of me, because I am meek and humble of heart.' What did the teacher proclaim, this Son and Wisdom of God through whom all is made?... You were probably thinking that this Wisdom would say: 'Learn how I have made the heavens and the stars, how in me all things were ordered before being produced. Learn that in the power of immutable principles even the hairs of your head are numbered.' Didn't you think that Wisdom would speak like this? But not so. Rather and before all else he says, 'I am meek and humble of heart.'

"See, my brothers, what you have to understand. Surely it is not so much. We reach for the heights, but let us grasp lowly things and we shall be magnified. Do you wish to grasp the majesty of God? Grasp first his humility. Deign to be humble yourself, for God has deigned to be humble, not for his own sake, but for yours. Take on, therefore, the humility of Christ, learn to be humble and turn away from pride. Confess your weakness and lie patiently before your healer. When you have put on his humility, you will rise with him. He will increasingly be comprehended by you. Your understanding was in the beginning uncertain and unsteady; now you have come to understand with greater certainty and clearness." (Sm 117-17) If God is kenotic or self-giving love, then humility is not just the route by which understanding comes, it is that perfection in God which is to be understood. Since the incarnation is the humility of God, those who are proud, however subtly, are in no psychological state to understand the logic of God in the meekness of Christ. God resists the proud, but gives grace to the humble.

Do we not also recognize this, if tacitly, in the compassionate Buddha? Why is the *bodhisattva* never so near the divine *śūnyatā* as when he is pouring out life in a suffering questing for the enlightenment of others? Because the annihilation of egoism (*anātman*) and its complementary evenminded compassion for others reflects, since it is like-minded to, the Buddha-nature which is at the primordial center of the world. Surely this sympathetic nature quietly corresponds to the *śūnyatā* nature. In a key statement such as, "The perfection of wisdom is nonclinging," does not our subjective experience correspond to the objective reality? (MPCl 655) For the *tathāgata* to know no self-being, to know universal relativity, and the quiescence of all plurality—is this not somehow through personal humility to know the ultimate humility? *Śūnyatā* is a deeply humbling doctrine as it touches self, world, and ultimate; and persons cannot know its truth who have not undergone that subduing where they are drawn out of passion into universal compassion. We begin to see why Madhyamika will not permit argument to touch absolute truth, for imperious logic will find an impervious real. It seeks to enter *nirvāṇa* by violence. But only the humble can cross over into the divine emptiness, and no egotist can perceive real truth because none can know the modesty of universal sympathy. *Śūnyatā* is a quiet truth, understandable only by those who come in quietness.

V. Detachment

The four preceding virtues now bring us to a conclusion which profoundly commingles participation and detachment. These virtues cast out the forces of prejudice; they purge the self-seeking attachments through which we err. They chasten us into renunciatory detachment. They bring us to a sort of passion in one's subject which results from love and which so increases critical sensitivity that one loves truth, and hates error, in and for religion. In a passionate dispassion, the self is cooled even as it is warmed by truth. The fullest existential senses of this still lie ahead of us, but we have already reached the sense in which it operates necessarily in every student of ultimate truths. How do I, in the Buddhist phrase, "course in wisdom"? By ceasing "the course in I-making and mine-making." In this way we have to understand an exchange between Buddha and Subhuti. "Subhuti: 'How is perfect wisdom marked?' The Lord: 'It has nonattachment for a mark.'" (AP 237m) The compassionate *bodhisattvas* are "disinterested demonstrators of the spiritual dharma." (MPCl 336)

1. Disinterested interest

"Truth alone wins and not untruth," cries Sankara, exclaiming that the master virtue in any inquiry is truth. (MuU 3-1-6) Religion too is a scientific inquiry, in the sense that it is a patient effort to see reality as it is, devoid of our bias. "For this was I born, and for this I have come into the world, to bear witness to the truth." (Jn. 18.37) If you are unable to endorse that intention, you cannot undertake religious inquiry, whatever you may come to think of Jesus during the course of that inquiry. "O Truth," joins Augustine, "he is your best servant who endeavors not to hear from you what he wants, but rather wants what he hears." (Co 10-37)

Buddha's opening word to each *bodhisattva*, seated at Vulture Peak, is that, with "being" given over to "enlightenment," remembering the etymology of *bodhi-sattva*, "he should develop the dominant 'I shall come to understand the not yet understood,' the dominant of understanding." (MPCl 1493ff) To see and not to be deceived, *vidyā* instead of *avidyā*, is the goal of Vedanta, "the end of wisdom," which is reached only in "detachment" (*vairāgya*) and "dispassion" (*uparati*). "The highest function of the soul of man," sings Ghazali, "is the perception of the truth; in this accordingly it finds its special delight." (Al 27) Truth is God; idolatry is allegiance to any other god. "I am certain that I am, that I know that I am, and that I love to be and to know." (CG 11-26) Such is Augustine's nonnegotiable passion for truth.

"To thirst after a comprehension of things as they really are," remarks Ghazali during his review of the denominations that he had explored, "was my habit and custom from an early age. It was instinctive with me, a part of my God-given nature." He wanted more than the Christian, Muslim, Jewish, or Zoroastrian education. "What I am looking for is knowledge of what things really are." (D1 21) Augustine recalls, when reading Cicero, "I was delighted by the *Hortensius* because its words stimulated me not to love, seek, and embrace this or that sect but merely to follow wisdom itself, wherever that might lie." (Co 3-8) That attitude not only prescribes a critical reception of other's creeds, but it proscribes a partisan and protective love of one's own creed, difficult as this is to implement. "There is no greater impediment to truth than a life devoted to passion"—"than the interested life," we might almost translate. (VR 3) *My* truth modifies *the* truth with dangerous interest, unless I have broken all my pride in self or creed.

So each saint accordingly steels himself against biasing loves, against self-serving, lest his love for truth be bent by his love for self. Augustine writes: "To wish one's own mistake covered up, even if others are led to error, is to be guilty of a perverse love of self.... I am not an uncritical receiver of my own opinions." (Ep 224) Ghazali recalls, "Never have I spoken to anybody and paid the slightest attention to whether God would reveal the truth through my words or through his." (Ih I, I, 65) "The debator should seek the truth as does the person searching for a lost object, never minding whether it is found by himself or his aides, regarding his companion as a friend not an adversary, and thanking him whenever he points out a mistake." (Ih I, 1, 114a) Buddha warns: "My disciples must not love the Dharma, they must not be attached to the Dharma, they must not show partisanship. They seek only the stopping of suffering, freedom, and true Dharma past vain discussions." (MPCl 65) In religious inquiry, not to ask "mine" or "thine," but only "true" or "false" is to let neutrality avail for the kingdom of God.

"He who begins by loving Christianity better than Truth will proceed by loving his own sect or church better than Christianity, and end in loving himself better than all."[7] Each of our saints knows, with Coleridge, how we hold truth fallibly, despite convictions, and that our grasp of it rapidly worsens unless we are more concerned with *the* truth than with *our* version of it. Any possessiveness that slips into religion is subtly betraying. The search requires calm intellection with the passionate resolution that truth must come, devastating or exacting though its impact be. Few phrases are more participatory and yet few urge more detachment than "truth for truth's sake," for this bids attachment to truth by forbidding all self-interest. Such an unreserved interest in truth emerges as Augustine soliloquizes further over a remark we earlier noted, that he desired to know only God and the soul. "Do you say with certainty that you desire to know the soul and God? *That is my only desire!* Nothing else? *Absolutely nothing!* What? Do you not want to know truth? *As if I could know these except through its means! It is first to be known!*" (S1 1-27)

Religions have what we may call a universal intent. Given that intent, the pragmatic observation that Islam has historically worked for Muslims must not be confused with a truth judgment. When we say a thing like that, we grasp only the personal pole so as to loosen our grasp on the cosmic pole. Truth just *for Muslims* is not their *islamic* concern to submit to ultimate truth; truth just *for Catholics* is not their catholic, universal intent. God or the Absolute, the precedent terminus of the relation, is fixed. The subsequent terminus, our apprehension of God or the Absolute, is flexible. "True knowledge...is conformable to its object and does not depend on the will of man, but merely on what really and unalterably exists." (VS 3-2-21m) "Thus true knowledge of all existing things depends on the things themselves, and hence the knowledge

---

[7] S.T. Coleridge, *Aids to Reflection* (London: George Bell, 1884, p. 66m. Compare a judgment from Doestoevsky: "If anyone could prove to me that Christ is outside the truth, and if the truth really did exclude Christ, I should prefer to stay with Christ and not with truth." *Letters of Fyodor Michailovitch Dostoevsky* (New York: Macmillan, 1914), p. 71.

of Brahman also depends altogether on the thing, i.e. Brahman itself." (VS 1-1-2) "For our minds see this truth, now more, now less, and by this fact confess themselves to be mutable. But truth, itself abiding, does not increase when seen by us in greater measure, nor does it decrease when seen by us in lesser measure." (Lb 2-34) Unless "religion" is viewed as an approximation of what is "real," all our inquiry is only subjective vanity.

This attitude of open inquiry is quite liberating. Among the handsome features of our free spirits is their reckless investment in ultimate truth, across careers which are strewn with their withstood and abandoned beliefs. Ghazali greets the philosophers he is about to review with Aristotle's remark: "Plato is dear to us. And truth is dear too. Nay, truth is dearer than Plato." (In 4; *Nich. Ethics* 1096a) He also finds the truth dearer than the authority of Sunni Islam and plunges with abandon into his Sufi quest. Augustine, another erstwhile Platonist, also finds himself stung by his too-rash Manichean and Academic allegiances, and he is slow to embrace his mother's faith because he is careful in his search for truth, skewed though that is by his vices. He is like the patient who has been so much hurt by poor physicians that he is slow to trust even good ones. (Co 6-4)

Later, though deeply committed, he still remains quite wary: "Indiscriminate faith is not good.... 'Believe not every spirit, but try the spirits, whether they are of God.'" (SL 55) "Indisputably we must be careful lest the mind, believing something it does not see, feign something which does not exist, and so hope for and love that which is false." (Tr 8-4-6) As for Nagarjuna, he repudiates his rearing because he is driven by a thirst for learning, which has since become legendary in his criticism of the inadequate "emptiness" of every dogma, including his own. Sankara's career shows less reversal than the careers of the others, but he too reveals from his earliest renunciation an ear for the beat of a different drummer, which he holds steady against the religious din of India. *Jñāna*, knowledge, with *mokṣa*, freedom, is his version of a liberal education.

But this attitude is at the same time binding, for truth requires what we might call the detachment of an epistemic submission. When "the truth sets you free," there is a *freeing of* the *you* but this comes by a *freeing from* the *you*, which is now irrevocably *committed* to truth. "Knowledge will surrender nothing to man unless man surrenders his all to it." (Ih I, 1, 129) Ghazali's discipline for truth reminds us of a saying by Polanyi, "Thought can live only on grounds which we adopt in service of a reality to which we submit."[8] We tend rather typically to suppose that knowledge results in dominion. The trainer masters his horses, the musician his music, the scientist his world. But that is partly awry even on the empirical level; and such pride goes wholly awry before the sacred, where truth is rather by resignation to whatever reality one's lights best require. We must be bound over to truth.

These bindings and freeings, positively and negatively, are aphoristically put in Rahulabhadra's *Hymn to Perfect Wisdom*, from Nagarjuna's circle.

> "One is indeed bound who sees Thee;
> One who sees not bound is too.
> One again is freed who sees Thee;
> One who sees not freed is too."[9]

2. Faith and open and closed inquiry

But what can we say of faithfulness to a creed? The criticism will perhaps remain that our saints have made much too heavy investments in God, Brahman, and *nirvāṇa*, in Jesus, Muhammad, Buddha, and the Vedic seers, in Scriptures and dogmas. Creedal and institutional orthodoxy and orthopraxy effectively close their inquiries. In religion an individual becomes an ideological captive, as did all our commentators. Their corporate and personal attachments invariably waylay any authentic disinterest. The culprit here is faith, which is usually mind-closing to truth outside traditional channels. Some will also complain that we have not escaped this even in the nonsectarian climate of this study. Do not these epistemic virtues we have commended dispose a person to a classical

---

[8] Michael Polanyi, *The Tacit Dimension* (Garden City, N.Y.: Doubleday, 1966), p. xi.

[9] Edward Conze, ed., *Buddhist Texts Through the Ages* (New York: Harpers, 1964), p. 148.

sort of religion, rather than, say, to a more modern, naturalistic or humanistic form of faith? Have we asked whether truth might be altogether uncongenial to love, faith, purity, and humility? The universe might be hostile or indifferent or absurd, but, blinding us to that fact, adopting the virtues we have been discussing would direct the mind into classically religious results. This sort of complaint brings us back to the earlier lament about our being conditioned for truth.

The modern temper is swift to praise open-mindedness, and to damn closed-mindedness; but reflection on the extremes here reveals that gaining truth is a discretionary opening of the closed and closing of the open mind, conversion of the prejudicial thinking process into the judicial thinking process. If we are in error, except as we become open to that possibility, we cannot replace it by truth. "He who does not doubt does not investigate, and he who does not investigate does not perceive, and he who does not perceive remains in blindness and error."[10] Such an openness must come through humility. On the other hand, to obtain truth is to close the mind, for every affirmation carries with it a thousand negations.

No one who is rationally satisfied with the Pythagorean theorem is any longer altogether open-minded about it, for he or she afterward presumes it to be true. We can demonstrate analytically little or nothing about the world, but we nonetheless arrive at some well-formed synthetic convictions. That the world is round, that the seasons come and go, that my mother has loved me—these are essentially nonnegotiable judgments. So far as we take reason and experience to settle anything, they close the mind. Since the wholly open mind has no judgments at all, it is empty and infantile. At the other extreme, only an omniscient God, whose judgments are perfected, can be rightfully entirely closed-minded. Like the all-out "liberal" who possesses nothing to conserve, perpetually unsettled, or the static "conservative" so unfree as to have nothing alterable, "open" and "closed" are terms with which we can be too reckless.

---

[10] Ghazali, cited in Smith, *Al-Ghazāli*, p. 17.

We must struggle here with partial and double countercurrents, mixedly good and bad. Against prejudice, we do need openness; but on the other side, mature judgment brings closure. The one movement is the obverse of the other. In this light we have to consider the traditional nature of faith. Vis-à-vis the sacred, we find ourselves, our saints tell us, with a falsifying self-enclosing of which we are at first unaware. Religions open up that closed mind by expanding the self and re-enclosing it on the sacred. This is a judicious process which involves the individual, but also one which is corporate, since religions become classic and communal. Few or no persons are up to this alone. In this process, what we have termed a systemic faith is always provisional, leading to the individual's interiorizing of it and passing then to an ontic faith, a seeing of that reality to which the religion points. Then inquiry necessarily increasingly closes. Augustine, Sankara, Nagarjuna, and Ghazali do not afterward hold borrowed belief, but they speak for their institutions only as they have entered into and found them to be existentially profitable and promising. The cumulation of such witnesses as they give is the manifold religious heritage; and no person now comes to faith in the absence of this sort of influence.

These saints to whom we have here been trying to listen converge on faith, love, purity, and humility as virtues which refocus the self on the sacred. The elimination of prejudice only superficially involves a kind of neutral epistemic climate in which we are equally open to all options. The movement we need is not to sheer openness, but rather we must be offset from self-closedness by a gravitation toward the sacred. Unless there is some rebiasing, some other disposing, we will be neutrally indisposed. One affection must dispel another; and we learn to judge not by being insensitive but by trial sensitivities, which these virtues provide. Faith leads to an accumulative inquiry, closing out much but closing in on its object. Faith limits but focuses. On the basis of past insight, partly ours, partly ancestral, it adjusts us for perception. Certain things are of such kind that they are visible only to an instructed vision, and they vanish from sight when looked at with eyes instructed otherwise.

The structure of response becomes unyielding, but so far as one is on the right track, that is a virtue. So long as this also remains critical, it becomes an asset, for such a tropic faith permits richer awareness than is possible under promiscuous, open inquiry. Fitting us for probable response, faith sensitizes and innovates, while the unfocused mind, says Ghazali, is like the unchanneled stream and soon lost. (Ih I, 1, 129) Total openness is not disposition to everything, but to nothing, not sentience but insentience. By contrast, in genuine discovery we do find what we look for; we look further where we have found; we believe a paradigm. Epistemically much more fertile than bare openness is a judicious faith which looks for truth from its likeliest directions. As we shall be saying in the next chapter, which we are now approaching, we must gain a perceptual set to see, and yet such a set biases us to see from our personal and cultural confidences. This is what Augustine means when he exclaims, "Faith opens up the way for the understanding, while unbelief closes it." (Ep 137-15)

Faith prevents *uninterest* and provides *interest*, not only broadly in truth but by specifying a direction of interest, when, inseparably caught in some particular educational process, we risk rewards. Faith alerts us to prospective truths, often inlaid in a traditional, institutional system, a system of faith with its paradigms, as these are judged to have served well in the past and to promise to serve further. Where they are wrong we are misled, where they are right we are led, and so faith may blind and prejudice us, but it may also focus sight and enable judgment. Nothing ventured, nothing gained. This participation we may call faith's heuristic, *attaching thrust.*

But there is more to be said, an opposite truth. Faith prevents *interest* and provides *disinterest.* For all the massive ecclesiastical, liturgical, and historical superstructures here, the form of faith in every system we consult is one designed to open up the person out of self-closure. With denominational differences, the root epistemic trouble everywhere is Luther's *homo incurvatus in se,* man closed in on himself. Though we fear an unjustified closure due to credulity, we have as much and more to fear from the closure caused by self-interested attachment. In the life which aspires to and is supplied with the noetic virtues developed in this chapter, faith closes in on what best opens up the incurved self. Who is less likely to rationalize than those who pursue righteousness, holiness, morality, and love, together with whatever faith seems best to supply them? What closes inquiry more to our detriment than the self that is unwilling to answer the demands for such virtues? What most opens inquiry is not noncommittal open-mindedness, but rather a genuine movement off self-center in the quest for the eternal. Only the faith which seeks understanding permits such an adventure, while skepticism rather closes it off. This kind of participation we may call faith's heuristic, *detaching thrust.*

When critics allege that these virtues condition the saint to find the sacred, we reply: Amen! They do! And for the better not the worse! Like the psychoanalyst who cannot judge the adequacy of psychoanalytic truth until after he has undergone self-analysis, the saint has another kind of psychoanalysis required for larger truth. Religious aspiration is by no means immune from the powerful sway of rationalization. Indeed none are so blind as those who in spiritual disguises seek their own material interests, unless it is those who think they do not have to reckon with their interests at all. What would be the sort of conditionings provided by uninterest in the sacred through self-interest, or by unfaith and secularity, by misplaced trusting, by nontrusting and indifference, by impurity and unrighteousness, by pride and self-confidence?

Precisely against these anoetic illusions, so inimical to our being right, all these higher faiths insist on these noetic virtues so that prejudice can be rectified to judgment, so that the closed mind may be opened for faithful conviction and a proper closing of inquiry. All this is gathered into Augustine's confession: "My weight is my love, by it I am carried wherever I am carried." (Co 13-10) Self-love weights us for error, but these epistemic virtues counterbias us for truth. And that the truth will make us free, rather than crush us, that too is a matter of faith.

Chapter 3. Perception, Conception, and Reality

Having examined the place of *virtues*, we are next ready to consider the place of *words* in the spiritual life, for it is in or through these words, however they may accord with the correspondent religious character, that truth may be thought to lie. They are the score which records the music. But when those who go on religious inquiry speak the truth, they do so pleading that in religion, as in music, we must remember the participant origins of what we can symbolically and linguistically express and record, the experiences for which we can register a score.

Here the concept is a sort of map of a perceptual terrain, such that the *perceptual* and the *conceptual* elements form complementary spiritual poles. Augustine hopes for "the power to conceive and to perceive God." (Tr 8-6) But Nagarjuna advises, "The wise person is not one who conceives because he perceives true reality." (Ka 26-10m) On the placing and misplacing of perceptual truth on a conceptual map, our witnesses differ. Yet there is a similar intent to use without abusing language to lead to ultimate reality, a relative word with which to feel for the absolute.

We first hear the relevant Latin, Sanskrit, and Arabic accounts, and afterward we explore them. Does speech so abstract as to distort the felt intimacy? Alternately, how far is the intuition untrustworthy until tempered by rational criticism? Again, when discourse is publicly shared with other persons who are isolated from the private generating experiences, is understanding possible? If the proposition always has its personal backing, can there be detachment of the known from the knowing participant, a thesis without a life?

I. Through Comprehension to Apprehension

When faith passes from teacher to disciple, the disciple apprehends the real by comprehending the master's religion, moving primarily through *conceptions* into *perceptions*. He gets by speech some idea of what to look for and then finds it. But the upward steps of religious education are a backtracking of the initial spiritual formation, similar to the way in which map-using reverses map-making. Retracing the effect, "religion," the follower secures the cause, "the real." The disciple's pedagogical repetition reverses the existential origin in the innovative master who primarily moves from *percepts* to *concepts*. The pathfinding savant finds something and then tries to express that discovery for others. Let us first consider this instruction in, and recovery of, religious wisdom as reported in our four traditions. Then we will explore the primacy in the master of what the student gains last.

1. *Sravaṇa* through *manana* to *nididhyāsana*
Yagnavalkya, a seer of the *Upanishads*, advises his wife, "The Self, Maitreyi, is to be known. Hear about it, reflect upon it, meditate upon it." "The true realization of the unity of Brahman is accomplished," adds Sankara, only "when these means, viz., *hearing, reflection*, and *meditation*, have been gone through." (BrU 2-4-5m) This becomes a much-treasured threefold means and governs the structure of the very extensive *Brihadāraṇyaka Upanishad* and its *Commentary*. First, there is primarily a hearing of the Vedic witness (*upadeśa*); secondly, there is intensive reasoning over it (*upapatti*), and, third, the conclusion is devoted to meditation (*upāsanā*). (BrU introduction and passim)

(a) Initially there is *hearing* (*śravaṇa*). The term itself immediately points us to language and asks a willing exposure to what
the seers have *said* (*śabda*, speech, revelation), a listening to the
Vedas and *Upanishads*. This is a receptively conceptual stage, with
perceptual activity yet minimal. What we earlier called a systemic
faith operates here, for without a conviction that what is said is
worthwhile, we listen inattentively. So we hearken. But with that,
conceptual preaching begins to strike a responsive perceptual
chord. Whoever has ears to hear begins to hear, hidden in the midst
of this transitory speech, the abiding voice of the Eternal. The
guru, who embodies the faith sought and who keeps words close to
life, communicates with the disciple metaverbally as well as verbally. He actualizes in the present moment the ancient tradition.
But there must be both words and the virtuous guru; no truth can
be educated without a linguistic input from the master to disciple.

(b) Afterward, there is deepening *reflection* (*manana*). The
term literally means "thinking" and indicates its rational character.
That which has been heard is interiorized through vigorous intellectual verification. The tenets of Advaitan belief are tested for
their coherence and the student undertakes the science of the
interpretation of texts (*mīmāṃsā*). Brahman is described as being,
consciousness, bliss (*sat-cit-ānanda*) and is also distinguished doubly with and without attributes, *saguṇa* and *nirguṇa* Brahman. Our
daily experience is analyzed as *māyā*, appearance; as *avidyā*,
ignorance; as *adhyāsa*, superimposition or mirage, by which we
mis-take the world. The empirical self, the *jīva*, is distinguished
from the *ātman*, the eternal Self. The inherited Advaitan world-
view is thought through; or, perhaps better, through it one learns to
think in world view.

Are we reasoning our way into Brahmanic perception? No and
yes. Vedantic religion is a coherent system but only as a viewpoint
from which one looks out, not as a logical system isolated from the
outlook. We do not reason before we enter, but as and when we
enter. We think as we go, testing the concepts against one another,
but that cannot be done except as we test them against their
production of perceptual sense. We are drawn into a sense-making
system; the cognitive element precedes the emotive element, yet
fails unless it can draw emotive support. The puzzle pieces are

mutually supportive of each other and the resulting picture is discovered and endorsed because it maps a terrain that is familiar, or is becoming so with the unpuzzlement. This second stage, *manana*, provides the internal picture coherence. It will not by itself supply the accordant perception by which the picture is composed or makes sense. Thus, in a phrase to which we must return, Sankara posits "reasoning as a subordinate auxiliary of intuitional knowledge." (VS 2-1-6) Sankara's work is almost entirely commentary, in order rationally to appropriate a legacy. But we are not to suppose that reason remains external to the system we explore; we learn how to reason by trying on, by trying out the logic of this *darsana*, this view. In India, philosophy is always a way of *seeing* as well as a way of *thinking*; the thinking is a function of the indexing perception. Analytic reflection is always en route to mystic experience.

(c) This last stage requires constant meditation (*nididhyāsana*). "By meditation we understand the lengthened carrying on of an identical train of thought," progressing on from partial understandings until we are able "to intuit the sense" of what was at first incompletely understood. This is *darsana* or spiritual perception. (VS 4-1-7; 4-1-2) "The knowledge of Brahman...terminates in a perception (*anubhava*), the intuition (*sākṣātkāra*) of Brahman." (VS 2-1-4m) "The science of Brahman is the most brilliant of all the sciences...and can be comprehended only by immediate perception (*pratyakṣa*), like the feeling of pleasure." (BhG 9-2m) The deeper self dissociates from the superficial play of *māyā*, the illusory world, in order to penetrate to the underlying pure and universal consciousness. The differentiation of multiple things ceases when one realizes the nonduality of cause and effect, of you and me, of self and world, of *ātman* and Brahman, and at last there is liberation, *mokṣa*, and wisdom, *jñāna*. "It is a hundred times better to reflect on the truth of Brahman than merely to hear about it from the scriptures. And meditation is a hundred thousand times better than reflection. But complete absorption (*nirvikalpa samādhi*) is infinitely the best of all." (VC 87m) The climax is wholly participatory. The conceptual elements have been altogether exceeded in perceptual experience. But, curiously, this participation is not without detachment, since the ego, having become disinterested in the apparent world, has been loosed from its subjective bias to see reality as it objectively is. Though we shall later worry about the trance states involved here, we are concerned now only with the conviction that the end state is a veridical perception, a steady "seeing" (*vidyā*) through and beyond this world into another level of reality beneath it.

2. *Īmān* through '*ilm* to *ma'rifa*

In retrospect Ghazali reviews the levels that were involved in his progressive *Deliverance from Error* and finds that they are the typical ones in religious education: "Certainty reached by demonstration is knowledge ('*ilm*); actual acquaintance with that (revelational) state is immediate experience (*dhawq*); the acceptance of it as probable from hearsay and trial is faith (*īmān*). These are three degrees. 'God will raise those of you who have faith and those who have been given knowledge in degrees.' " (Dl 62; S 58.11) These degrees of knowledge are the *traditional*, the *intellectual*, and the *experiential*. They correspond roughly to the ways we know someone is at home. We may trust someone else who is an informant, or conclude from our own overhearing of his voice within, or see the person inside his house, although the religious analogue of this seeing is complex and with varying clarity. (Ih III, 1, 115)

(a) *Īmān* is what we have called systemic faith. This does not cover all that Augustine means by *fides*, but only the traditional element. It is borrowed belief. The dominant component here is "following the authority of others" (*taqlīd*), either naively or with some intelligent awareness of what is involved. Ghazali intensely criticizes arrest here where advance is possible, but he knows that there is no other entrance into Islam. There is a child-like state of faith. We naturally accept parents and teachers; we sometimes give ready and rational adherence to mediated truth. The *Revivification*, I, 2, *The Book on the Foundations of Belief*, although it follows I, 1, *The Book on Knowledge*, reveals this chronological and catechetical priority of *īmān* over '*ilm*, the next kind of knowledge to which we turn. In the second book Ghazali is amply creedal, as in the first book he is amply discursive. In both books he tutors and argues. Creedal discussion is the gateway to all the ensuing books which bring us to the religious life (*dīn*).

(b) The second degree, *'ilm*, is intellectual knowledge. Here the root component is a demonstrative logic. The claims of reported prophecy are comprehended, and the result is a science, *kalām*, theology. This knowledge is the kind that Ghazali can put into his books, not the whole of religion, as he repeatedly warns us, but its conceptual transcription. We expect this knowledge to make sense; we search the faith we inherit for its reasonableness, and we estimate critically where we are headed. But, as with Sankara, this is never by a strong, autonomous logic which pushes us within, which forces conclusions upon the nonparticipant. That hope was the *Incoherence of the Philosophers*, exposed in that work. Argument here is rather by a modest, dependent reasonableness drawing us inward, satisfying us with logical coherence as we enter. The sense of Ghazali's use of "demonstration" is not an apodictic proof, but a softer *'ilm* which certainly makes intellectual sense. Religious knowledge is not brought by logical violence, but neither must we violate logic by its coming.

(c) The consummate gift is *intuitive knowledge (ma'rifa)* or *immediate experience (dhawq)*. Both these words attest a perceptual intimacy; *ma'rifa* is personal disclosure and *dhawq* is literally "tasting." "The pleasure of the knowledge of God Most High...is a kind of perception and perception demands a thing perceived and a power of perceiving." (Ih II, 8, 230) This is a "spiritual vision," where "the power of internal perception is like the power of external vision." (NN 46m) The peak moments are of an episodic "passing away" (*fanā'*) into God, but the constant result is an ever-present apprehension of God in a life lived in steady Godward reference, which Ghazali calls trusting (*tawakkul*) and which is fully parallel to the deepest senses of Augustine's *fides*. The prophets are given "revelation" (*waḥy*, major inspiration), while the saints and the pious are called to "awakening" (*ilhām*, minor inspiration); but both have this immediate experience of God.

Ghazali recognizes increasingly sophisticated levels of epistemic awareness. At the simplest is physical sense, sense perception, which we share even with animals. Beyond this there is a mnemonic level, at which sense perceptions are integrated in memory. Then, as may begin in children, the simpler memory advances to a level of discrimination involving inductive logic and habitually correlated perceptions. Still further along, phenomenal knowledge matures with adult intellectual development, including deductive logic and conceptual analysis of discriminated sensations. But, at the highest level, a person's noumenal wisdom comes when "another eye is opened by which he beholds the unseen...and other things which are beyond the ken of the intellect." (Dl 64) Even in the common life persons often make nondiscursive judgments, of which poetic and metrical criticisms serve as examples. We will examine Ghazali's account of these in detail in chapter five. Here it will be sufficient for us to recognize how he finds a suprarational and perceptual element crucial in religion. Ghazali's whole orientation here is gathered into the following passage from the *Niche for Lights*.

"Why should it be impossible that beyond reason there should be a further plane, on which appear things which do not appear on the plane of the intelligence, just as it is possible for the intelligence itself to be a plane above the discriminating faculty and the senses?... Consider the intuitive faculty of poetry, if you will have an example of everyday experience, taken from those special gifts which particularize some men. Behold how this gift, which is a sort of perceptive faculty, is the exclusive possession of some; while it is so completely denied to others that they cannot even distinguish the scansion of a typical measure from that of its several variations.... Were all the professors of music in the world to call a conference with a view to making such a person understand the meaning of this musical sense, they would be quite powerless to do so. Here, then, is an example taken from the gross phenomena which are easiest for you to understand. Apply this now to this peculiar prophetical sense. And strive earnestly to become one of those who experience mystically something of the prophetic spirit; for saints have a specially large portion thereof.

"If you cannot compass this, then try, by the discipline of the syllogism and analogies,...to be one of those who have a knowledge of it scientifically. But if this, too, is beyond your powers, then the least you can do is to become one of those who simply have faith in it.... The province of mystic experience is feeling; of knowledge, ratiocination; and of faith, bare acceptance of the creed of one's fathers." (Ni 82f,m) A Qur'anic verse recalls Moses' experience of God at the burning bush, and how, on his return, "Moses said to his people, I have see a fire, I will bring you tidings of it, or I will give you a flaming brand that you may warm yourselves." (S 27.7) Ghazali first accepted the report of Moses, later he reasoned from the flaming brand. In the end he was warmed, indeed, consumed by the sacred fire. Such an epistemic order is a provocative one, and we will steadily be keeping Ghazali under cross-examination about it.

3. From *scientia* to *sapientia*

Augustine's religious education moves from knowledge (*scientia*) to wisdom (*sapientia*), a distinction he develops in the later books of the *Trinity*. "The intellectual cognition of eternal things pertains to wisdom, but the rational cognition of temporal things belongs to knowledge." (Tr 12-25) All sorts of empirical knowledge form the various sciences, and some are more and some less distant from religious import. Religion too makes use of knowledge, science, empirical facts. Christianity educates by beginning with a temporal, historical base. By believing, the disciple in the earliest stages of faith grasps knowledge; later on as a student his faith rationally cognizes that knowledge; and finally a deepening intellectual faith is elevated to understanding. Understanding is an intellectual recognition of the eternal, and thus "understanding is the reward of faith." (GJ 29-6)

   (a) Using what Augustine calls first-level reason (*ratio inferior*), a person can survey the natural and historical realms to produce empirical knowledge (*scientia*). One paramount result of this is our power as agents in the course of events. A great deal of common faith operates here, as we believe in reason, in sensation, in colleagues, and in predecessors. This sort of science includes also the biblical data, the historical evidence of Israel and Christ, as well as the dogma and tradition of the church. We are formed religiously by discernment through such knowledge which leads on to wisdom. "Christ is our knowledge and the same Christ is also our wisdom. He himself plants in us faith concerning temporal things. Through him we proceed on to himself; we stretch through knowledge to wisdom." (Tr 13-24) Exposed by the church to Christ, satisfied with the integrity of this witness, the disciple gains *scientia*, mediated linguistically, in which *sapientia* is enshrined.

Augustine gives us an example of this double-leveled truth: "There was a man sent from God, whose name was John." John in history with his preaching is *scientia*; to see that he was sent from God is *sapientia*. Scripture mixes both, so that comprehending one we may apprehend the other, learning that "he came to bear witness to the light." (Tr 13-2; Jn. 1.6f) In keeping with Augustine's account of faith which we examined in the previous chapter, historic *scientia* is ever "temporally believed," never technically "understood" or immediately intellected. "There are some matters of belief the sight of which is no longer possible. Christ can never again be seen on the cross. But unless we believe that which once happened and was seen, though there can be no expectation of its happening or being seen again, we can never reach the everlasting vision of the Christ." (Tr 15-49)

(b) With what Augustine calls higher thought (*ratio superior*), we confront eternal reality to gain wisdom (*sapientia*). The paramount character of this is contemplation, a contemplation quite as participatory as action. This is the full Augustinian *understanding* (*intellectus*), which denotes all our mental reckoning with the nonempirical or the nonsuperficial. It contains elements both of comprehending and apprehending. (CI 3) *Sapientia* too is a "tasting," from the Latin root *sapio*, and so Augustine is one with Ghazali in choosing the sensation which provides the nearest analogy to religious learning.[1] "Understand, savor what you have heard, think how great and of what quality this is, and feel greater things about God." (Sm 28-5) The cognitive component is *cogitation*—discursive and conceptual—found both in science

---

[1] Cf. *savor*, Latin *sapor*, and French *savoir*. The root of *scientia* is *scio*, to divide, essentially analytic. Tasting, by contrast, is synthetic and joins knower and known.

and also in wisdom. But wisdom is a perceptive, faithful seeing of the invisible, and involves more than the calculatory reason. Intellection is not what it might superficially appear, simply a logical process. It felicitously combines the conceptual and the perceptual elements. Thus there are in Augustine two powers of mind: *intellectus* adds intuition to the more simply discursive *ratio*. (CG 11-2)

In the *Literal Commentary on Genesis* Augustine recognizes, at the simplest, physical vision which we share with the animals. Higher up, there is mental vision, seeing by the rational life, which (confusingly to a non-Latin reader) Augustine calls "spiritual vision," though he is referring to psychical not to religious facility, to ratiocination and imaging. Lastly, by *intellectual vision* we perceive the nonempirical, including the sacred. For example, in the commandment "Love your neighbor as yourself," I physically see the written words; by recollection and analysis I psychically see what "neighbor" means; by intellection I understand this self-sharing love and its divinity. (LG 13-11-22) Augustine is working here in the Platonic climate, where the mind, arching over sensory data, sees the ideational world, whose prime characteristic is its intelligibility. It is always by our intelligible penetration to the universals behind the superficial data that we find beauty, law, meaning. These never lie there for common sight, whether this is sensory or calculatory. So too, supremely in the highest of intellectual acts, a perceptive faith in God matures out of the traditional belief which we first inherit.

Neither in science nor in wisdom do words communicate truth in the complete absence of the things signified. But temporal things may be readily presented for sensation. There is an easy correlation, and words are more apt and public in science. In wisdom, by contrast, intelligible realities cannot be put on public display. Words find their references more privately, by the intellectual rather than the physical vision. Still, this occurs by using knowledge, for example knowledge about Jesus in history, indicating and disclosing the transempirical. There is here a double pointing: We first learn the empirical references of words, and then we must learn the sacramental references which may be hidden in that *scientia*. Meanwhile, Augustine cannot map all he sees. He laments to noncomprehending, although willing readers, "Oh, if they would only see that internal eternal light, which, having tasted, I have been sorely grieved because I cannot show it to them." (Co 9-10)

We are left no doubt here that the Real is the source of all intelligibility. There is a noumenal Mind lent to and incarnate in the phenomenal world. Language fails us, but not wholly so, and where there is silence, it is "before Him" who is the transcendent, intelligent ground and goal. We come nearest to the ultimate in the *Word of God*, but this is a person not a proposition. This is the mind of Christ. Proportionately more than the others, Augustine is historical and less mystical, since he must first appropriate history through "scientific" thought and then stretch on to wisdom. No other of our saints makes it so clear that the felt spiritual end is pure intelligibility. Indeed, next it may seem that we turn full round in the silence of *śūnyatā*, reached only by the radical repudiation of language. When Augustinian wisdom goes beyond words, we know its direction; but when Madhyamika wisdom goes beyond words, by negation and incoherence, the direction is less clear. But we are ahead of ourselves and must now let Nagarjuna locate for us his relative religion which ferries us to an absolute wisdom.

4. From *samvṛti-satya* to *paramārtha-satya*

Nagajuna's quest for *śūnyatā* is one which empties language of its capacity to describe reality. "Calm, inexpressible through words, exempt from conceptualization, of not many meanings— this is the definition of *tattva* (reality)." (Ka 18-9)[2] Speech "comes to a stop by emptiness,... the domain of thought is dissipated." (Ka 18-5ff,m) But because we are not easily deconceptualized Nagarjuna provides us with a dialectic, a catharsis removing initial dogmas (*dṛṣṭi*) by destroying them critically. Then, when logic has cleared itself away, we realize emptiness. While we are en route, there is the teaching or *dharma* of the *Kārikās*, a view leading to viewlessness, but, when we arrive, Gautama "taught the real *dharma*, the destruction of all views." (Ka 27-30m) That is the

---

[2] Translation by Narain, "Śūnyavāda: A Reinterpretation," p. 324.

Mahā-Prajñā-Pāramitā-Śāstra, the *Science of the Wisdom that Has Gone Beyond*. When Nagarjuna is asked, "If all views are false, what is the ultimate view?", he replies, "That way transcends speech and stops and destroys all activities of mind.... There speech is at an end, thinking has ceased, and that unborn, undying *dharma* is as *nirvāṇa*." (MPCl 45)

(a) The one truth appears to us to be twofold, and our spiritual formation is by the using and undoing of this duality. "The teaching of the *Dharma* by the various *Buddhas* is based on the two truths; namely, the relative (worldly) truth and the absolute (supreme) truth. Those who do not know the distinction between the two truths cannot understand the profound nature (*tattva*) of the Buddha's teaching." (Ka 24-9*i*) At the level of *relative truth* (*saṃvṛti-satya*) we gain knowledge of the common world, which is the proper domain of language. But no amount of rationality will take us to any absolutes. Like Kant's first *Critique*, Nagarjuna's *Kārikās* find metaphysically incoherent and dismantle all the categories that empirically serve us so well: change, permanence, identity, causation, motion, space, time, sensation, existence, nonexistence, and the self. Yet in the midst of these empty doctrines, there is a curious one which, although it is as void as all the rest, is spiritually cleansing. The doctrine of *śūnyatā*, creedlessness, presses on to truth beyond, not to describe it but only to point there. Having first destroyed these secular forces that presume to know too much, Nagarjuna turns his dialectic next against all the sacred propositions, and, concluding the *Kārikās*, finds even the holy Buddhist truths, those about the *tathāgata*, and *nirvāṇa*, to be also discursively empty.

Earlier in his discussion, *śūnya*, "empty," is roughly a synonym for the great Theravadin watchwords: *anitya*, the impermanent nonultimate world; *anātman*, the fluxing unreal self, and *duḥkha*, the disease of the common striving for pleasures; and so, negatively, *śūnya* empties phenomena. But later on, Nagarjuna's innovation in Buddhism is to force *śūnya* to serve also as a predicate of *nirvāṇa*, of Buddha, of *prajñā*; and here its meaning shifts to verbal emptiness, to the failure of words. "The inexpressibility of all *dharmas* (truths) is their emptiness." (MP 410) Lastly, positively in the *Commentary*, if hardly in the *Kārikās*, *śūnya* hints of a resplendent and indeterminate nonduality. Thus Nagarjuna teaches that even Buddhist conceptuality, to say nothing of any other, is empty, that is, discursively fails of the absolute. Did not Buddha say so? Nevertheless, we have first to exercise these Buddhist truths and in due course to collapse them for a perception beyond.

R.H. Robinson puts the Madhyamika genius this way: "Emptiness is not a term outside the expressional system, but is simply the key term within it.... Like all other expressions, it is empty, but it has a peculiar relation within the system of designations. It symbolizes nonsystem, a surd within the system of constructs."[3] So "the highest sense of the truth is not taught apart from practical behavior." "The transcendental is not preached save *vis-à-vis* the empirical." (Ka 24-10m)[4] "Saying 'emptiness' is for the purpose of conveying knowledge." (Ka 22-11m) "Strictly, the undivided is the unutterable; but the unutterable is yet uttered on the mundane level in a nonclinging way." (VR 251m) Positively put, here heavenly treasure is hid in an earthen vessel, and the conceptual vessel must be shattered before the perceptual treasure can be had. Or, negatively put, when medicine is given to purge the stomach, after it has worked, it must itself be expunged, else it will make the patient sick anew.[5] So all creeds, and lastly the Buddhist, must be expurgated. Only the thoroughly emptied patient is healed.

(b) So far as language is concerned, we are powerless to denote this healing *absolute truth (paramārtha-satya)* except by a nonconnoting emptiness. So our heads are set swimming; but that is the point of the regimen, when, discursively dizzy, we are stopped on the threshold of *prajñā*. Through the vacuity or *śūnyatā* of phenomena, we rise to the undivided *śūnyatā* of the real. That "emptiness" is first ontological, meaning that the real is indeterminate, void; but then it is semantic, meaning that words about the real are devoid of meaning. Here deconceptualization destroys itself and only silence remains. "The death of thought is the birth of *prajñā*, knowledge

---

[3] R.H. Robinson, *Early Mādhyamika in India and China*, p. 49m.

[4] The first translation is by Streng, the second by Narain, p. 335.

[5] The analogy is from the *Ratnakūṭa Sūtra*, see Stcherbatsky, p. 50.

devoid of distinction."[6] "Deep, O Lord, is this perfection of wisdom, hard to see, hard to understand, inaccessible to reasoning and discursive thought, calm, subtle, delicate, to be felt only by the learned and discerning." (MP 359)

This emptiness does not mean that we know nothing, but that we know all. The *Great Sūtra* calls it repeatedly "the knowledge of all modes." But while perceptually absolute and vast, this wisdom is conceptually nil. It is first convicted of and then abandons dualizing sophistry (*prapañca*), so that the converted come to taste sheer nonverbal intuition. "The *dharma* that is called *prajñā-pāramitā* is most profound, difficult to comprehend. In it all thoughts and all activities of mind come to an end, there is not the clinging even to *prajñā-pāramitā*, all kinds of speech come to an end, and therefore it is called Peace. With the realization of the excellent taste of this *prajñā* one realizes a permanent fulfilment of heart, and there is no more any hankering left." (MPCv 118f,a)

We must tear up our maps not only when arriving but in order to travel, though there is one "nonmap," the emptiness of all maps, through the use of which we must arrive. The land of our arrival is absolutely unmappable, and final wisdom, *prajñā*, is mapless being there. Needless to say, those of us who are not yet there, along with any saints who find that maps inform their arrival and intelligent being there, will insist on Nagarjuna's cross-examination. But no one will doubt that Nagarjuna's inquiry is spiritual to the core.

II. The Evasive Perceptual: Intimate and Expansive

We cannot map without a journey, and those who first speak have been there. This outflowing of verbal knowledge—the saint's discourse welling up from springs beneath—reverses the flowing in of learning when a disciple hearkens to a master. At the corporate level in traditional faith, every doctrinal heritage flows down from springs upstream. But language production always marks less than is known, owing both to an intimacy and to an expansiveness.

---

[6] Murti, *Central Philosophy of Buddhism*, p. 140m.

Much of life cannot cross our lips. We must now try to get some feeling for what we cannot specify, an account of these primitive and pervasive elements which are missing in speech and why they cannot be registered there.

1. The primitive percept

Metrical perception, Ghazali was just saying, underruns the intelligent capacities of discourse about it. If a nonauditor were to be present at a conference of professors of music, he would find baffling their chatter about tune, lyric, meaning, and rhythm. "Mark how extraordinary is this intuitive faculty in some others, insomuch that they produce music and melodies, and all the various grief-, delight-, slumber-, weeping-, madness-, murder-, and swoon-producing modes! Now these effects occur strongly in one who has this original, intuitive sense. A person destitute of it hears the sounds just as much as the other, but the emotional effects are by him only very faintly experienced, and he exhibits surprise at those whom they send into raptures or swoons." (Ni 83) Those are *primitive* modes—to be glad, sad, mad, sleepy, weepy, dizzy; and not incidentally are they allied with music. We can name them, but the word reflects a remembered impression. Ghazali would have enjoyed a remark made by Louis Armstrong. When asked to define jazz, Armstrong replied, "If you have to ask, I can't tell you."

Time, continues Augustine, is something we can undergo, but are able to put into words inexactly. We may meter time and philosophize over it. (Einstein did this in relativity theory with more success than Augustine could have dreamed.) But all this discourse illuminates only those who first perceive time's passage. All the spoken words are derived from a sensed *duration*. This derivation of a concept from a percept is an instance of a general principle. "There are but few things that we state properly (*proprie*), and many that we state improperly, but what we mean is understood." (Co 11-26) If this is so even for temporal things, how much more is it so when we touch eternity. In a rather variant vein, we are talking about Nagarjuna's conceptual emptiness over all the categories which we so regularly perceive—change, identity, causation, motion, time, space, existence, the self. It is only with some incoherence that we can fix these in words! Those who recognize these terms as names for the stormy philosophical disputes of many centuries, West and East, will have already some taste of this Nagarjunan emptiness.

At the level of *sense* perception, Augustine is here pointing out a sort of bedrock level of earthy experience. Even an empiricist, unless a completely skeptical one (a phenomenalist), will grant the objectivity of our perceptions here. Our impression is *of* something. But it is not easy to express these sensory experiences in words. The linguist is weakest with smell and taste. We do not name dozens of savors that we can perceptually recognize; many that we do name—wines and teas, for instance—we can scarcely further describe. Our capacity to correlate words and experiences becomes stronger with touch and sound. But the ornithologist will find it impossible discursively to separate the calls of warblers, although he knows them well. We can best describe what we see, though an aspiring botanist will grope for a fully adequate taxonomic terminology. Beyond this he finds the picture worth a thousand words.

We can make and use nonverbal maps of various kinds which scan a spectrum from highly abstract diagrams and graphs to photographs which more or less reproduce elsewhere in time and space the original sensations. The closer these come to the photograph, the less conceptually mediate and the more perceptually immediate they become, the less maplike and more like the memory of being there. With the yellow of a lemon, or the smell of sassafras, or the taste of pineapple, we merely name such things, point, and invite the experience. We could never really learn what the moon looks like, says Sankara, merely through the vision of someone else who reports it. (VC 42)

At the level of sacred perception, we leave the earthly and reach the divine. Sense perception is animate, shared even with the beasts, but sacred perception is angelic, reserved for saints and shared hardly with insensitive persons. Any who doubt that there is such a thing as a religious percept should ponder that not all perception is of bare sensory things. We undoubtedly perceive beauty, value, rightness, love, fear, the humorous, the tragic; and surely, if problematically for the empiricist, we perceive space, time, causation, identity, and the world. Similarly there is no obvious reason to think that some persons do not perceive the numinous. Religious impulses are held, almost crudely, at a sort of gut level. To say, "I feel..." is not at that level of use to report a loosely founded opinion. To feel is to know that the needle is sharp, or the landscape of beauty, or the person of worth, or the Eucharist sacred. But the intimate truth has not yet been conceptually processed, and we may be reticent in our linguistic transcriptions and unsure of our capacity to bind and commit others to what we have felt. Just this *taste* of truth, like that of raspberries, is real enough, even though it strains our talk of truth. Besides using the imagery of taste, we also come repeatedly to resort to our richest organic mode of sensitivity and speak of the religious perspective as, simply, a *view*.

"For my part," writes Augustine as though he were speaking for all, "I am nearly always unsatisfied with what I can speak. For I desire something better, which I often inwardly enjoy before I begin to unfold my thought in spoken words. But when I find my powers of expression inferior to inner apprehensions, I am sorely disappointed that my tongue has not been able to answer the demands of my mind.... This arises basically because intellectual apprehension floods the mind, as it were, with a sudden flash of light, while the expression of it in speech is a slow, drawn-out process of a vastly different nature." (CI 3) This "inward word" is recessed in the "memory," a rich Augustinian storehouse of non-verbal knowledge, over the surface of which rational cognition operates.

To a question about the character of the religious impulses, Ghazali replies that the nature of these impulses "cannot be answered in writing and in speech. If you attain the religious state you will know what they are; and if you do not attain it knowing them is impossible; for whatever is known by experience cannot be described in words, as with the sweetness of the sweet or the bitterness of the bitter." (Ay 62a) Names here only recall judgments which are too primitive to be given more than ostensive definition. How comic it is to try to discuss the comic in the absence of any sense of it! How tragic it is to forget when speaking that the sacred presence is too elemental for speech! This is what prompts the Madhyamika saint to exclaim, "Not in letters is the perfection of wisdom.... The enlightenment of the Tathāgatas cannot be talked about, it is incommunicable." (MP 210)

2. The pervasive percept

The religious impulse is not only too *primitive* for words; it is also too *pervasive* for words. We are often quite adept in our capacities to recognize overall configurations, yet such a facility resists analysis. We meet a friend and recall the character of her face and the tone of her voice, knowing through decades a persistent pattern, although we can hardly say how. Our best computers are largely inept at the recognition of what are called "facies," aspectual tones. Perhaps this is owing to the poor programming of fuzzy sets or to a computer's electronic limitations. Nevertheless, persons do this readily. We respond holistically to "my country," to "the truth," to "the church," or to "modernity." Often when dealing with these terms we desperately need a good Socratic analysis, but even after that, concepts such as "the good" and "the just" will have to be shaped by an extensive living through them.

We need now to recognize that in religious awareness a *pervasive* gestalt constructs and integrates all the contributing components. Perhaps in the case of Nagarjuna's and Sankara's dissolving of world appearances, we can rather say that it "destructs" and dissolves them. Such a depth structure is required for intuition, but it is necessarily absolute and uncomprehended, too suffused for conceptual fixing. Later, albeit inadequately, these do become paradigmatic concepts, but earlier they are arch-percepts that edit and govern thought.

"What is that through which, when it is known, everything else becomes known? Brahman." (MuU 1-1-3m) As we hear whole melodies, not single notes, so specific perceptions take their tonality from the Brahmanic whole. "Various particular notes are not heard apart from the whole, but in the total sound all its notes are heard.... So, through the knowledge of the Self, Pure Intelligence, all things and beings are known." (*BrU* 2-4-8f,*p*) "All beings as well as the whole of this universe are woven in Me, as a cloth in the warp, as clusters of beads on a string." (*BhG* 7-7m) Brahman is the universal melody, the weave of the cloth, the string through the beads. But all this is ill said, and nondual wisdom is finally felt, too monist for words. "Brahman is beyond speech and thought." (BhG 13-12) Brahman is not in a genus, where words may apply, for words only delimit apparent things in the world. The genus and the word have edges, but Brahman is nonspecific, the overarching All, the receptacle, the ground. "Brahman, which is the Light of Lights, is alone true, and everything else its modification—a modification that exists only in name, having speech as its support." (MuU 2-2-10)

Sūnyatā supplies the believer with a similarly pervasive gestalt. "It is by keeping oneself in harmony with the apprehension of the complete *śūnyatā* that one keeps oneself in line with the knowledge of all forms." (MPCv 266m) "When truly comprehended, the determinate entities, form, etc., enter into *tathatā* (suchness); there all things are of one nature devoid of particular natures." (MPCv 256m) "Even as it is the very nature of water to flow down, by reason of which all waters return to the great ocean, blend, and become of one essence, just in the same way all determinate entities, all natures general and particular, return ultimately to fundamental reality (*dharma-dhātu*), blend, and become of one essence with it.... The mind seeks the true nature of things and thus gets to *tathatā*." (MPCv 264m) When this becomes explicitly absolutist in the *Commentary*, we may grow suspicious that Nagarjuna has been reunderstood by later Madhyamika followers. But so far as it is anything at all past silence, even the less entified *śūnyatā* of the *Kārikās* is that space, an empty void, where all the phenomena take place.

Even there, an interpreter like Stcherbatsky can find an emptiness of the parts cohering in a silent Integral Whole, a curious positive summing up of differentiated zeros.[7] Actually, however, Nagarjuna's dissolution, like that of the earlier Buddhists, usually works in a reversed fashion, dismantling the whole into its parts

---

[7] Stcherbatsky, *The Conception of Buddhist Nirvāṇa*, p. 43.

and the parts into fluid emptiness. In either case, the consummate character of the end state vision remains, for Nagarjuna's *śūnyatā* vision undoubtedly makes *saṃsāra* and *nirvāṇa* cohere, and ineffably so. "When emptiness works, then everything in existence works. If emptiness does not work, then all existence does not work." (Ka 24-14m) A synthetic percept, *śūnyatā* empties out all the analytic views that pretend to be absolute, when they are merely relative and finally unreal parts. Beyond, in *prajñā*, the real is felt to be too enveloping and too undifferentiated for words.

Ghazali can be found thinking along parallel lines. "I have never seen a single object, but first I saw Allah. I only see objects in and through Allah. I see Allah in and through those objects. He is with everything every moment and by him does everything appear." (Ni 66f,a) "The Light is the visible One by means of whom all visibility exists." (NN 123) The ineffable passing into God which the Sufi seeks is not merely episodic but flows into a residual contemplation (*mushāhada*) or an apprehension (*mulāḥaza*) that pictures God in all, and all in God. Ghazali's use of meter and music as an analogy also suggests a scanning capacity which is required for listening to God, and here again the sweetness of trusting in divine union (*tawakkul* in *tawḥīd*) is both too intimate and too consummate for words.

Augustine is similarly fond of saying that God is nearer and surer than self, friends, or everyday things. He can say this so confidently that a bafffled nonbeliever might even worry about the church father's sanity. He means that God is his abiding gestalt, without which there is only perceptual vanity. Of themselves fugitive things do not make any intelligible sense, though they may make scientific sense. Calculations may succeed but all evaluations will fail, until we *understand*, that is, discern the immutable God midst the mutable world. "God is the intelligible light in and from and through whom all things intelligibly shine, if they intelligibly shine at all." (S1 1-3) In his favorite epigram, God supplies *form*, *order*, and *disposition*. (LG 4-3-7ff) Contrasting with his intimate, inward look in the *Confessions*, the *City of God* shows this expansive, outward look. All the historical creation is brought within the scope of the heavenly kingdom.

God is the only principle adequate to explain the presence of wisdom in the human mind. All argument for God is underrun by this arching divine impulse, which is too deeply dominant and in the Platonic sense too ideational for speech. Augustine knows a sort of depth grammar which he cannot bring to the surface. "I found no form of words adequately corresponding to such understanding as I had reached—though even in that understanding I am aware of more endeavor than success." (Tr 15-45) We "speak of subjects which cannot altogether be expressed in words as they are conceived in the mind, while even our thought falls very short of him about whom we think and it is unable to comprehend him as he is." (Tr 5-1)

"He is before all things, and in him all things hold together." (Col. 1.17) Augustine would have endorsed a remark by Wittgenstein, "How everything hangs together, is God."[8] Light is a universal symbol of the absolute because we see it and everything else with it. As empirical perceptions are *in* space and time, so spiritual perceptions are *in* God, *śūnyatā*, Brahman. We do not know space and time only inferentially from moving things; we rather know them experientially. We do have a sense *of* space and time, pervasively, primitively. So too, and more so, it is puzzling to specify just how we perceive God, Brahman, *śūnyatā*; nevertheless the saint has a sense *of* these ultimates. This comes with an immediate, consummate perception such that, while discourse rises from it, speech fails to capture the seen. It only calls to memory, whether for criticism or re-enactment, the scene the percipient has lived through.

The pervasive, governing character of a gestalt here may be crudely illustrated by the kind of drawings which are employed in the psychology of perception. The beholder may see, alternately, a vase or two faces in profile. He may see alternately a stacked set of six or seven cubes, or a beautiful girl oscillating with an old hag. Someone ponders what is at first a senseless black and white rorschach, then awakens to a portrait suggesting classical represen-

---

[8] L. Wittgenstein, *Notebooks, 1914-1916* (New York: Harpers, 1961), August 1, 1916.

tations of Christ. In each case, the regnant percept controls the way the subsidiary lines, curves, and spaces go together. If one switches the master mesh, the subsidiaries regroup, systematically reperceived. Here *seeing* is *seeing as*. But the scheme itself is read out of, not into the data (except perhaps in the last example). Subsequent argument is apology. The proposition "Her nose is upturned" makes sense only if a person can see the young woman. So far as any concept takes its significance from this experience alone, statements will approach irrationality in the degree to which the indexing perception is missing. If someone says, "That hag has a ziptic look," whoever misses seeing the hag cannot know the meaning of "ziptic." In the case of aspiring observers, concepts to some extent precede percepts, as when a tutor invites us to look for a "hag." But to see is not to invent, only to find, and when the concept triggers the perception, the perception at once becomes dominant.

But are these four master lights of all our seeing, recommended by our different saints, uniform? Perhaps Allah, Brahman, God the Father of Jesus Christ, and *śūnyatā* are multiform? Are they compatible? That inquiry still lies ahead of us, though the psychological analogy which we have just used foreshadows trouble. What if *śūnyatā* or Brahman orchestrate the world for some other melody than we hear in God? Worse, what if the theist can hear nothing at all of the Eastern harmonies? What if the Advaitan and the Madhyamika saint hear dualizing discordances in Allah and the Father of Jesus Christ? Then will not any efforts at ecumenical conversations run athwart of a perceptual discrepancy? That two of us have ineffable perceptions—one tastes strawberries, the other ginger— does not mean that we have the same perceptions. But for the present we are only identifying this impressive *scenic* character which is expressed by all the variously paradigmatic and presiding predicates: *nondual, gracious, absolute, loving, empty, indeterminate, one, infinite, sat-cit-ānanda, unitive, communicant*. All these terms inexactly name judgments of lyric, subliminal timbre.

III. *Expression and Impression: the Escaping Inscape*

The map never tells it like it is. Even a geographic map abstracts from both the intimacy and the pervasiveness of the actual world, to err as it informs. Music never freezes into the score. Even more so, religious words, forming spiritual maps, involve a kind of "impressive expression," such that their expression never altogether registers the impression. We now continue, from another direction, to explore this refusal of experience to rest immediately in any words. We will first use a passage from Ghazali to distinguish intellectual study from existential experience, next explore the spiritual significance of silence, and finally analyze the forcing of language into religious paradigms. The sum of this inquiry is that the spiritual life springs out of a kind of *escaping inscape*. That is, it catches an inwardly significant quality of reality which is known only by blended observation and introspection, and quite difficultly expressed.

1. Intellect and experience
"When I had finished with these sciences (of philosophy and logic)," reports Ghazali, "I next turned with set purpose to the method of mysticism. I knew that the complete mystic 'way' includes both intellectual belief and practical activity.... The intellectual belief was easier to me than the practical activity. I began to acquaint myself with their belief by reading their books.... I thus comprehended their fundamental teachings on the intellectual side, and progressed, as far as is possible by study and oral instruction, in the knowledge of mysticism. It became clear to me, however, that what is most distinctive of mysticism is something which cannot be apprehended by study, but only by immediate experience (*dhawq*—literally 'tasting'), by ecstasy and by a moral change.

"What a difference there is between *knowing* the definition of health and satiety, together with their causes and presuppositions, and *being* healthy and satisfied! What a difference between being acquainted with the definition of drunkenness—namely, that it designates a state arising from the domination of the seat of the intellect by vapours arising from the stomach—and being drunk! Indeed, the drunken man while in that condition does not know the definition of drunkenness nor the scientific account of it. The sober man, on the other hand, knows the definition of drunkenness and its basis, yet he is not drunk in the very least. Again the doctor, when he is himself ill, knows the definition and causes of health and the remedies which restore it, and yet is lacking in health. Similarly there is a difference between knowing the true nature and causes and conditions of the ascetic life and actually leading such a life and forsaking the world. I apprehended clearly that the mystics were men who had real experiences, not men of words, and that I had already progressed as far as was possible by way of intellectual apprehension. What remained for me was not to be attained by oral instruction and study but only by immediate experience and by walking in the mystic way." (D1 54f)

Obviously sincere, is Ghazali profound or confused? When we say that a petrologist knows (about) rocks, the preposition is immaterial to meaning. But it begins to matter when we remark that the jockey knows (about) horses. Double senses clearly emerge, owing to inwardness, when we say that a physician knows (about) a disease. "Knows (about) medicine," or "knows medicine" we say, inattentive to the "about" so long as reference is to mastery of a science. But the knowledge of illness is no longer a matter of science when the query is about the qualitative life-impact of cancer. Physicians may be sensitive to that effect too; but such medicine is an art, when by sympathy the doctor is "there" with the suffering patient. In these areas, the preposition "about" tends to mark off a second-level knowledge.

External knowledge may be had with high genius, as with medicine. But a "theory about" is always detached and nonparticipant, and thus only approximates the experienced reality. Further, tomorrow the theory may be altered, although the experience itself remains unchanged. Consider Ghazali's now quaint "scientific account" of drunkenness—fumes rising from the stomach and clouding up the brain! From one point of view, illness and inebriation may seem to be exemplary cases where we can know a process behaviorally in order to cure and prevent misfortunes, and where we can disregard any accompanying inwardness. If so, we might retort to Ghazali: A theory of alcoholism is far superior to being drunk! Heaven help the physician who must catch a disease to cure it!

But Ghazali has not chosen his analogies lightly. He has another point of view. He desires "to set forth upon the Sufi path and to drink of their wine."[9] It is the ecstasy and exhilaration, not the hallucination which makes drinking a relevant analogy. Ghazali elsewhere carefully specifies sober reason as needed to correct errant Sufi intoxication. Using medical analogies frequently, Ghazali speaks of salvation as healing for the diseased. Nagarjuna writes of suffering (*duḥkha*) and its extinction (*nirvāṇa*), and Augustine comforts and blesses those who mourn. Drunkenness and disease, sobriety and health, pain and pleasure have been selected rather carefully as helpful secular analogues because these are notoriously impossible to describe to those who have not experienced them. So too is the mystic perception.

Still, such a move inward may invite the further retort that the participant gains his authority at the cost of retreating to subjectivity, a pyrrhic victory. Believers claim some experience, for example, an experience of God. The subjectivity of their experience may be undenied, while the objectivity of their experience is denied, and what can the believer then say? But here is the nub of the argument: Minimally, the claim is that the objective world makes sense under a gestalt which escapes transfer to the inexperienced student, who is a poor judge of a missing perception. If God is mirrored in the healthful, exhilarant, purified soul, then perhaps such souls do have a privileged and nontransferable access to God.

To use a familiar distinction, *know-how* superintends *know-that*. The education of the Christian, says Augustine, is like learning to walk. "It is as if a man wishing to give rules for walking should warn you not to lift the rear foot before you set down the other one, and then should describe in careful detail the way you ought to move the hinges of the joints and knees. What he says is true and

---

[9] Related by al-Subki (d. 1370), cited in Smith, *Al-Ghazālī*, p. 18.

one cannot walk in any other way. But people find it easier to walk by executing these movements than to attend to them while they are going through them or to understand them when they are told about them." (CD 2-55) Not one bicyclist in a hundred can tell what he is doing when he rides, nor has one in a thousand a scientific theory about it. (Tending to fall, the wheel is veered to bring centrifugal force counter to gravity.) Yet the rider, responding appropriately, has "learned" something about force and mass. Kinesthetically, a player "judges" a fly ball. If the coach talks to him about how to do it better, his criticism is tributary to and returns to enrich the act. Similarly, when religion first rises to speech, it does not go straightway to the detached proposition, but rather surrounds religion with music and rite, law and love, art and sacrament, chant and meditation, all of which supply syntax with a perceptual precedent. When Martha Graham was asked what a dance meant, she replied, "Darling, if I could have told you, I wouldn't have had to dance it for you." Something like that is at work here; at least these saints are doubtful of any talking to or by those who are unwilling to dance.

Language is willy-nilly conceptual, for propositions can be unfolded from every speech act. Still, there is a sort of language which always hovers near an enactment of it. What if our religious traveling through the world should be like walking, or cycling, or dancing through it, only in infinitely more depth? There is something oversimple about likening religion to experiencing a salty taste, and we should not forget that our doctors put religion beyond, not on this side of, intellection. There is no religion without discourse, and our language feeds and makes possible religious experience. Still, this analogy with taste is where we must begin, and where we must return. In religion, as Aristotle remarked of ethics, "the decision rests with perception."[10]

2. Inward to silence

Augustine finds present in genuine spirituality what he calls an "inward word,"en route to a still deeper spiritual silence. Some-

---

[10] *Nichomachean Ethics*, 1109b.

what like the flesh which the divine Word embodied in Jesus, our speech is a bodily sign of our mental thought, making possible communication and criticism. "It is possible therefore to understand what a word means, not only before it is spoken aloud, but even before the images of its sounds are remembered in thought. For there is a 'word' which belongs to no language. When we speak what we know, there must be born out of the knowledge retained in our memory a word which corresponds to the knowledge from which it is born. The word spoken in our heart is not in Greek or Latin or any other language. But, when we need to convey it to those to whom we speak, we employ some sign with which to indicate it. So the word in its outward sounding is a sign of the word that is inwardly luminous. To this latter the name of 'word' more properly belongs, but when spoken aloud, the word is not spoken as it really is." (Tr 15-19f,a) Knowledge may be lodged in memory which is not being presently recalled, for instance, on an occasion when the musician is discussing geometry. When we do call it to thought, for example, when the musician turns to discuss harmony, we diffract an inner meaning. In theology, we are "speaking of things that cannot be spoken, that we may somehow say what we cannot at all say fully." (Tr 7-7) Augustine laments to himself, "You too have been able to perceive it, although you could not and cannot adequately express in speech the truth which you have but scarcely seen." (Tr 15-50)

Augustine is perhaps insufficiently aware of the dependence of thought upon language. Still, recent researches have revealed a wide sweep to nonverbal understanding. Is the taste of cherries more like raspberries than that of cheese? Her face most resembles which of her sisters? Is that melody from Wagner? Should I take this pitch or let the ball go by? Augustine notices how we may try to recall a forgotten name and be able to reject false candidates, although we do not know the correct one consciously. It remains subliminal in the memory. (S1 2-34) Or, consider Blake's remark that "He who does not prefer form to color is a coward." None of these thoughts proceeds without words, but none is right there in the words either. This is even more true in judging the loving, the right, the beautiful, the Christ, the *Logos*. Our faculty of *intellec-*

tion using what Augustine calls the *superior mind* advances over our capacity for verbal *ratiocination* with the *lower reason*. Religious thought, like the deepest levels of much everyday thought, has a sort of depth syntax, or depth grammar, which runs under and runs ahead of our verbal skills. Though such skills may be necessary, they are insufficient for it.

Theology, pleads Ghazali, is like a precious fruit with a double husk. The outer husk, its verbal expression, is all that the detached observer sees. The inner husk is reached by those who probe further and gain a partial entrance, for example, when a participant wrestles in faith with what the words of a traditional creed mean. Protected by these husks, the kernel itself is tasted only in *tawḥīd*, unification with God. What is seemingly a public outer husk hides at the same time that it identifies. It covers and circumscribes the inner pith. (Ih I, 1, 85) When Luther lectures on the *Psalms*, again and again he laments in honesty, "I do not yet sufficiently understand this." But he comes at length, reflecting over the "*in iustitia tua libera me,*" to an experience of grace and reformation. Then he exclaims, "Then I understood the *grammatica*, and I truly tasted the *Psalms*."[11]

By this approach we can empathize with the even deeper Eastern preferences for silence. Sankara can write commentary at great length, but he also knows that the saint ends in silence. "Bahva, being questioned about Brahman by Vashkalin, explained it to him by silence. He said to him, 'Learn Brahman, O friend,' and became silent. Then, on a second and third question, he replied, 'I am teaching you indeed, but you do not understand. Silent is that Self.'" (VS 3-2-17) The highest Brahman is *nirguṇa*, without predicates; that is to say, we are reduced to silence there. The *Great Perfection of Wisdom Sūtra* is one vast sermon from Buddha, delivered at Vulture Peak. But again, in lieu of a sermon there, Buddha holds up a flower, a silence that Nagarjuna much celebrates. "Though, Lord, you have not uttered a single word, all the votaries have been satisfied by the teaching of the doctrine." (CS 1-7)[12] Thus the

---

[11] M. Luther, *Werke* (Weimar: H. Böhlaus, 1883), III, 257; III, 14; *Tischreden* (Weimar: H. Böhlaus, 1912), V, # 5247. See Ps. 71.2.

[12] Translation by Muri, *Central Philosophy of Buddhism*, p. 282.

śūnyatā symbol, an empty, open circle, conceptually nil, descriptively zero, symbolizes so well this silence, the final meaning of emptiness.

Ghazali cannot take his language about Allah literally. Even using the blessed names of God, we know by means of light veiled with darkness. When all the veils are gone, Ghazali can predicate nothing whatever of the God he then beholds. Correcting a Muslim tendency toward Qur'anic literalism, he reminds us that persons imitate God by having an inner speech which is silently precedent to Arabic or any tongue. (Ni 94f) Augustine does not quite reach Eckhart's aphorism that "He speaks best of God who in the fullness of his inner riches can best keep silence."[13] Still, Augustine says of the apprehension of God that "God must not even be described as unspeakable (*ineffabilis*), since by the very use of this term, something is spoken, and thus we are led to a curious contradiction, by which the unspeakable is and is not what can be spoken of, a contradiction rather to be avoided by silence than explained by speech. Yet God, though nothing can be worthily spoken of him, accepts the service of the human voice, and wills us to rejoice in praising him with our words." (CD 1-6)

Augustine's silence before God is in some ways near and in some ways far from Nagarjuna's silent emptiness. "Those who describe in detail the Buddha, who is unchanging and beyond all detailed description—those, completely defeated by description, do not perceive the *tathāgata*." (Ka 22-15m) "About the absolute (*paramārtha*), the saints remain silent!" (Ca 138m) Alike, all our saints detect the error of literalism, which supposes that the concept maps the percept without distortion, and that the percept in turn reproduces without loss the real. They know that any felt sense of the sacred is rough-hewn if it is at all cut into *sūtra*, myth, symbol, poetry, vision, parable, history, *mantra*, hymn, or precept. The most studied and thoughtful of our phenomenal, verbal expressions stretch but loosely over our noumenal encounters.

At the same time, our saints do have unlike gestalts which control

---

[13] *Meister Eckhart*, trans. R.B. Blakney (New York: Harpers, 1941), p. 37, quoting Dionysius.

intellection, a fact which, already foreshadowed, will increasingly beset us from here onward in this study. To take only two of them, Nagarjuna's real repudiates speech, silences thought, and his intellection is extinguished in *nirvāṇa*. But Augustine's silence is before the intelligent ground of all thought; he would "perceive by pure intelligence the immutable substance of God." (Ep 181) Augustine does require a transverbal intellection which "oversees" verbal conception; but speech is redeemed and made a helpful but inexact sign of the divine intelligibility. By our thinking we image God, not less than we do by our loving and by our righteousness. Thought too is essential in the Platonic *ideal*. The resulting symbols are, in Nagarjuna's hands, the subliminal *śūnyatā* of *śūnyatā*, sheer silence, which is not without love and rightness; and in Augustine's hands, the supraliminal *Logos*, the Word of God, reserved to an incarnate Person, just because it escapes propositional expression.

Our perspectives on language and thought are not unallied with those we have on world and self. We take the world and the self, as we take language and thought, to be samsaric and void or created and creative; and hence we have these differing accounts of whether language has any significant use in mapping the real.

3. Paradigm and conviction

Nevertheless in all our traditions, concepts break this silence to sound out and spread abroad an inward illumination. Such concepts may seem straightforwardly to express perceived truth for public review; but when we press them at an insistent core, we fray this appearance. For instance, there reappears a funny sort of *is*.

(a) *Ātman is Brahman*. Has the celebrated equation of Svetaketu in the *Upanishads*, "That art thou," a routine grammar? We routinely use *is* to predicate, but this is no simple case of predication. Nor do we use *is* to make the *ātman* an instance in the class Brahman, nor do we take a part for the whole, a weakness of the favorite analogy that the spray droplet is the ocean. (BrU 2-1-20) We sometimes use *is* for numerical or linguistic equation, as in "2 plus 2 is 4," or "IV is 4." But not here. We sometimes identify a subject through roles, or trace a single referent through two appearances, as in "The bank president is my father," or "The morning star is the evening star." We sometimes follow a cause into its effect, as in "The water is the ice." But the Advaitan rejects any Brahmanic transformation (*pariṇāma*). Sometimes an *is* corrects mistaken appearances, as in "The snake is the rope." Such a usage Vedanta knows elsewhere, but here is no mistake (*vivarta*), rather a central truth. Some say that this *is* means, "Ātman is not other than Brahman," but such a double negation, not-twoness (*advaita*), only returns us to the puzzling identity.

"In their literal, superficial meaning, 'Brahman' and 'Atman' have opposite attributes.... Their identity is established only when they are understood in their true significance." (VC 69) In that true significance, Sankara concludes that the equation has not so much a rational as an "intuitional sense," a nonduality that no specific *is* can designate. (VS 4-1-2) Rudolf Otto concurs: "The word 'is' in the mystical formula of identification has a significance which it does not contain in logic."[14] The mystic copula paradoxically forces together two disparate concepts, the self and the All. We are left conceptually breathless, but converge them to gain the intuitive perception in which meaning lies. It is comparatively difficult, and finally impossible, to specify this relation of the *jīva*, the ego, the *ātman*, self, and Brahman, oscillating as it does between a suicide and a divinizing of the I.

(b) *Nirvāṇa is saṃsāra.* When he closes the *Kārikās*, Nagarjuna rises to this greatest puzzle of the Madhyamika mind, joining what are unmitigated antitheses in Theravada Buddhism. "There is nothing whatever which differentiates *saṃsāra* from *nirvāṇa*." (Ka 25-19m) The *Great Sūtra* reaches the same climax for the penetrating *bodhisattva*. "When he thus does not discriminate, they, i.e. Saṃsāra and Nirvāṇa, become exactly the same." (MP 650) The possibilities for the meaning of *is* which we have just rehearsed all fail. *Saṃsāra* is not a predicate, an instance, a part, a transformation of, or synonymous in meaning with, *nirvāṇa*. The *is* is one of redescription, but of what sort? There is no subject which remains in constant continuity under predications which follow in chrono-

---

[14] Rudolf Otto, *Mysticism East and West* (New York: Macmillan, 1970), p. 104.

logical sequence, as when Jones found to be now a friend is no longer an enemy. *Nirvāṇa* is not ex-*saṃsāra*. The assertion is of a simultaneous perception, as though heaven is found to be hell, black to be white, or the ball red and green all over. That the conditioned is something other than the unconditioned is relative truth, and that is sayable. But here in the absolute truth that is voided; and it is now resaid that the voided conditioned, when seen through, is the unconditioned. Still, this is not quite, indeed, not at all sayable, but rather felt.

"The mundane is not different from the transmundane and vice versa, the mundane is itself the transmundane and the transmundane is itself what appears as the mundane. In the ultimate truth there is no difference between them. All the different views disappear, all the activities of mind return to enter the original void, all words cease; the world (*saṃsāra*) is itself beheld in its true nature as Nirvāṇa and not anything different." (MPCv 122a) That holding and erasing of the distinction is accomplished by the predicate *śūnya. Saṃsāra = śūnya = nirvāṇa.* The *is* is thus by an equation (as it were) through zero, and therefore contentless. The *emptiness* which was a lament against *saṃsāra* is carried on, but now used in praise of *nirvāṇa*, to consume both. We will later protest that there is equivocation here. But the Madhyamika saint rather believes he has made an equation, forcing toward convergence two disparate concepts, until speech stops.

(c) *Jesus is both God and man.* From Augustine's trinitarian struggles, too complex for us here, we may isolate rather starkly his incarnational creed, remembering how the patristic doctor lived immediately adjacent to Chalcedon and Nicea with their confession that Jesus is "fully human, fully divine, one person." What sort of *is* operates when we say that the humanity of Jesus *is* the divinity of God? In the various heresies—docetism, adoptionism, intermediate natures, modalism, similitude—we might specify some *is* of appearance, of transformation, of combination, process, or likeness. But this creedal formula, which serves as a signpost against heresies, rejects bad doctrines with more success than does it designate a good one. It insists *that* in Jesus is Immanuel, God-with-us, to leave unspecified *how* God is with us in him. Can we specify exactly this nonduality of Jesus with God? Augustine admits that he cannot couple the two natures by specifying some strong rational connection. He knows something of what he means as a result of his encounter in Jesus with both humanity and divinity without diminution of either. More is meant and believed than can be verified and understood, but the Augustinian believes en route to understanding. In the religious pilgrim's own life, through trusting, he comes to know something of an "I, yet not I but the grace of God." Taken at the pitch and uniquely in Christ, this is the way the human and the divine are joined in Christ. This forms a subjective basis of the objective witness, an inner word which superintends the outer word. This is, in its essential form, the Augustian soul which images the Trinity. The Christian believes that by the incarnation Christ perfectly forged together two disparate concepts, man and God, and that the believer in the course of discipleship imperfectly imitates this unity. In Augustine's discerning of the eternal divinity in the humanity of the man from Nazareth, the immutable seen there in the midst of the mutable, he deepened the philosophical intellect, received from Athens, by adding to it a spiritual vision, received from Jerusalem. He eventually found all the wisdom of God in the Chalcedonian conjunction of God and man in Jesus.

When we are told that x is y, the word *is* seems simple. But its meaning depends in fact on an experiential and conceptual background which backs up any understanding of the *is*. We must have some idea not only of the *is* but of the x and y, some idea how the things hooked up might converge, how the disparate terms might really be the same. If these terms are very disparate, as in these religious equations, an air of mysticism haunts the identification.

We could trace this "escaping inscape" in its Islamic form by inquiry into the Sufi union of passing into God. But Ghazali, with whom we began this section, has said enough for the present. Whoever tries to join heaven and earth, the sacred and the secular, the self and God, the eternal and the temporal, the finite and the infinite, will find that by a *coincidentia oppositorum* he pushes logic so far that the concepts without a subtending percept are empty.

IV. Conceptual Education of the Perceptual

But are not percepts without concepts blind? (Kant) Naive and unlettered, our spiritual perceptions, like our sensory ones, are variously confused and clear, appropriate and inappropriate, false and true. Realizing that there are indistinct spiritual landscapes, our doctors next ask for what we call a conceptual education of piety, a term chosen for its *leading out* (*educo*) of our powers. Doctrine *educes* awareness, but does not *induce* it. It excites vision, but does not insert it. But thought also disciplines feeling in a sort of refining process which purifies, as in metallurgy, not to generate and to create the metal, or the spirituality, but to transform it. Our talent becomes sophisticated with our education, but it is not supplied by education. Maps may correct misjudgments of direction, distance, and elevation, or sensitize us to see certain features of geology, hydrology, or climate. We do not suppose that perceptions are incorrigible, least of all in religion. Conceptual criticisms may correct them, yet that is by leading us to better perceptions, in religion as in so much else, so that a perceptive being there remains primitive.

1. Critical conception

Much of our human genius lies in a capacity for analysis which assists our perceptual powers. Each of our saints is simultaneously an intellectual giant, and each has insisted on critical phases (*manana*, *'ilm*, *scientia-sapientia*, and *saṃvṛti-satya*) which direct vision. Words help us to see. We watch them now as by turns they find criticism to be variously corrective of perceptions, helpful in an analysis which feeds a synthesis, to be clarifying, and relatively necessary.

(a) Immediate experience, *ma'rifa*, must be educated by passing through, not in bypassing, logical knowledge, *'ilm*. "If the soul has not been exercised in the sciences that deal with fact and demonstration, it will acquire mental phantasms that it will suppose to be truths descending upon it. Many a Sufi has continued for ten years in one such fancy before escaping from it, whereas if he had had a sound scientific education he would have been delivered out of it at once."[15] Such Sufis misdescribe their primitive experience. Al-Hallaj did this when, having indeed encountered God, he gave an exaggerated report of his experience, claiming, "I am the True One," reporting as *inherence* in God what was only *nearness* to him. "When that drunkenness abated and they came again under the sway of the intelligence, which is Allah's balance scale upon earth, they knew that that had not been actual identity, but only something resembling identity." (Ni 60m) "Nothing which reason has concluded to be impossible can become evident when one is in the state of (Sufi) election. To be sure, something may become evident of which reason falls short in the sense that it cannot be reached by reason alone." (NN 137f,m)

Though Ghazali disparages rationalism in lieu of religion, the advanced Muslim is quite necessarily an intellectual savant. "Nor does his belief become complete and his religion upright until his intellect matures." (Ih I, 1, 223) We must call such a person a scientific mystic, and know that a nontheological religion is laden with pitfalls. "He who first acquires versatility in tradition and learning and then turns to Sufism comes off well, but he who takes to Sufism before learning exposes himself to danger." (Ih I, 1, 52) Sufism never excuses us from learning but rather requires it, and literate Sufism is all too rare. (Al 27)

(b) Notice Augustine engaging in philosophical study: "By some kind of inner activity of mine, I am able to analyze and to synthesize the things that must be learned; and this power of mine is called reason. What needs to be analyzed is just that which is supposed to have unity, but as yet has none or has less than we believe it may have. Why do we synthesize except to make things one, so far as possible. Both in analyzing and in synthesizing I seek oneness, I love oneness. When I analyze I seek a simple unit; when I synthesize I look for an integral unit." (Or 2-48) Here he is in theological contemplation: "To comprehend him all at once is quite impossible. God is an object for the mind, he is to be understood, while a physical body is for the eyes, to be seen. But do not

---

[15] *Weighing Deeds (Mīzān al-'Amal)*, trans. A.J. Arberry in *Revelation and Reason in Islam* (New York: Macmillan, 1957), p. 110.

think you wholly take in even a physical body by the eye, for you never see the whole. You cannot see a person's face and back at the same time. When you see a part not seen before, memory recalls what you have left behind. You handle it, turn it on this side, and work round to see the whole. Putting together the remembered parts, you fancy that you have seen the whole, not by eyesight but by memory. What then can we say of that divine Word? How much more is this so as the eye of the heart comprehends God?" (Sm 117-5a)

In passages like these, Augustine is pondering the pieces to fit them into the puzzle, looking for their contributions to a gestalt. His faith put him to literary work, and across the decades he studied scripture, doctrine, history, science, critically to specify the units of that integral perception which began in the garden vision. By dissertation on the *City of God*, the *Trinity*, by *Narrations on the Psalms* and *Homilies on the Gospel*, he seeks "to bring the separate parts of the problem one by one into the light." (Mg 40) Thought is the scrutiny of memory, where once-immediate perceptions are recollected so as to be integrated in the intellect. Corrective doubt cannot work in sheer immediacy, but only by consulting memory to judge whether one experience sits well or ill with another. (Tr 10-14) Superbly an intellectual process, conceptual education is the cyclic induction of all into, the deduction of all out of, the governing divine perception. This is not a circular activity so much as it is an encyclopedic one. To Augustine, as much as to any other, we owe the conviction that the world's intelligibility lies in its divinity.

(c) Intuitional experience, explains Sankara, carries the highest degree of directness, but the lowest degree of conceptual clarity. In this light we understand his chosen career as an interpreter. The *Brihadāranyaka Upanishad* deals initially with revelation and mystic experience (as these are reported by and urged in scripture) (*upadeśa*), but after that it proceeds to logical explanation (*upapatti*) and conceptual truth. "Self-knowledge is also established as such by argument; it is decided by both scripture and argument, and seekers after immortality should adopt this means." (BrU 4-5-1a) "Should nonduality be admitted only on the authority of scripture, or should it be accepted on logical grounds as well? It can be known on logical grounds as well." (GaK 3-1m) Sankara's commentaries are laden with arguments designed to disentangle lesser understandings, *apara vidyas*, and he hopes that reasoning about the perceptual witness attested in the *Vedas* and *Upanishads* will help us correctly to gain, certify, and clarify it. "The scriptural passages enjoining thought (*manana*) on Brahman in addition to mere hearing (*śravaṇa*) of the sacred texts show that reasoning (*tarka*) is to be allowed to take its place. The passages must not deceitfully be taken as enjoining bare independent ratiocination (dry, pure *tarka*), but must be understood to represent reasoning as a subordinate auxiliary of intuitional knowing (*anubhava*)." (VS 2-1-6m) *Manana* supplies conceptual coherence, but only when this is hung onto the presiding perceptual set.

(d) Not even the ruthless *dharma*-slayer can ignore misconceptions. Admittedly, Nagarjuna in some moods collapses all relative truths indifferently: "Everything is true; everything is false; everything is both true and false, both false and true. Such is the true character of Dharma." (MPC1 46) But such groping for truth is of no help grading it, and Nagarjuna himself, on Buddha's warning, elsewhere seeks the mundane right view, opposing the mundane wrong view. He remembers what Buddha taught Subhuti: "The Lord: 'A Bodhisattva, who courses in perfect wisdom, makes definite distinctions between *dharmas* (both things and teachings about them), although they are all like a dream, nonentities, with nonexistence for their own-being.' Subhuti: 'It is wonderful and astonishing that the Bodhisattvas should, when all *dharmas* are absolutely empty, yet make a definite distinction between *dharmas* which are wholesome and unwholesome.' The Lord: 'So it is, Subhuti. They nevertheless make a definite distinction between *dharmas*.' " (MP 574a) So Nagarjuna teaches that, as samsaric descriptions, impermanence (*anitya*) is truer than permanence, and suffering (*duḥkha*) truer than pleasure. That the world was created is a gross perversion, while that it was beginningless is relative truth. That the soul is, is less true that that it is not (*anātman*). (MPC1 2101ff; MPCv 217ff)

Buddhist belief, it seems, is to be kept right up to the last stage for what they term its *skill-in-means*, its leading capacity toward truth. All other belief is soon discarded, and only lastly is the Buddhist belief left, for it is vital to go out with this emptiness, which alone works to save. If emptiness is misunderstood it can destroy "like a snake wrongly grasped or magical knowledge incorrectly applied." We have to beware the "counterfeit perfection of wisdom." (Ka 24-11m; MP 264) Nagarjuna can quite baldly question and then reprimand an opponent: "In what Sūtra has the Buddha, the world's honored one, taught such a doctrine? It is not to be found in any Sūtra, for it is not correct teaching." (Ek 307m) When the *Prajña-Pāramitā-Sūtra* comes to a close, Buddha entrusts to Ananda its letters, words, and verses, noticing how everything hangs on this scripture, "the inexhaustible store-house of dharma for the Tathāgatas." (AP 268) We begin to suspect that "emptiness" is a kind of map after all, although not descriptive like the rest.

Now let us gather in overview the insights which we have been accumulating across this chapter. Adapting a distinction from Michael Polanyi, we say that we *attend to*, explicitly, some analysis only as we *attend from*, implicitly, a general gestaltic knowledge.[16] We ask the meaning of a single word, but out of other words where meaning is for the moment unchallenged. We cannot talk about everything at once. The larger, the more unwieldy is the concept. Spiritual discourse reaches logically for the whole which is encountered psychologically. It is drawn into these presiding categories— Brahman, God, Suchness—and, eventually beginning to *respond* rather than to *reason*, we shade back to an apprehending perceptual set where we had hoped for focused verbal comprehension. We do not have the rational prowess to attack that expansive stream at once, but only piecemeal. Although they complement each other, perception is synthetic and diffuse, while conception is analytic and precise.[17]

---

[16] Michael Polanyi, *The Tacit Dimension* (Garden City, N.Y.: Doubleday, 1966), p. 10.

[17] Some maps enable us to see wholes with ease, although with corresponding loss of intimacy, rather like global seeing at a distance. In this they are nondiscursive, graphic, synoptic, themselves nearer percepts than concepts. Maps and concepts differ in picturability.

Language always limits, but proportionately the more severely where there is an exact argument. Close logical control is achieved by selectivity. Working through the components in a religiously perceived whole, verbal criticism steadily educates, modifies, and corrects perception, but the cognitive act always has below its surface logic a depth grammar in life. It is the tip of an iceberg. Truth here is never held afloat simply by exposed conceptuality, but rather by a much larger tacit embodiment of it. Just as it is *with* reason that we think *about* reason, it is also *with* religion that we think *about* religion. This does not inevitably involve a mere surface rationalization of what we subliminally believe anyway, for comprehension is an immensely satisfactory part of piety. But rather, neither saint nor skeptic can think in independence of a perceptual set operating beneath the threshold of any particular conscious cognition. Logically put, we cannot argue except from premises that, sooner or later, we cannot get by argument.

Each part is judged from the floating whole, and any exposed surface is modified when it is no longer submerged. There is always an inner penumbra which we cannot illuminate without altering it, any more than we can turn on light to catch soft-lighted detail in the shadows. We dip buckets of water to see what the river is like. Articulated reasons are cogent only as they coincide with inarticulate feelings. Argument here is best interpreted not as inference from world-statements to God-statements, but as a transcription from percept to concept. Argument will thus be rational not in the *strong* sense of compelling us to move from the world to God, a move which is made only by sacramental experience. Argument is rational in the *weak* sense of showing that the world is intelligible under such a presiding paradigm.

Thus, with Augustine, arguments for God are really faith in quest of understanding, a *proving* or *approving* of what one already perceives or hopes to perceive. Always deeply apologetic, religious argument is *ad hominem*. If rational damage can sometimes be heavy, as with Augustine when he reflected on his Manicheanism, this is only where reason tests a spiritual vision. Analysis notoriously shows us where we are wrong, more than how to be right; it checks intuitive insight that it cannot make. Further, all this mixing of percepts and concepts is deeply compounded by the refractoriness of value to logic, and the mixing of the right with the righteous. Analysis cannot reach up to truth; rather, that is the synthetic genius of perception. Perhaps we should say that truth-finding is for saints and saviors, while its verification is for scholars and thinkers. Mature inquiry combines both.

Apparently, every superior faith can be made impressively rational within its axioms. It is doubtful whether logic ever so disproves a sophisticated faith, or so proves a competing one, as to necessitate changing faiths. Conversion occurs with biographical factors operating as well. Things cohere under another intuition, and that too becomes rational, given the new awareness. Or, during loss of faith, they fragment to a disintegrating nihilism. Thus we can say that faith is *defensively* rational, but never *offensively* so, for faith does not necessitate by some logic which is independent of what we have called correspondent truthfulness. This kind of account allows for the power of reason, yet recognizes that a simple rational persuasion is not what supports faith. We are drawn to a religion, and kept there, not merely by its logic, but also (as we are to music, to art, to persons) by larger synthetic critical judgments which are perceptually superintended. That is why the logic of belief operates differently on outsiders, who do not possess this experiential buoyancy. Employing a Christian term, and that not incidentally, we contend that, even when most deeply critical, religious rationality still remains *incarnate*.

Nagarjuna hopes by a sort of "spiritual ju jitsu" to trip his opponents under their own weight.[18] If this means that Nagarjuna believes that he can show that no faith is rational in our strong sense, then Nagarjuna will be joined by the other three saints we here consult. But, especially in the *Kārikās*, Nagarjuna is more ambitious than this, trying to assume what his opponents assume and demonstrate their contrary, to show that no conceptual system can, under criticism, remain rational in the weak sense. His approach may be useful in testing inferior religion, but he does not show that every possible belief, however refined, is inherently

---

[18] Murti, *Central Philosophy of Buddhism*, p. 132.

inconsistent, empty. His pitiless condemnation *en masse* of all other systems has convinced few opponents and does not succeed. His ju jitsu dialectic is itself operating in the perspective of a faith, we must remember. No abuse *of* or *in* other religions can establish one's own, even when one also tries to rid one's own religion of these same abuses.

If Nagarjuna only warns us that we literally state exactly nothing about ultimate reality, the rest will join him again. But the inadequacy of our rational and critical powers is one thing, their complete emptiness is another, which not even Nagarjuna can quite affirm. All advanced perception entails, not less than it escapes, some conception, whether that entailment is drawn or not.

2. Catalytic conception

In those classical formative processes with which we began this chapter, the conceptual system educates though it cannot generate an intuition. This happens corporately when beliefs flow from master to disciple. But further, as we now wish to say, this is true individually, as speech enables the saint to be religious. In an accelerated inquiry, the novice is prevented from retracing some of the false routes through which his predecessors have groped. The student inherits the tested distillation of much genius. Thus, in the history of a religion, a doctrinal maturity evolves to express a primitive perceptual set which has grown critically reflective. But also, in the individual, refined doctrine can elicit faith, although it is itself a precipitate of such experience. It is conceptuality which makes corporate religion possible. Although the child cannot receive the *wisdom* of his parents, he can receive their *knowledge*, through which he may stretch to wisdom. The pilgrim travels with a map that the pioneers did not have. As the infant in the womb undergoes the key stages through which the race has evolved, guided by the genetic encoding of its parents, so religious learning educates tacit stirrings which are seeded within us, and brings them to fruition with a speed and competence otherwise impossible.

Still, every tradition insists that propositional expressions in religion are so personally backed that we may not transfer the concepts except in the presence of an indexing structural awareness. Never imparted verbally from without, wisdom is unfolded only from an apprehension within. "Our hearer, if he himself also sees those things with his inner and pure eye, knows that of which I speak by means of his own contemplation, but not through my words. Accordingly, even though I speak the truth and he sees it, I still do not teach him. For he is not taught by my words, but by means of the realities themselves which God discloses to the inner soul." (Mg 40) That is the paradox which Augustine develops in *The Teacher*, toward which we are headed in a later chapter. The *Vedas*, continues Sankara, "aim not at enjoining knowledge, but merely at directing our attention to it, as do imperative phrases such as, 'Listen to this! Look at this!' Even when a person is face to face with some object of knowledge, knowledge may either arise or not; all that another person wishing to inform him can do is to point it out; knowledge will then spring up in his mind of itself." (VS 3-2-21a)

Ghazali's way of saying this is that only as the outward, public Arabic comes to signify Allah's inner speech can we say that the Qur'an is the Word of God. No more than fire is in the Qur'an because the word "fire" occurs there, is the eternal speech of God literally there. God is heard as the Qur'anic grammar fires a meaning which privately corresponds to the public language, as the Arabic provides "pointers" and "leads." (DP 57ff) This is what we judge to be the authentic thesislessness of Nagarjuna, that no absolute truth is ever so captured in verbal truth that it can be handed over to the nonperceiving aspirant.

This catalytic effect of speech is not only in the pupil's reproduction of religion, it is also in the master's production of it. It is doubtful if any being unable to speak has the capacity to be religious. While we know no religion coextensive with speech, we know no religion that has not passed through speech. Language provides us with the intellectual capacity to entertain religious perceptions. Sensory perception is perhaps pre-verbal, but spiritual perception is never pre-verbal, despite all that we have said about its exceeding verbal expression. Our religious speaking is not simply the result of being there, but we speak in order to be there, even though being there is much more than we can speak. Here, without concepts there are no intelligible percepts.

Conceptualization so re-feeds the experience which generates it that deepening experience is not possible without this conceptual looping, even though these concepts are inadequate to catch that experience. Our reflection cooperates with our perception. Seeing *as* requires seeing *that*. Though the map never tells it like it is, without maps we never really know where and who we are, nor in what environment we find ourselves. Notwithstanding Nagarjuna, there is no mapless being there, for the maps enter into our being there. Our speech, then, is a sign of and for our being there.

In Augustine, intellection is being there and mapping for fuller being there. His verbal maps facilitate but are inadequate to our presence before the divine Logos. The lyrics are set to music. Moving through Ghazali and Sankara, we find that they make descending judgments about the adequacy of speech, although both maintain its necessity in the preparation for religious experience. The predicates of Allah fail in fullest light and the mapped Brahman (*saguna*) dissolves into the mapless Brahman (*nirguna*). Lastly, even Nagarjuna must speak in order to go there, in his relative preparation for an absolute truth, though when he is there he "empties" the speech that brought him, and, in the *śūnyatā* presence, intellection stops for mapless being there. The music has no lyrics. But that puzzling intelligibility confounds us, for to despise speech is to despise the self and God, though to reduce the self or God to what can be spoken likewise despises the self and God.

A critical education, while necessary, is never sufficient for perceptual experience. The virtues of purity, love, trusting faith, and humility are also needed to inculcate the sensitivities of spiritual perception. We have to alter not only our argument but our premises, not only our logic but our psychology. Prayer, meditation, discipline, liturgy, sacrament, art, and communal fellowship must serve to provide the environment of disclosure for a tacit sensing of what is explicitly taught. But we do need to be wary of catalytic mechanisms that replace this passage through critical conception, cultivating all the while those spiritual exercises that provide a perceptual base for conception. The Sufi way requires practice beyond intellectual activity, Ghazali insists, but then he adds, "Keep your wits. God has never had a saint who was mentally deficient." (Ih IV, 3, 32)

There is some current research investigating a polarity in the human brain, one which perhaps provides the physiological basis for a double mode of consciousness. The left cerebral hemisphere, dominantly involved in logic and language, processes information sequentially. In contrast and complement, the right hemisphere processes information by simultaneously holistic and diffuse screening, and is primarily responsible for orientation in space, for artistic talents, body awareness, and recognition of faces. "The complementary workings of our two thought processes permit our highest achievements, but most occupations value one mode over the other. Science and law, for example, emphasize linear thought and verbal logic. The arts, religions, and music are more present-oriented, aconceptual, and intuitive. The unfortunate result is that many intellectuals often disparage the nonverbal mind, while many mystics and poets often disparage the rational mind.... But a complete human consciousness should include both modes of thought.... We must not ignore the right-hemisphere talents of imagination, perspective, and intuition, which in the long run may prove essential to our personal and cultural survival."[19] Any correlation of this kind is likely to elude a simple formulation, but we must wonder in closing whether the perceptual and the conceptual poles we have developed here coincide with our cerebral hemispheres, as complementary epistemic modes in the single mind.

Like religious systems, maps are something we see with, indispensably helping us to make our way around in the world. Religion is the struggle to obtain, by inheritance and by composition, a vision of the universe that satisfies. In ensuing years, one tries to clarify and deepen that vision. Various maps result from differ-

---

[19] Robert E. Ornstein,"Right and Left Thinking," *Psychology Today* 6, no. 12 (May 1973): 87-92, citation on p. 92; cf. Michael S. Gazzaniga, "The Split Brain in Man," *Scientific American* 217, no. 2 (August 1967): 24-29.

ently selected areas of experience. None tells it like it is, and none fully tells what the mapmaker has seen. Maps and their makers may err, and what if the maps conflict? Some adjudications can be made by recalling the nature of projections. We must map onto a plane a round and roughened world. There is a more complex error when the ultimate is projected onto the relative. But there may also be discordant perceptions. Then an inquirer must take in hand the pilgrim's journal, and take the journey. But that presumes that the coordinates of mapping and the orienting gestalt make sense enough for us to travel by and to verify them. Whether multiple journeys are possible will become our most troublesome inquiry.

Chapter 4. Subjectivity, Objectivity, and Beyond

We have now reckoned first with the *virtues* and secondly with the *words* of this correspondent truthfulness which we are developing. This has prepared us for an account of the central and basic element in religious knowing: the sensed *union* in and out of which the saint knows his ultimate. We next undertake this through the categories of subjectivity and objectivity. Even the conventional epistemic process is puzzling enough, but when the self asks of the ultimate, there is much compounding of participation and detachment. Lodged in persons, knowledge is analytically a subjective process, for no percept is without a perceiver, no concept without a conceiver. Even corporate knowledge is still intersubjective. But, far from being a trivial or obvious matter, this opens up many questions.

At best, what we catch depends upon the nets with which we fish. At worst, we skew what we see, and murder to dissect. In objective knowledge, diligently sought in the modern West, we magnificently intend to see things "as they are." But that demands reckoning with the knower's contribution, and only the naive suppose no subjective outreach. We will first ask of the knower and his troubling subjectivity, and after that ask of the known and its peculiar objectivity, inquiries that will take us on to a knowledge that is beyond subjectivity and objectivity.

I. *The Knower: the Epistemic Subject*

Most philosophies, if not all, contain the conviction that things are not finally, not merely what they simply seem, but that the untutored know only superficially, and that reality is variant from or grander than what meets the unreflective eye. Religions add that we are mistaken due to our subjective unregeneracy. The world we see reflects our mental condition, for our interpretation of the world constitutes that of the self, and vice versa. Invited by religion to perspectival reformation, we are promised some breaking out of this subjective prison to know the objectively real, a blessed passage out of anthropocentrism toward ultimacy.

Even conventionally, the mind heavily contributes to its recognitions of natural and historical things. The genus *Rosa*? Do I uncover or choose its boundaries? Some of both, as every taxonomist knows. My understanding is by means of cause, effect, law, class, or aspect, but I invent as I find abstractions such as these. I recognize paleontologically "from the Pleistocene period" "a mammoth," rather than, as did a Neanderthal man, "a totem." The brahmin and I do not see a cow in Delhi streets the same; or, we can almost though not quite say, we do not see the same cow. It is not Tuesday, 9.00 a.m. E.S.T. in "the United States" except my system makes it so, nor even "day" except from here.

Einstein has revealed that there is no objective simultaneity in time; there is only intersubjective convenience. How curiously the search for objectivity has thrown us into an epistemic relativity! Our cultures and sciences can alert us to the question of perspective; and the human genius, conceptually sophisticated, does escape from a primitive acquiescence in the senses. But perspective, although expanded, is never escaped, and every global, cosmic estimate is "from here," so that, as surely as we must think in some language, we must see from somewhere. Such an inescapable observer's standpoint is vastly more crucial in religion. We will next review how this is so in our four saints and their classical traditions.

1. The clinging subject

According to Madhyamika, the impact of the ordinary subject, the person, on its object is total, so that we virtually construct our world. "Thus the ignorant people construct the conditioned things; that is the source for existence in flux (*saṃsāra*)." (Ka 26-10m) Nagarjuna's account of what the West calls creation is that the world is our corporate mirage. "This universe like a magic play comes from nowhere and goes to nowhere; being due to mere mental bewilderment, it does not stay anywhere." (Rv 2-13) Candrakirti, his disciple and commentator, expands this: "Common mankind, whose power of vision is obstructed by the darkness of ignorance, imputes to separate entities a reality which they do not possess, a reality which for the saint does not exist at all.... The separate entities of the phenomenal world have never originated and do not exist." (Ca 138f,m)

A favorite metaphor is that the world is a dream, suggesting solipsism, but the prevailing mood is rather a sort of phenomenalism. We do not invent the phenomena; they are given to us. But we swiftly add their reality and articulation. Phenomena are, Nagarjuna insists, "not real," "empty," insubstantial, a mock show that we fall for, or fall into. In another favorite metaphor, like the whirled firebrand that we mistake to be a wheel, the world is a whir that superficially seems real. This peculiar genius seems alternately almost insane and to come to conclusions remarkably like those on the frontiers of physics. We know well enough what matter is, in transience, for tables and chairs; but ultimately it has evaporated on us. It is some kind of spin and not much of anything. To seek its essence is like peeling a banana tree, or an onion. We do not know what is there; there is nothing (*śūnyatā*) there.

On the logical level, the mismatching of language with reality can be noticed from this Madhyamika subjectivity. Like the coordinates of latitude and longitude, like map contours, or amperes, volts, and inches, all our words are an articulating overlay on reality. This allows scientific stability, for Nagarjuna nowhere means to deny empirical knowledge. But words only apply to these appearances, to jars, rocks, and trees; and the objects which answer to our names, the denotations of our connotations, are unreal. Language stops there and can go no further, for articulation cannot touch the inarticulate whole. Outside *prajñā*, we have no access to reality undressed of this conceptuality we have hung upon it. Like Kant's *Critique of Pure Reason*, the *Kārikās* analyze and prove ontologically incoherent all those philosophical categories—existence, cause, space, time, matter, motion, self, world—which have promised to lead us to what really is.

But every logical ill is at depth a psychological one, and the deeper trouble is the clinging self. "All things are devoid of substantiality; they so exist that they are not absolutely existent. In regard to these, the common people, on account of their clinging, owing to the thirst of passion, give rise to perversions and imaginative constructions. Comparable to children, such people do not get beyond life in the limited sphere; they do not dwell in the noble way. Lacking the power of skillfulness, they are called 'the clinging.'" (MPCv 90a) "These realities (*dharmas*) do not exist in such a way as the foolish common people are wrong to suppose.... But foolish people have settled down in ignorance and craving. They have constructed realities out of their ignorance and craving." (MP 107f,m)

This "clinging" or desire composes the self with the world as its counterpart, for we gain our consciousness, not nakedly or autonomously, but only in the presence of this supposed other. We articulate a subjective self in encounter with an apparently objective world. " 'The one who forms' is himself being formed magically; and the act performed by him is like a magical form being magically produced by another magical form." The world is a trick (*māyā*) of the ego, but that ego is in turn another mirage. "Desires, actions, bodies, producers, products are like a fairy castle, resembling a mirage, a dream." (Ka 17-32f)

Buddha teaches this in a dialogue with Subhuti: "The Lord: 'Are then I-making and Mine-making isolated and empty?' Subhuti: 'Yes, they are.' The Lord: 'Is it because of I-making and Mine-making that beings run and wander about in (the *saṃsāra*-world of) birth and death?' Subhuti: 'So it is, O Lord.'" (MP 441) Candra-kirti comments, "Obsessed by the unreal devil of their 'ego' and their 'mine' the obtuse men and common worldlings imagine that they really perceive separate entities which in reality do not exist, just as the ophthalmic person sees before himself hair, flies, and other objects which never did exist." (Ca 188m) We bifurcate the world into "I" and "It," then view the other as a means to our pleasure; only, alas, that thirst becomes rather the source of our suffering. *Saṃsāra*, the world, is the product of our attachment to the "I."

The common interconnections in emptiness (*śūnyatā*) of world impermanence (*anitya*), self-unreality (*anātman*), and suffering (*duḥkha*) become clearer now. To stop the clinging, thirsting self is the same as stopping the whirl of *saṃsāra* and its hurt, since the world is extinguished by the extinguishing of the sources of our attachment. It becomes dissolved and diffused when the self is dissolved and diffused, and vice versa. Here world-objectivity is a construction of the subjective mind. To seek to know as truly real the world of objects is like chasing a rainbow, for the self is looking for something it is significantly composing. When, during our reformation, the subjective/objective line blurs, with this non-dividedness we begin to escape the perspectival self. All this insists, in its own curious way, that the true nature of things (*tathatā*) ought not to be altered by one's subjective fantasies, and is not so altered in perfect wisdom.

2. The individuated subject

Although they differ as to what underlies the person, as well as his world, Sankara and Nagarjuna have closely allied accounts of the superficial self. Sankara's self also effectively constructs the world which it finds in illusion (*māyā*) and appearance (*vivarta*). "*Saṃsāra* is only based on *avidyā* (mistake) and exists only for the ignorant man who sees the world as it appears to him." (BhG 13-2m) "Just as an illusory city in the sky—appearing to be full of shops, replete with vendable articles, houses, palaces, and villages, bustling with men and women—is seen to vanish suddenly before one's eyes, so for the wise this whole universe, this entire duality, is viewed as unreal." (GaK 2-31a) But a further crucial concept, superimposition (*adhyāsa*), distinguishes the Advaitan from the Madhyamika subject, when phenomena are constituted by the self upon something which is really there.

We do not mis-take phenomena but we mis-take the real. Sankara does not find adequate the Buddhist explanation that the appearances are grounded in nothing, but he holds that we would not superimpose a snake (the world), if there were really no rope (Brahman) to ground the illusion. In a modern analogy, a motion picture cannot be projected into empty air, but there must be a screen. Though the projected detail is all apparent, there is a substrate, a screen, under the fluid impermanence of the movie. We do not compose the "thatness," only its "whatness." The color, multiplicity, and evanescence are all of our manufacturing. There is finally only "*nirguṇa* Brahman," not an empty nothing but a "qualityless greatness."

The Madhyamika account finds only silence, being unable to say whether anything is there. Negatively, there is only emptiness; or, positively and rarely, this will deferentially approach a thesisless "thatness" (*tattva, tathatā*). The Advaitan account finds an Absolute, and affirms it, then rests in a kind of semisilence. Beyond appearance (*vivarta*) there is such a splendid reality (*sat*) that description lapses. Both our Indian saints negate subjective plurality, but the one finds as a residuum an Absolute, while the other can find only emptiness. Sankara criticizes Madhyamika for missing this other reality on which the empirical world is based. "It is not possible to negate the empirical world without the acceptance of another reality; for to negate an error is to accept the general truth on which it is based." (VS 2-2-31)[1]

Sankara is of a mixed mind himself whether the subject is the sole contributor of this false surmise about there being a plural world, for he can sometimes ground the world-mistake in Brahman. Nature (*prakṛti*) is "emitted" in the indifference and purposeless "play" (*līlā*) of Brahman. (VS 2-1-33; 2-3-17) "The highest

---

[1] Translation by Murti, *Central Philosophy of Buddhism*, p. 312.

Lord...by means of ignorance manifests himself in various ways."
(VS 1-3-19m) "The Lord is fictitiously connected with *māyā*." (VS
2-2-3m) From whom is the illusion? From us or from Brahman?
Both! "The One thought, may I be many." (VS 1-1-5m) The *māyā*-
illusion is eternally "produced by" Brahman. (VS 2-1-9) Yet, "the
opinion of the entire phenomenal world is based on the (mistaken)
individual soul." (VS 2-1-14m) "The waking state is only a pro-
longed dream. The phenomenal universe exists in the mind.... The
mind of the experiencer creates all the objects which he experiences." (VC 58f)

Sankara steadily sublates objective, creationist, cause and effect
models of Brahman and the world by his greater development of
subjective, projectionist models where the self superimposes an
apparent world. We will postpone the considerable problems
here, but we cannot forget them; indeed we will eventually judge
that they contain an incoherence. But we need now only the belief
that the world is "mutually determined" when a nonagentive
Brahman uses our agentive mistake. (GaK 2-13) If *māyā* comes
from Brahman, it operates by our dreaming, for Sankara is everywhere clear that we fall for or into illusion. There is no route to
Brahman which lies in these dreamed-up outward phenomena, but
access to Brahman is only by moving inward into the self. We do
not then find that the disvalued phenomena are revalued; they are
only dissolved.

The mistake is again a logical one. Language bifurcates the
world into a subject who knows about an object. Sankara admits
that the empirical world is the rightful domain for this kind of
reasoning, and he has a detailed conventional epistemology, which
we overlook here. But such an analytic, differentiating power
becomes a vice when we move to the noumenal level, for it
prevents the synthesis of the knower and the known. Our logic
works while the ego searches its world; but when, in overview, we
need to see through this duality into oneness, our discourse lapses,
like the eye which cannot be used for the observation of itself,
though it readily observes others. Logical and linguistic criticism
requires distance, articulation, and categorizing. But none of this is
truly so. To speak is to determine, to separate, to name, to focus on

a part. But reality is indeterminate. What is definite cannot be infinite, what is defined cannot be the Infinite.

Still further, as with the Buddhist clinging, the error may be more deeply described as egoism (*ahaṃkāra*), the sense of agency. (BhG 13-5) "The ego is your enemy.... Man drinks the wine of Māyā, becomes deluded, and begins to see things as separate from each other, so that he talks of 'you' and 'I'." (VC 78, 91) The deluded mind "also causes us to discern objects. It is endowed with the power and faculty of differentiating objects by giving them various names.... When, in the enlightenment of the Ātman, a man transcends the mind, the phenomenal universe disappears from him. When a man lives in the domain of mental ignorance, the phenomenal universe exists for him." (VC 58) The ignorant have fallen into the Hindu form of the fallacy of misplaced concreteness. Sound knowing can correct this by dissolving the individual subject and its projected world. "Just as the normal state of a man, afflicted by disease, consists in his getting cured of the disease, similarly the normalcy of the Self, stricken with identification with misery, is regained through the cessation of the phenomenal universe of duality." (MaU 1) The diverse world is a disease of the ego.

3. The proud subject

Earlier we contacted Augustine's epistemic mixing of pride and error, of humility and truth. We need now to return to that and see error as a subjective mistake, born of our chief sin. Augustine defines "the proud" as "the self-pleasers," and adds, "Certainly it is good for the heart to be lifted up, not to oneself, for this is pride, but to the Lord, and only the humble are capable of such obedience." (CG 14-13) Proud knowledge "puffs up" the sense of self. (GJ 27-5) The self-loving are unable to go Godward in trust or to go to the world in self-giving love, and therefore a subjective bias prevents our knowing God and the world objectively, as they are, the one the sacrament of the gracious presence of the other. "Vanity and truth (*vanitas et veritas*) are directly contrary to one another." (NP 118-12) The proud, subjective self is not disinterested, not humbled enough for objective truth.

There exists for Augustine an objective world known with an appropriate *scientia*, which comes by "the rational cognition of temporal things." (Tr 12-25) The sciences of nature and of humankind, the arts of culture, histories, including the Christian story—all merit objective study, nor is wisdom otherwise possible. These things in their eventful sequences are with Augustine the creation of God, neither (as in India) the constructions of our ignorance nor superimpositions upon a homogeneous Absolute. The illusion and appearance, the mirage and dreams are replaced here by a divine fiat of a real, good world. Theism and creation posit, if distance between God and Earth, also their intimate connection, and there is a resulting legitimacy to phenomena that is absent in Nagarjuna and in Sankara.

The Augustinian subject's knowing of nature and history is with markedly less mental contribution. We do know things as they are, and not merely as they appear. They have, independently of our cognition, reality by which they are plural in their distinguished integrities given by God. Accordingly, *scientia* is encouraged; and as a result we have the modern sciences, not incidentally. Such knowing in the objective mode is by cogitation, not by intellection, and, in sheerly empirical investigations, Augustine finds that the distortion due to pride is minimal. As with unenlightened persons also in Nagarjuna and Sankara, the unregenerate can gain objective common knowledge, for the lower reason (*ratio inferior*) is not adversely affected in its capacity for analysis. But progressively as we move toward synthesis of the whole and our emplacement in it, the perspectival bending due to pride becomes more dominant. Though the sciences are objectively true in a limited sense, when in overview they are put under *hubris*, in our search for intellectual wisdom (*sapientia*) we are not so smart as we think.

The Augustinian subject is suffering from a kind of illusion, nevertheless. To call it the pride of the concupiscent self is comparatively very like those egotisms which trouble us in Nagarjuna and in Sankara, though later we shall need more deeply to reflect on their variant meanings here. The autonomous, carnal self does not create *the* world, but it does create *this* world, this distorted world into which by its desires it falls. Jerusalem, the city built by

God, is by pride demolished into Babylon, that vain, evanescent city in which the aggrandizing self utilizes its world in search of happiness, finding but little. There are two epistemically biasing loves, the one is rectifying charity, the other is debilitating concupiscence. The noble love is "the affection of the mind which aims at the enjoyment of God for his own sake, and of one's self and one's neighbor for God's sake"; the base love is "the affection of the mind which aims at the enjoyment of one's self, one's neighbor, and physical things without reference to God" but rather in the pride of self-fulfillment. (CD 3-16) However clever the subjective self is in its science, the self fails of wisdom, until it gains that meekness which alone can be taught by God, because such meekness is itself the character of God. So the saint confesses, "You do not draw near to any but the contrite of heart, and you are not found by the proud, not even if they could number with cunning skill the stars and the sands, and measure the constellations, and plot the courses of the planets." (Co 5-3)

How to correct our subjectivity becomes the dominant epistemic concern when we seek wisdom, the "intellectual cognition of eternal things." (Tr 12-25) Because the Christian stretches through *scientia* to *sapientia*, he is less tempted than the Indian to set aside the empirical and the historical worlds, and by this is gained much protection against exclusive subjectivity. There is no wisdom without objective knowledge. But neither is science sufficient for wisdom, and the root trouble is that pride puts knowledge under the bias of self-love. Sooner or later, egocentrism causes us (now rejoining Sankara and Nagarjuna) to mistake the world. Tumbling into the secularist fallacy, we do not see the world as a sign which points to God, but as a thing to be pressed into our service. The world is real. Hence the possibility and necessity of *scientia*. But it is not ultimately real, and cannot be wisely known except in its derivation from God.

The Earth can be studied in its secondary regularities without God, but cannot be valued in its primary significances except in God, since our concupiscence will invariably color that evaluation. Science begins in objectivity, but, without faith, ends in a utilitarian prostituting of the world to human lust, which misses not only the world's author but its essential integrity. Nor can philosophical and religious minds, if proud, go further, for the world, like God, is seen purely only in purity. The meek inherit the Earth, and the pure in heart see God. By a subjective reformation for objective truth, by a psychological healing for higher logical truth, not through mere cogitation but through a more advanced intellection, the faithful self proceeds in search of understanding.

4. The self-impulsive subject

Ghazali does not so deliberately provide us with an account of subjective distortion, but nevertheless he is sometimes explicit and everywhere implicit over the same terrain. Born with a natural disposition (*fiṭra*) to be *muslim*, submissive to God, the person comes to dwell in the times of ignorance. This indisposition Ghazali calls self-impulse (*hawā*), of which the contrary is the religious impulse (*al-bā'ith al-dīni*). The *Niche for Lights* is an extended meditation on mystic epistemology, evaluating the degrees of illumination in which various inquirers stand. Those who understand nothing are in a class "veiled from Allah by pure darkness," of which "self-absorption is the characteristic." "This veil is, as it were, their self-centered ego and their lusts of darkness; for there is no darkness so intense as slavery to self-impulse (*hawā*) and self-love." (Ni 89ff) Though intermediately there are many translucent veils which hide God, all our final opacity, complete ignorance, is invariably produced by this passion.[2]

The predicates which describe this impulsive, non-Islamic subject are the successive vices of the *Iḥyā'*, Quarter III: perversions of the heart, sensuality, malice, envy, worldliness, avarice, status-seeking, terminating in arrogance and conceit. Ghazali joins Augustine here: Pride is the final result of *hawā* and the antithesis of trusting submission (*islām*). (Ih III, Books 1-10, B 201ff) On the other side, the attributes of the converted Islamic subject are those epistemic virtues of Quarter IV: courage, gratitude, fear and hope, poverty and self-denial, trust, love, and yearning, consummating

---

[2] See Ali Issa Othman, *Concept of Man in Islam*, pp. 71-114, esp. p. 91; see also Ih III, 1, 167ff; I, 1, 85.

in resolve, sincerity, contemplation, and self-examination. (Ih IV, Books 1-10, B 311f) In the one quarter, the vices which flow from *hawā* guarantee ignorance; and in the other, the virtues which detail the Islamic disposition (*fiṭra*) permit knowledge (*maʿrifa*). We should notice too how the "Reviver of Islam" never disjoins Sufi ecstasy from integrity in the common life, nor character from cognition, and how he insists that we know only in self-mortification, which quiets self-impulse.

Ghazali is not uninterested in conventional epistemology. He outlines various advancing levels of sensation, discrimination, and intellection. With Augustine he is a realist; we can know God's created Earth in our intelligent capacity as his vicegerents (caliphs). That licenses the sciences, which Ghazali ever recognizes and sometimes praises. Though often incidentally, he reveals much appreciation of the natural scene. Still, we are for Ghazali citizens of two worlds, the sensuous-visible one and the spiritual-invisible one. These are comparable to Augustine's mutable and immutable realms, to Sankara's phenomenal *māyā* and noumenal Brahman, to Nagarjuna's relative *saṃsāra* and absolute *nirvāṇa*. In contrast to the natural world, the supernal world is known only through religious apprehension, beyond any secular epistemology, and this requires reformation of the self.

All faith must *surpass* the sensory world in order to know the sacred. But in his undoing of this self-impulse, Ghazali has much inclination to *suppress* the natural world. The senses always darken our spiritual sight. "The senses preoccupy the soul, drag it back to the Sense-world, and turn a man's face away from the world of the Invisible and of the Realm Supernal." That is why he thinks that spiritual vision is sleep-like, or even occurs in sleep; for in both states sensory input is stopped and psychic insight is more freely allowed. "The only effect of sleep in this and similar visions is to suppress the authority of the senses over the soul." (Ni 79)

We will have later to puzzle over Ghazali's valuation of the present, sensory world, though he does not deny it reality. We need here to notice only his disciplining of sensuality so as to check self-impulse, if the Muslim is ever to see the common world *sub specie aeternitatis*, panentheistically. Ghazali's Sufism sometimes, and unhappily, meditates on the physical world for its dissolution. It also and always—the key point here—operates on the impulsive, passionate psyche's appetite (*hawā*) for that world. This latter operation does not necessarily scatter the objective world, but may rather by subjective reformation try to see it as it truly is, hung in God. In any case, no one can see rightly in sensuality and egoism.

Despite their divergences, the Madhyamika phenomenalism, the Advaitan idealism, and the Christian and Muslim realisms concur that, when our inquiry approaches ultimacy while yet uncorrected, *I* interrogate the world *with care*, a troubling care. The logic with which this subject operates on its object is a product of its affections, of its striving, and its defense. Always, *I* reason. Freud was to this extent right; we rationalize the world in projection of our *libido*. This attempt to know fails of universal interest, of right placement of both self and other relative to *śūnyatā*, Brahman, and God. Although their prescriptions and remedies differ, the East and the West both diagnose how we shall surely remain mistaken until there is reformation, even deformation of the I. Unregenerate knowing intensifies the ego in its distance from the world. As objectivity, it-ness increases, so does its foil, I-ness, subjectivity. No technological prowess will rectify this, for the dichotomy between subject and object provides the paradigm, the technique, with which we see. Enlightened knowing comes only with the kind of disinterest that will allow a true interest in the other, and this does not come by a neutralizing passivity, but by a sacrificial outreach that discerns something transcending and consuming the subject and its object.

Whether we are remiss, or right, we see through what we are.

II. The Known: The Epistemic Ultimate

Knowing is also analytically an objective process. One must know something, as to see is to see something. But, as with the knower's subjectivity, far from being a trivial or obvious matter, this introduces many puzzling questions. At the range of ultimacy, the real is a difficult epistemic object, and what is known "about" and who it is known "by" confuse and fade. The sacred all-ness and oneness, its outreach and its inreach disturb the knowing process. We can get neither the nearness nor the distance, neither the participation nor the detachment requisite to bring it into focus. There is a peculiar hiddenness to anything like an ultimate object. We next try to catch the sense of this in the faiths we are studying.

1. The transcendent ultimate

Boldly put, the ultimate is not an object at all, and therefore cannot be "objectively" known. In the East, this is the crux of nondual knowing, alike in Brahman and in *śūnyatā*. "Brahman is that whose nature is permanent purity, intelligence, and freedom; it transcends speech and mind, does not fall within the category of 'object,' and constitutes the inward Self of all." (VS 3-3-22) Vedanta's purpose is "to show that Brahman as the eternal subject is never an object, and thereby to remove the distinction of objects known, knowers, acts of knowing, etc., which is fictitiously created by ignorance." (VS 1-1-4m) "Brahman is clear to the knower whose conviction is that Brahman is not an object of knowledge. Whoever, on the other hand, believes that he apprehends Brahman as an object does not at all understand the nature of Brahman." (KeU 2-3)[3] Brahman is in no genus, not one thing among others, but is the One without a second, so that the whole objectifying process is inappropriate here. Brahman is so spiritual that the whole corporeal element is dismissed as illusion (*māyā*). The way we know in religion varies greatly from our routine knowing of things; it is access to the transcendent ground, our nondual intuition of the indeterminate Greatness, and hence the irrelevance of sensation. "Only a differentiated object, which is within range of the senses, can be perceived, but the Self is the opposite of that." (BrU 3-9-26) Brahman is pure consciousness in which objects disappear.

Nagarjuna has his parallel point, but he pushes further to say that reality will not become even an Absolute, much less a God. We search for an Object only to find emptiness, no-thing or non-being subjacent to phenomena. Transcendent to thing-hood, event-hood, and every empirical category, the real (*tattva*) cannot be

---

[3] Translation by M.K. Venkatarama Iyer, *Advaita Vedanta*, p. 28.

reified, or made an object. *Śūnyatā* is overarching suchness (*tathatā*), too recessive for any predicates. So thesislessness follows from the nonobjectivity of *śūnyatā*. The symbol of *śūnyatā*, an open circle surrounding emptiness, catches this quiet, inarticulate splendor. Even when Nagarjuna breaks into praise before a personified focus of his faith, we retain this deference, as in his hymn to Buddha being. "Thou art neither big nor small, neither long nor globular. Thou hast reached the state of the limitless. Homage unto Thee, the unlimited One. Thou art neither far away nor near, neither in the sky nor in the earth, neither in the cycle of existence nor in Nirvāṇa. Homage unto Thee, who dost reside in no place!" (CS 2-6f) We can sense relative things as the "appearance" of supreme reality, but what is absolutely so is hidden beyond any apparent objects. "But even if Thy appearance has been seen, it cannot be said that Thou hast been seen. When the object has been seen, Thou art well seen, but reality is not the object of vision." (CS 1-17) That is the *beyond* of "the wisdom that has gone beyond" (*prajñā-pāramitā*), that is, beyond the questing for an objective real which characterizes all lesser wisdoms.

In the West, theism knows an objective God. Nevertheless its God is no object. Ghazali's form of this is to deny God all resemblance to an objective entity. "He resembles no entity and no entity resembles him; nothing is like him and he is not like anything." (Ih I, 2, 2m) That is the recurrent Muslim witness that "God is greater" (*Allāhu akbar*), for there is no thing with which God can be compared; he is transcendently greater than any empirical object, and hence the supersensory quest we have already noticed in Ghazali. Augustine continues this line of thought, warning that "God is not said to fill the world in the sense that water, air, and even light fill space, so that with a greater or smaller part of himself he fills a greater or smaller part of the world. He is able to be everywhere present in entirety. He cannot be contained in any place. He can come without leaving the place where he was. He can depart without abandoning the place to which he had come." (Ep 2-4) To locate him as an object, objectively to locate him is to make a category mistake.

This is to say that God is pure spirit, and only understanding this,

Augustine confesses, did he begin to make sense out of Christianity. Plato helped him here with his concept of an intelligible world superintending the sensible. Nearer like mind than body, God is a subject not an object, and is to be known by subjective correspondence. "Approach to God is not across intervals of space, but by likeness, and withdrawal from him is by unlikeness." (Tr 7-12) "If the soul reaches him, it reaches him by a sort of incorporeal and spiritual touch, and that only if it is pure." (Sm 117-5) Augustine does not give us an Oriental nondualism, still he finds there is no dichotomy between subject and object; rather there is dialogue, the I encountering an Eternal Thou, never an It. (Buber) So the West too transcends the objective mode of knowing, on account of the character of its ultimate.

2. The immanent ultimate

Transcendence sometimes passes unawares into immanence. The very distance of the ultimate, its nonlocation and its spirituality, next swing round to become its nearness, its composition of all, its omnipresent location, its subjective or inward pervasiveness together with its objective or universal pervasiveness. "That is far off, That is very near; That is inside all, and That is outside all." (*IsU* 5) God is light and veiled with light, in a prime symbol for Ghazali, being hidden because so obvious, transcendent because so pervasive, invisible because we do not see it, so much as we see in it and with it, for we are seldom cognizant of sheer light, but usually rather of things lighted. "This very intensity is the direct cause of its invisibility, for things that go beyond one extreme pass over into the extreme opposite." (Ni 66) The search for God, in Ghazali's more homely metaphor, is like the dullard who is riding on his ass while looking for it; God is right at us, supporting us, while we are looking for him. (Ih IV, 6, 678) Similarly, Brahman is so with us that to miss it is like forgetting to count oneself in tallying the number of persons present. (TaU 2-1-1)

This immanence is objective, actually there in the world. While there is no thing that *is*, there is no thing that *is not* Brahman, or God, or *śūnyatā*, when the world is seen through. "The entire aggregate of things is nondifferent from Brahman." (VS 2-3-6m)

"There is one God hidden in all beings, all-pervading, the Self within all beings." (VS 2-3-17) The doctrine of appearance (*māyā*) bears witness that Brahman is the final substrate of all. Augustine's God, we have just heard, is able to be actually and everywhere present in entirety. Islam is often considered a religion of transcendence, yet by a passing over into contraries, Ghazali finds such sheer immanence as to broach pantheism. In this way Sufi Islam merges with Sunni Islam. Allah's divine unity permeates and even undoes all pluralism; the world is filled with his signs, and more, there is nothing that does not resolve into Allah's omnipresence.

Though more recessive, *śūnyatā* is not less pervasive, but is always there and here. Consider this rare positive mood: "This *tathatā*, universal reality, is in all. It is in the Buddha, it is also in the *bodhisattva*, for it is one, undivided. It is therefore that the *bodhisattva* is considered to be the same as the Buddha. Apart from and devoid of *tathatā*, there is nothing; there is nothing that does not ultimately enter the *tathatā*.... Even in the beasts there is the *tathatā*. But they have not yet fulfilled the necessary conditions to realize the ultimate reality in them. They have not yet brought to light the *tathatā* in them." (MPCv 262m)[4] Mahayana came, in later years, to say that there is Buddha-essence in all. But this pervasiveness is not lost even if such positiveness is dissolved into negativity, as it usually is in Madhyamika. Even with the undoubted Nagarjuna all things enter *śūnyatā*. We will presently catch this negative pervasiveness in the likeness of *śūnyatā* to space.

Now, owing to the interfusing of extremes, we can move from the objectivity or universal occurrence of this ultimate to enter its subjectivity or inward presence. "Where is your God? But the soul's God is within, and is within spiritually, and is lofty spiritually; not as though by spatial intervals, as places are higher through such intervals. For if altitude of this kind is in question, the birds excel us in approaching God. But the soul does not reach him, except as it passes through itself." (NP 130-12) The divine subject has its nearest analogue and contact in the human subject, not in the study of

---

[4] Though it is taken from the *Mahā-Prajñā-Pāramitā-Śāstra*, we may wonder whether the positive tone is quite that of Nagarjuna himself.

external objects. So we discover that we ourselves are the image of this God we wish to know, a patristic antecedent for the epistemic methodology which Kierkegaard was later to recover. "God is a subject and therefore exists only for subjectivity in inwardness."[5] When Muhammad is asked, "Where is God? In the earth or in the heavens?" he replied, "In the hearts of his believing creatures." He further recalls how God says, "My earth cannot contain me, nor my heaven, but the tender and tranquil heart of my believing creatures contains me." (Ih III, 1, 111) Two much-loved Qur'anic verses notice how "God stands between a man and his heart," and how Allah says of man, "We are nearer to him than the jugular vein." (S 8.24*a*; S 50.16*a*)

Not by a hair's breadth is Brahman other than the self. "He is my very Self, dwelling within the lotus of my heart. Smaller than a grain of rice is the Self; smaller than a grain of barley, smaller than a mustard seed." (*ChU* 3-14-2f,*p*) Knowing this self is more like self-knowing than like other-knowing, nearest to pure, nonobjectifying consciousness, a discovering of the lamp, not of something it illuminates, of the seer, not the seen. "This Immutable, O Gargi, is never seen by anybody, not being a sense-object, but it is itself the witness, being vision itself.... So also it is never thought, not being an object of the mind, but is itself the thinker, being thought itself. Similarly, it is never known, not being an object of the intellect, but is itself the knower, being intelligence itself." (BrU 3-8-11m) Even for Nagarjuna, the puzzling finding of emptiness in the stead of the egoistic self is, so paradoxically, just the coursing of the *tathāgata* onward into the immanent *tathatā*. Despite their differences, do not all these saints gather around an intimate ultimate whose very immediacy makes it epistemically evasive?

3. The consummate ultimate

An axial real will be exhaustive both in its outreaching beyond us and in its inrushing within us. So we say that God, Brahman, and *śūnyatā* are consummate. What in the two previous sections we

[5] Søren Kierkegaard, *Concluding Unscientific Postscript*, trans. D.F. Swenson and W. Lowrie (Princeton: Princeton University Press 1941), p. 178.

differentiated into transcendence and immanence, we can now integrate into a staggering inclusiveness, further to register the epistemic intransigence we have been developing. Religious inquiry in its universal intent has the maximum possible cognitive assignment.

First, the comprehensive ultimate is, almost analytically, incomprehensible. Comprehended by it, we cannot comprehend it. The divine exaltedness escapes our reach, though we find no escape from it. Since believers search the unsearchable, there is in religious inquiry a humility and reverent mystery, which is often read by the proud or the puzzled as a dodge and put-down. "We are speaking of God; is it any wonder if you do not understand? For if you do comprehend, he is not God. Let there be a pious confession of ignorance, rather than a rash profession of knowledge." (Sm 117-5) "This is not God, if you have comprehended it, but if this is God, you have not comprehended it." (Sm 52-16) Augustine thus finds true the Latin aphorism, *Deus cognitus, Deus nullus*. Ghazali does too: "The end result of the knowledge of the knowers (*'ārifīn*, those with *ma'rifa*) is their inability to know him, and their knowledge is, in truth, that they do not know him."[6] Such warnings as these fail to recognize some partial comprehension, else our doctors are incoherent; but we want now only their encounter of a frustrating *mysterium*. Such an encounter guarantees rather than questions the divinity which has been met. The finite, spiritual mind stands on the shores of the infinite, divine ocean, and the saint finds God to get lost in God.

Eastward, this tendency toward agnosticism advances even more. Brahman is apprehended, never comprehended, that is, existentially known but never cognitively explored. "He is incomprehensible, for he cannot be comprehended." (*BrU* 4-2-4p) "Him the eye does not see, nor the tongue express, nor the mind grasp. Him we neither know nor are able to teach. Different is he from the known, and different is he from the unknown." (*KeU* 1-3f,p) Brahman with attributes (*saguṇa*), comprehended, is not Brahman

---

[6] From NN, an opening section untranslated by Stade. Translation by Shehadi, *Ghazali's Unique Unknowable God*, p. 37m.

without attributes (*nirguṇa*), the incomprehensible, except as we introduce error (*māyā*) and approximation (*neti-neti*). Similarly for the Madhyamika saint, perfect wisdom is vastly beyond us. Buddha warns Subhuti: "Subhuti: 'Hard to know fully, O Lord, is the perfection of wisdom!' The Lord: 'Because the perfection of wisdom has not been seen by anyone, nor heard, nor felt, nor discerned, nor fully known.'" (MP 301) *Emptiness* is where all our concepts collapse in awareness of the incomprehensible, the comprehensive Void, and *prajñā* is unthinkable arrival. So we see how absolute truth cannot be made relative without thereby being made empty, and now we may more favorably return to the Buddhist denial of "intellection" and "activities of mind" in *śūnyatā*. We are back at the silence so universally found at the sacred frontiers.

Secondly, this obscurity of the ultimate lies not only in its escape from our powers but also in its intimacy, its inescapability. Every saint invites us here to consider the epistemic oddness of light. In Augustine's and Ghazali's illumination, similarly to the way in which the sun shines for vision, the divine light bridges knower and known. The Buddha too radiates light to fill the world, and "enlightenment" is Buddha's prime symbol. (MP 38ff) In Brahmanism, "the manifestation of this entire world consisting of names and forms, acts, agents, and fruits has for its cause the existence of the light of Brahman; just as the existence of the light of the sun is the cause of the manifestation of all form and color.... Whatever is perceived is perceived by the light of Brahman only." (VS 1-3-22m) Ghazali continues a theme we have already heard: "Praise then be to the one who is concealed from mankind by his light, the one who is hidden from them by the degree of his manifestness!" (NN 112)

It matters little whether the thought here is in Latin, Arabic, or Sanskrit. For all, the oddness of light helps us see the intimacy of knowing the divine. Even in *science*, routine objective knowledge, we know by divine light, perhaps unawares. The way we can see an empirical object unmindful of the solar light in and by which it is seen is an analogy of this. In *wisdom*, we trace the lighted object back to its illuminating source, the enveloping Light in which all proceeds. To be aware of such a fundamental light is demanding in its intimate reflexivity, since we quit the ordinary objective mode to inquire into our elemental epistemic condition. This lighting of the grounds by which all illumination takes place is rather like trying to see the light with which we see, to think about the logic with which we are thinking. Augustine and Ghazali suppose an entified light, a God who lights himself, but is hidden in that consuming light. So too with Sankara and Brahman. Even in Nagarjuna, where there is no comparable entity, still there is non-dual *seeing into tathatā*, an *illumination* elusive for its hidden intimacy.

In another metaphor, God, Brahman, and *śūnyatā* are like space, which suggests an environmental comprehensiveness. "That Brahman is truly the space (*ākāśa*) which surrounds mankind." (*ChU* 3-12-7m) "In being the universal principle of accommodation, while not yet being a specific thing, space (*ākāśa*) is the prototype of the ultimate reality (*śūnyatā*)." (VK 206f) God, the creator of space and time, is as enveloping as these and yet is so omnipresent as to transcend them both. Like the fish looking for water, or the child for air, so is the person who is in search of the encircling God. "It is hard to discover where he is, still harder to discover where he is not." (Qu 77) Whether it is by the spirituality and immensity of God, or by the inarticulation and the attenuation of Brahman and "thatness," the sacred real is consummate in its simplicity, in its depth, its embrace. It is extensively and intensively pervading.

4. The critical ultimate

The spiritual real is never gently within except as it is also a radical presence. It comes with violence, though it brings peace; it is demanding though rewarding, exhausting though fulfilling. We journey there on its terms, it does not come on our terms. It requires submission (*islām*), self-emptiness (*śūnyatā*), the losing of life to find it (*kenōsis*), renunciation and detachment (*vairāgya*). This ultimate which we seek is nonnegotiable, absolute; before it we negotiate and yield, even if meanwhile and humanly speaking we adjudicate our estimates of what is ultimate. Although God is persuasive and loving, God is also a coercive, judging power with whom we sooner or later must reckon, willing or not. Both Christ in his love and Buddha in the *bodhisattva's* compassion search those who are searched for. Since, East or West, the inflexible ego is our main epistemic barrier, to possess any truth about any ultimate reality is to be dispossessed from that possessive ego-center.

"We do not judge truth; truth judges us," says Augustine. The critic who thinks himself a discoverer realizes that he is the discovered. (VR 56) We reverse the scientific method, typified in "I examine that object," and find rather the spiritual awareness, "Thou God seest me." (Lb 2-34) The hunter becomes the hunted, the lover the loved, the judge the judged, the master the mastered, the knower the known, when Augustine finds that his *Confessions* are to One who, being sought, rather found him. Similarly, Ghazali's *Deliverance* is as he becomes first a sinner, then a penitent, then a saint, and finds how the path to God leads through the dark night of the soul. At the level of sacred knowledge, our convictions convict us, our judgments judge us, and we find here that truth is trying and incriminating.

If we go further eastward, we may not be permitted to speak of a personified searching by God as an active inquisitor, for activity and intentionality are not ascribed to Brahman or found in *tathatā*. Yet there too the known still effects an excruciating search of the knower. Nontheistic truth is quite as critically invasive, quite as fully prosecuting of the defendant ego, if not more so. The renunciation which is demanded as a condition of inquiry into Brahman, or the perfections (*pāramitās*) stipulated for the *bodhisattva*, are amply judgmental. The ignorance (*avidyā*) of which we are convicted by Hinduism and Buddhism is less rebellious than is sin before Almighty God, but this no less finds us guilty of sophistry, of egoism, of blinding desire. The self-deformation which is demanded for critical knowledge, as this is derived from the exacting character of ultimate reality, is never more grave than it is in India. With this, we are pushing ever more deeply that understanding of personal truth which we began in chapter one, with its inward, evaluative, expansive, and disclosing natures. With this too, we return to humility and purity as these were found to be conditions of judgment in chapter two. Every real puts the self right by a difficult, critical passage.

In the religious quest there eventually collapses the treasured detachment of scientific objectivity, for this sacred "object" of study will not stay "out there" so that we may compass it about; it rather presses "in here" compassing us about. *From* this ultimate there is no detachment, for it invades even as it evades those who seek it. Yet this very sort of encroaching provides us a detachment *in* this ultimate, for by it we are criticized that we might become more discriminating, released from self-attachments and thus given a new detachment into truth. Relatively, we may be the critics; but, absolutely, we are the criticized, and the really crucial question is this crucial questioning of us. A real religion, as has been remarked of a real book, reads us. After initial and superficial contact, serious inquiry into a noble religion is always into some proposed real which is found to be probing us even as it is probed, to be offensively forcing and eroding our defenses. To inquire about religion is to find oneself inquired about, and to investigate here is to become the subject of investigation.

Looking for God, Brahman, or *śūnyatā* is a little like looking for beauty. Setting creative artistry aside for the present, let us consider our enjoying of presented beauty, as with the fall foliage or with the symphonic performance by an orchestra. Beauty is there before the beholder's arrival; it is given to the listener and to the viewer, yet in its perception it is odd to say that the beauty is either or neither without or within us. To shut our ears or eyes is to find that the beauty ceases, yet it is difficult to say, undergirding the perception, what if anything is objectively there; and even in the perception the beauty is not there in any routine sensational way, but is received at some nonscientific level.

The presented beauty is, perhaps we can best say, "in" the dialogue—or the nonduality—of knower and known. Its reception requires a judge whose being is "up to" what is presented, whose life the beauty also feeds and judges. In religious inquiry, the location of the sacred has even more of this sort of elusiveness. Antecedent to my psychic awareness, the cosmic real is discovered as soon within as without, found ever here and there, if earlier unawares, later in consummate embrace. In this embracing, objectivity and subjectivity are intimately wedded. We will next try to be more specific about this.

III. Knowing: Beyond Subjectivity and Objectivity

Our consideration of the disordered seeker to be unbiased by the peculiar reality of the sought has prepared us for a sort of gnostic truth reached in embrace and synthesis. As we now hear such a witness from each of our spiritual quadrants, we need to be cautioned that these are not entirely uniform. We still have to puzzle over differences between Brahman, *śūnyatā*, Allah, and the Father of Jesus Christ. Yet they will be in concert about a needed passage beyond subjectivity and objectivity, however envisioned, about a sort of inquiry apt for synoptic intuition, without antithesis, when our personal inwardness is engulfed by an environing reality. The self is flooded by the real. After this, we will conclude this chapter by cross-examining our doctors on the themes with which our study is titled, on participation and detachment.

1. Advaitan pure consciousness (*turīya*)

"The fourth (and final knowing state), say the wise, is not subjective experience, nor objective experience, nor experience intermediate between the two, nor is it a negative condition which is neither consciousness nor unconsciousness. It is not the knowledge of the senses, nor is it relative knowledge, nor yet inferential knowledge. Beyond the senses, beyond the understanding, beyond all expression, is the fourth. It is pure unitary consciousness, where awareness of the world and of multiplicity is completely obliterated." (*MaU* 7m,p) That is Sankara's *advaitan* (nondual) consciousness, past either separate self or separate other, past subject or object. The states of consciousness advanced in the *Māṇḍūkya Upanishad* are (1) the waking state, (2) dreaming sleep, where objects are but apparently real and separated, (3) dreamless sleep, where there is, by Hindu presumption, consciousness devoid of any phenomenal scene, and (4) pure consciousness (*turīya*).

The last state is doubly enigmatic. Its approach using the analogy of dreams and sleep suggests to the outsider, first, sheer subjectivity and, then, unconsciousness. We may justifiably ask whether there is any such psychological state and what it has to do with cosmological knowledge. But, for the moment, let us listen to how the progression of knowledge states is intended to rid us, not of consciousness, but of objects. When we rise above the objective mode, objects vanish. Advaita Vedanta means "to intimate only the annihilation of all specific cognition, not the annihilation of the cognizer. For there is no destruction of the knowing of the knower." (VS 1-3-19m) Why then do we not tumble into barren subjectivity, which, however pleasant, is disconnected from reality and therefore not veridical? Because by the Advaitan account this consciousness finally "sees through" objects and is no longer "of" anything. The realization that the phenomenal world is fugitive is what the dreaming analogy intends to teach us. About such a riddance of objects, we shall express some concern; still, every passage to ultimacy, East or West, dissolves the permanence and autonomy of multiversal things and passes beyond plural objectivity into a universal real.

We err if we think that the knowing of Brahman is objective, like the knowing of some conventional thing in the waking world. That world is but illusion (*māyā*), to be dispelled before we gain access to Brahman. But we equally err if we think this fourth level of knowing is subjective, like the knowing of the waking self, set oppositely to its parade of objects. There is here a radical plunge to a deeper Self, about which, Sankara insists, there is nothing individual or personally subjective. For there the *jiva* (ego) with its subjectivisms has been dismantled, and we reach the divine presence subjacent to the subject, as we also reach omnipresence subjacent to the phenomenal mirage. We have risen above the subjective mode, for the empirical self must as much be "seen through" as have been empirical objects. So individuality vanishes and we are elevated to a superconsciousness. "When the individual soul which is held in the bonds of slumber by the beginningless *māyā* awakes, then it knows the eternal, sleepless, dreamless non-duality." (VS 2-1-9m) That true "awakening" is what the dreaming analogy intends, though it conveys it somewhat unconvincingly.

There is thus a reflexive dissolution of the subjective self and of the objective world. "This doctrine of the individual soul having its Self in Brahman...does away with the independent existence of the individual soul, just as the idea of the rope does away with the idea of the snake, for which the rope had been mistaken. And if the doctrine of the independent existence of the individual soul has to be set aside, then the opinion of the entire phenomenal world—which is based on the individual soul—having an independent existence is likewise set aside." The "cognition of unity" removes the "cognition of manifoldness." (VS 2-1-14) When *advaita* (nonduality) replaces *avidyā* (not-seeing), even the metaphor of a mirror, which supposes that the local self reflects the great Self, is too dualist. "As the reflection of the sun in water enters into the sun when the water is removed, so this self gets wholly established in the supreme immutable Self." (PrU 4-9m) Absolute nonduality (*kevala advaita*) is what Sankara finds so metaphorically attractive about deep sleep. "When the division of subject and object is eliminated by enlightenment, there is only the all-pervading and intrinsic bliss that is one without a second." (TaU 2-8-1m)

Such an inner discovery, following as it does the obliteration of our sensory input, worries us with its implications about world illegitimacy, and it correspondingly reduces any objective criticism of our subjective states. No one ought so to hasten beyond subjectivity and objectivity that he bypasses the critical prowess which can be gained while passing through these categories. Still, in religious inquiry we may well expect that an ultimate self-discovery will have to supersede sensation and intuit the sacred union of the subject self and its divine object. Any who believe that the psyche is a key to things must discover the Real within. Whoever plumbs the depths of the human subject will not be far from the objective reality of God.

2. *Prajñā-pāramitā* as nondual wisdom

More insistently than all the others, Madhyamika knows no objective real. More insistently too, it eventually has no knowing subject, no self. Yet the *bodhisattva* just as devoutly as the others aspires to know through a wisdom that goes beyond. Beyond

what? Among multiple answers, none is more crucial than: beyond
subjectivity and objectivity. Candrakirti writes in his commentary
on Nagarjuna, "Thoughts and feelings do not arise in the undifferentiated whole; there is no subject and no object of knowledge;
there is consequently no turmoil." (Ca 91m) Nagarjuna sings,
"From the standpoint of metaphysical truth there is neither knower
nor thing to be known," because the *tathāgata* has "perceived the
sameness of everything." He is "beyond any duality." (CS 1-3f; 4-4)
In an often-used simile, this knowing is like looking into pure blue
sky. You have nothing as your object, but rather stare into it, and
are absorbed to sense the expansive whole.

"In the Gnosis of perfect wisdom, subject and object are identical. Nevertheless, for the purposes of description, one can distinguish between perfect wisdom as a subjective, mental function
(*prajñā*) and its object, which is emptiness (*śūnyatā*)." (SP 61)
Edward Conze thus notes in Madhyamika a relative distinction
which ultimately vanishes. Accordingly, we will follow his lead
and focus first on the nonduality of the apparently subjective
prajñā-wisdom and then on the nonduality of the apparently
objective *śūnyatā*-void.

(a) In the ignorance of *avidyā*, world and self compose each
other, so that subjects and objects are overlaid on reality, all of
which is a dichotomizing bad dream. In enlightenment we see
through this. We cease to dream up these distinctions, awakening
to the evanescent character, or the emptiness, of the phenomenal
world and the phenomenal self. Seeing the subject-object bifurca-
tion to be hollow (*śūnya*), the *bodhisattva* discards it. "He courses
in ultimate reality, wherein the idea of duality does not exist." (MP
414) The first three of the twenty kinds of emptiness developed in
the *Great Sūtra* are "the emptiness of the subject, the emptiness of
the object, and the emptiness of both subject and object." (MP 144)
The *tathāgata's* cognition, his level of wisdom, passes beyond
"subjective-objective emptiness." (MP 102)

(b) Beyond to what? Refusing to say, Madhyamika will only
point with an attenuated, nondescript "real" (*tattva*) or "suchness"
(*tathatā*), and even that rather rarely. Usually Madhyamika prefers
to evade description with its arid *śūnyatā*. But in either case we can
transpose from (a) the psychic nonduality of *prajñā* to (b) the

cosmic nonduality of *śūnyatā*. But here to say more would reestablish that subjectivity and objectivity of which in *prajñā* we are rid. In this light we understand why Nagarjuna makes such a total investment in viewlessness. Every view must be "about," literally *from out*, and thus reconstructs the subject-object illusion. All concepts are as subjectivizing as they are objectifying; they force us into separating our subject selves off from our objects of thought. So reason must be deconceptualized and must give way to intuition as apt for fullest truth. Ordinary percepts are too perspectival, too composing of an ego and its world, except that there is precisely this extraordinary *śūnyatā* which can serve as the critical decomposing concept, the phantom that destroys other phantoms, when it reduces us to a viewless perception. In this viewlessness that results from *śūnyatā* there is no view from here, and therefore no one-sided subjectivity. So in the end we see things as they really are (that is, we see that things as such are not really separated, nor us from them), which was the initial hope of "objectivity."

In *śūnyatā*, *nirvāṇa* becomes nondifferent from *saṃsāra*. We enter the Madhyamika cosmic nonduality by telescoping the world and the ultimate, heaven and earth, into nondual oneness, or, better, into nondual emptiness. Such a coalescence is intended to protect us from worries parallel to those we have just expressed in the case of Vedanta. This knowing is not thought by Madhyamika to be so vapidly subjective as Sankara's fourth state. At the cosmic as well as at the psychic level, the divine and the mundane realms are brought into one embrace; and then the universal reality (*tathatā*) is found to be in all. By transfiguration an illusory world returns, redescribed and better experienced as the abode of the real. *Saṃsāra*, the ordinary world, is the dichotomizing of subject and object, but in *prajñā*, ultimate wisdom, this *saṃsāra* is de-subjectivized and de-objectified. Beyond the common world, the self empties into the ineffable real, into *nirvāṇa*. But that *nirvāṇa* is also here and now, and so *saṃsāra* is not left at all. One is not simply released *from* the duality of subject and object, but *into* the nonduality of *nirvāṇa* and *saṃsāra*, the beyond and the here. So we pass from *avidyā* (not-seeing) to *advaya* (nonduality).

This merging of the sacred and the secular brings the Madhyamika saint to bliss. But in those of us who may stand outside there is considerable bewilderment. What do we make of this awesome *śūnyatā* by which nonduality is obtained? Although intended to convey the fugitive nature of the objective world and of the subjective self, the imagery of trick and mirage, powerfully coupled with this master percept of "emptiness," very easily slips into a devaluing both of the apparent self and of the apparent world. Does this not tempt us to bypass, rather than to pass through, their relative witness to absolute wisdom? Does this not, alas, cause us to wonder, even if we could arrive there, about the worth of this nondual Void?

3. *Ma'rifa* as passing away (*fanā'*)

In the book of his *Revivification* which deals most with mysticism, that on music and ecstasy, Ghazali reveals how he cherishes the Sufi passing away into the Unity (*fanā' fī'l-tawḥīd*), a state of deep divine embrace, of being enwrapped in God. We will listen at sufficient length to find its implications for the passage beyond subjectivity and objectivity.

"Of such as are in this condition, the Sufis use the expression *faniya*, 'he has passed away from himself and come to an end' (i.e. he is oblivious to himself) and, whenever anyone passes away from himself, he must pass away from all besides himself. Then it is as though he passed away from everything except the One—the witnessed One. He passes away also from the act of witnessing; for the heart, whenever it turns aside to view the act of witnessing and itself as a witnesser, is heedless of the thing witnessed. But for him who is infatuated in a thing which he sees, in his state of seeking to plunge into the thing, there is no turning aside to his act of seeing, nor to his own self through which is his seeing, nor to his heart in which is his pleasure. A drunken man tells no tale about his drunkenness, nor he who is taking pleasure about his taking of pleasure, but his tale is only about that in which he takes pleasure. And an example of this is in knowledge of a thing, for it changes to knowledge of the knowledge of that thing, and the knowledge of the thing, whenever there comes to the knower knowledge of his knowledge, is turned from the thing.... This is the step of those who are faithfully true in understanding and in ecstasy, and it is the highest of the steps." (Ih II, 8, 716f,m)

Knowing is in first order union, not in subsequent reflection, as we are taken out of ourselves into what we know, passing out of our subjectivism into its objective reality. First, *we know* unitively; but when, secondly, *we know that we know*, the rationalizing, self-conscious ego has already broken the spell of intimate witnessing. The most intense theological posture is address; any who seek to express that witnessing have turned aside from its immediacy, as we pass from *ma'rifa* to *'ilm*, from *gnōsis* to *epistēmē*. There are vital differences between Ghazali and the Eastern nondualities, but they have the common conviction that the witness is so enwrapped in the witnessed One that self-conscious separateness is lost.

The relevance of *fanā'* for passage beyond subjectivity and objectivity is clear in a commentary on this passage by Kojiro Nakamura. "This is the ecstatic state in which the object, or 'the witnessed One,' has so completely permeated and absorbed the mind of the subject that he is not conscious of himself but only of the object. To be more precise, the subject does not have *his* consciousness of the object, since he is not conscious of himself. Nor is there consciousness of *his* witnessing of the object. Only the witnessed One occupies his mind. In this state, therefore, there is no disparity nor differentiation of the witness, the witnessed One, and the act of witnessing.... This is the goal of the Sufi way in the world."[7] The richest kind of knowledge we can enjoy is in the synthesis of the subject with its object, not in the analysis of an object by a subject.

Nevertheless, Ghazali analyzes this union, lest it be misunderstood for the lack of an adequate critique through rational judgment. Subsequent reflection, following "the passing away of passing away," will find that union to have been not identification (*ittiḥād*) or inherence (*ḥulūl*), in which the divine and the human essences coalesce, but rather to have been nearness (*qurb*). More than that, the experience was unification (*tawḥīd*) understood in

---

[7] Nakamura, *Ghazali on Prayer*, p. 17f; cf. Ih I, 9.

both a subjective and an objective sense. Subjectively, the mystic's consciousness is filled with God; the separated self has passed away and is absorbed. Further, objectively, the God-derivative life is sensed to be contingent on God, from God and one with God. The fugitive world is seen through; only God exists and everything is from and in him. "All things perish, except His Face." (S 28.88a)

In these moods, Ghazali accommodates what, out of context, looks like pantheism and perhaps was so in other Sufis. Sometimes, it even brings him close to Advaita Vedanta. But he is too Muslim not to check these absorptions in God with a denial of our identification with God. (Ni 60f) Our knowing unites the human subject and the divine object so that psychological separateness is forgotten, but it does not obliterate the logical or cosmological subject-object difference. Our resonance with God is not our identity with him. Some favorite metaphors here, on which we soon press Ghazali, are those of the lover and his beloved, the reflective mirror, and the crystal which borrows its color from the light it absorbs. Ghazali need not be one with Vedanta or Madhyamika to share their conviction that we must go beyond subjectivity and objectivity. (Ih II, 8, 718)

We can now return to questions left unsettled earlier. God, drunkenness, and health are all known "as they truly are" in unitarian and ecstatic enjoyment. But drunkenness and health, though initially suggestive, eventually fail as overly subjective metaphors, while Ghazali's talk of "tasting" better preserves the needed subjective-objective union. For all its critical necessity, knowing "about" reintroduces a distance between subject and object which ruptures primitive, intimate knowledge. The physician knows about a disease, the scientist knows about drunkenness, and on conventional occasions that may suffice, or even be preferred. But it will not suffice at ultimacy. The saint enjoys a kind of conjunctive tasting in which "about" passes away. Tasting is always of another; nonetheless in it one brings the other within. Is tasting a subjective or an objective experience? Both and neither, it passes beyond to unite taster, tasted, and tasting. So too when we taste of God.

4. Wisdom (*sapientia*) as recovery of the *imago Dei*

"We can recognize in ourselves an image of God (*imago Dei*). Of course, this is not an equal image but rather a very remote one. There is neither coeternity, nor, in a word, consubstantiality with him. Nevertheless, it is an image which by nature is nearer to God than any other created thing, and one that by reformation can be perfected into still closer resemblance." (CG 11-26) Augustine's care to distinguish the believer's capacities from the consubstantiality (*homoousion*) which he allows only to Jesus indicates what resistance he would have given to Advaita Vedanta. But, if God is ever known, this is only as we mirror the Trinity, instantiating in ourselves the Father's grace, the Son's humility, and the Spirit's charity. God is not known scientifically and publicly, but contemplatively and inwardly. The objective God is known by subjective correspondence, by the soul's synthesis with, rather than by its analysis of, God.

The African doctor's *Trinity* has as a dominating theme the search for psychological analogues of the trinitarian God. That account is too complex for us to judge here; its detail no longer illuminates the Trinity as convincingly as Augustine had hoped. But all we need for present consideration is the basic conviction, congenial to all Christianity, that knowing God is not like knowing about trees, where we study an objective other; rather, to know God is to experience the self as a grace-full image of God. Rightly to know oneself is to know God, for it is to know a personal God-likeness in which the self reflects God, catches God's grace, and so the external "about" is erased. In this inward subject-subject dialogue, we are past all external dichotomy of subject and object. Augustine's notion of our "participation in God" is an alternate description of this imaging. (Tr 14-20)

Consider the incarnation, in which "Jesus Christ became a participator in our mortality in order to make us participators of his divinity." (CG 21-16) In the new Adam we recollect the primal likeness lost in sin. The historic atonement repairs our alienation and reconciles the human and the divine. In Christ, we discover how the temporal is funded by the eternal, first in Jesus of Nazareth and then, derivatively from him, also in us. God the Father,

Creator of persons in his image, continues his presence historically in God the Son, Immanuel, God with us, in order to effect the pervasive, immanent presence of God the Spirit, God within us. All of life is a trinitarian participation, though we are cautioned, "It is one thing to be God, quite another to be a participant in God." (CG 22-30) Augustine's notion of *understanding* requires this subjective-objective conjunction. "This intellectual vision is the soul's apprehension joining the apprehending subject and the apprehended object." (S1 1-13) We can register anew here the force of a correct and corrective *agapē*-love as an epistemic virtue. This participation is by detachment from all subjective, proud love of self and from all biasing Babylonian loves.

"Participation," following the Greek *koinōnia*, fellowship, is a more felicitous metaphor for establishing world and self integrities than is illusion (*māyā*) or emptiness (*śūnyatā*), and thus Augustine is comfortable with a less rigorous nonduality than the Indians require. Although he too holds that the phenomenal scene is evanescent, still the mutable partakes positively of the immutable divine reality. Surviving in God, the world can be used sacramentally in a way foreign to Madhyamika or Advaita Vedanta; but it can be so used only by the noble person, and hence there is an Augustinian inward turn quite as necessary as any in Sankara or in Nagarjuna. When the world is hallowed, it points to God, among other ways, through man and woman as the noblest of creatures. "Among all the things which he created, nothing is nearer to God than the human soul." (Qu 77) But the soul only points this way for and in that person who, pure in heart, recollects and becomes himself this principal sacrament, this mirror of God. If not, if we lust through the world in selfish pride, Jerusalem decays into Babylon, and the world and the self point us nowhere.

Thus, at the apex of creation, the arrow to an objective God passes through the subjective self. "Man must first be restored to himself, so that, making in himself as it were a stairsteps, he may mount up and be elevated to God." (Rt 1-8-3) Though we shall later find a way in which the East-West differences are finally incommensurable, Augustine is together with all our respondents when he advises that we must come within to know the real. "Do not go outside yourself, but remain within yourself; for truth resides in the inmost part of man." (VR 72) "Ascend, but do not seek a mountain. Do all within. Even if you seek a lofty place, first be yourself a temple of God within, for he in his temple will hear him that prays." (GJ 15-25)

Augustine never seeks a contentless intuition of the One without a second, but rather a synthetic intellection of all in God. His sense of the trinitarian community in unity, as well as that of plural earthen creatureliness, protects him from a homogeneous nonduality. His concept of participation, *koinōnia*, makes Augustine synergistic, however odd that term may seem of him. Against Arius, he will not have any synergism of divine and human energies. But against monergistic Vedanta, he would insist on grace from God so as to establish the distinct and dependent self, not as God but in God. Augustine might even have complained that Advaitans stumble mistakenly into the root sin, the desire to be God, an ultimate ego trip after all, rather than content themselves with the more humble desire to be like God, the root of righteousness. Augustine is not lost in the ocean of God, but, with Paul, is made a new person in Christ, crucified to self but resurrected to newness of life in Christ. Still, even this communion, symbolized in the Eucharistic tasting, is one in which God is known beyond subjectivity and objectivity. We see reality "objectively," as it truly is, even where God is discerned in nature and history, only by a subjective reformation in which we participate in God. This is not by a sheer but rather by a clear subjectivity. This is the discovery within of a cosmic reality that arches us out to the objective whole.

IV. Becoming: Ultimate Participation and Detachment

"He who knows Brahman certainly becomes the fearless Brahman." That puts in pith, Sankara tells us, the whole truth of the *Brihadāraṇyaka Upanishad*, and it terminates our inquiry in integral knowing and being. (*BrU* 4-4-25m) We fuse ontology with epistemology, as we earlier fused ethics with it, a fusion found not only in Advaita Vedanta, but, if differently so, found also in the others. Finally in this chapter we turn to interpret this fusion of knowing and being for the complementarity of participation and detachment of and in the real, the self, and the world. "That art thou!" Splendidly but simply, such monism returns the knower into the known, and this cognition of unity is necessarily consuming, for to know that there is One without a second is to be that One. Thus for Sankara knowing is not *karmic*, an accessory act of the person, but *jñānic*, a constitutive conjunction of self and real. In nonduality, logically and psychologically, being and truth are the same word (*sattva*). More devotionally, the *Gītā's* knowing is by entering the divine being. (BhG 18-55) But this principle does not evaporate when the Absolute does, for the *Sūtra* and the *Śāstra* alike insist that understanding Buddhism is at last a matter of becoming a Buddha. Enlightenment takes place in fully completed being (*tathāgata*), in one who has gone (*gata*) to suchness (*tathatā*). "Therefore the *bodhisattva* should cultivate this wisdom that goes on to suchness (*tathatā-prajñā-pāramitā*). Cultivating this, the *bodhisattva* can fulfill the realization of the *tathatā*." "Skillfully to enter the ultimate reality (*dharma-dhātu*), this is what penetrating comprehension of the unconditioned (*bhūtakoṭi*) means." (MPCv 262f, m)

We have thus the Madhyamika equivalent of the favorite maxim of the Yogacarin *Sūtrālaṇkāra*: "The ultimate truth has not, as a matter of fact, been preached by the blessed Buddha, seeing as how one has to realize it within himself."[8] The *Kārikās* conclude, "A person's cessation of ignorance proceeds on the basis of 'becoming' through knowledge." (Ka 26-11m) Madhyamika truth is not a possession of the ego, but requires the ego's dissolution—we might almost say its un-becoming—into nondual silence. Nagarjuna cannot allow that truth is a viewpoint, because all conceptualizations, being tributary to possessiveness, prevent our highest knowing by substituting truth at a distance. "To know emptiness is to realize emptiness."[9]

Though a theist is more reserved about the divine union, in

---

[8] Asaṅga, *Mahāyāna-Sūtrālamkāra*, trans. to French by Sylvain Lévi (Paris: Honoré Champion, 1911), v. 2, p. 138 (XII, 2).

[9] Streng, *Emptiness*, p. 98.

theism too one becomes "like" God. "All knowledge according to species is like that which it knows.... Hence, so far as we know God, we are like him, but not so that similitude becomes equality, since we do not know him to the extent of his own being." (Tr 9-16) That is a troublesome "like," which we presently erode by finding the saint to reside in the divine being which is known. Ghazali too knows a marvelous reflective capacity of the pure heart in moral congruence with God, even though he warns us that we do not acquire God's essence, but rather his attributes, realizing our "portion" of the divine names. (NN 12, passim) To the lay Muslim, "unification" (*tawḥīd*) means only a belief about God, the belief that God is one; but to the Sufi it means more, it brings an intimate coming into gnostic union (*ma'rifa*).

We can at this point partially appreciate the recurrent "contentlessness" of Asian religious truth, for even these Western saints do not adventitiously "have truth" or "know an object." Rather, knowing is by intrinsic being; each is what he knows. In the admittedly difficult concept of wisdom as "pure consciousness," we may well wonder whether knowledge survives, and our Eastern seers concede that it does not in ordinary senses. But some of what is intended has an Augustinian parallel. Scientifically to know we must know something. To ask about *knowledge* is to ask how much a person knows "about" empirical items. But *wisdom*? Here we are more involved with a question of character, no longer quantitatively with the "contents" of a mind, but now more qualitatively with the sagacious state of mind. Wisdom is more broadly intransitive, cosmic, and not always with any immediate, particular thing in objective scope. Wisdom pervades our being, as knowledge does not, and accordingly the end of knowledge is action, agentive capacity in the world, while the end of wisdom is contemplation of the embracing divine environment. Unlike scholars, who know about things, saints know God by incarnating what they know.

We have now reached the culmination of the advancing obedience begun in chapter one, as this chapter has reached ultimate participation, deepening the binding of obedience into a *becoming*, a *communion* and *union*. In every noble religion the self is lost in, flooded by, filled with the real. No religion is more consum-mately participatory than Advaita Vedanta, with its "That art thou." Uncovering Buddha essence within, the *tathāgata* "enters *tathatā*," or if that "realizing suchness" is too affirmative, then we can rather say with equal, but negative, nonentifying participation that the *tathāgata* "enters *śūnyatā*." Madhyamika's very stopping of all theses, permitting us to *have* no truth, is out of conviction that we must *be* that truth. Like the One without a second for Sankara, thesislessness for Nagarjuna registers participatory intensity. For both, *nonduality* is the final Eastern synonym for *participation*. Indeed, the Western word which heads and-has been governing our inquiry here, "participation," is too weak for Asia. These Asians must have identity, nonduality, and silence. A Western critic may judge that for these more intuitively apt modes of knowing there has been traded a more considered and reliable verbal grasp on cognition. But the Eastern experiencer thinks to gain the trust-worthiness of an incumbent immediacy and intensity, at whatever cost to the analytic prowess of detachment and distance. At ulti-macy, where knowing is by being what truly is, "objectivity" is at once the most hoped for and the most hopeless category.

Now to take fuller account of theistic participation, we must for both Christianity and Islam remove the knowing by being "like God" to replace it with an abiding "in God." *Nearness* to God (*qurb*) is not the full truth, holds Ghazali; *unification* with God (*tawḥīd*) is still truer. "One who strips himself of passions and has no desire for anything except for God Most High, engrossed in Him, does become as if he were He, but not in the sense that he actually is He. The poet at times says, 'It is as if I were the one whom I love,' and at other times, 'I am the one whom I love.' The mirror in itself does not have a color; its only property is to receive the forms of colors in such way that it gives to those looking the superficial impression that this actually is the form of the mirror." (NN 133f,a) The crystal jar borrows the color of the wine it con-tains. We do not confuse the mirror and the light source, the jar and the wine. That is the mistake of identification (*ittiḥād*) and inher-ence (*ḥulūl*), which are Ghazali's synonyms for nonduality. Careful rational analysis will prevent our confusion here. Yet color and wine certainly "fill" both the mirror and the jar, which are otherwise qualityless. So the soul is filled with, receives, and passes into its God.

The Augustinian parallel is the divine grace which comes to us and by which likeness is achieved, for *we* do not imitate God, except as *God* is our gracious source. "This then is the sum of great knowledge, for a man to know that by himself he is nothing, and that whatever he is, he is from God and is for God." (NP 70-1-4) That is the great Pauline "I, yet not I but the grace of God." (Pg 14-36) This never produces a consubstantial union, but it ever brings a convivial one, ever a shared life. Augustine's grace (*gratia*) and trust (*fides*) are homologous with Ghazali's unification (*tawḥīd*) and trust (*tawakkul*), since both elevate us into the divine, not to the point of equality, but still with a participatory intensity that exceeds mere likeness owing to the divine presence within. For all their drawing back from a too thoroughgoing divine union, our two theists are only alternately participatory, not less so than our two nondualists. What a person who authentically knows God must sense is an energetic input, an aura that comes from deeper within, or from a transcendent without, but not merely from the common self.

We appropriate or assimilate (*iktisāb*, Ghazali) the divine in all our actions; every act of our will is the presence of grace (Augustine). In this light we can understand the heavy investments our devout theists make in predestination, for we are always carriers of the sacred presence. Such a theological determinism, where we are always funded by the divine energy, when this is found in Africa and Persia is, like the nonduality found in India, the final synonym for ultimate participation, for which synergistic "participation" is again too weak a word. This likeness so skirts and wants identity that it is tortured whenever it is sought to be explained, whether in the Nicene formula, in the *imitatio Christi*, in the Eucharistic presence, or in the Sufi *fanā*'. It is better perceived than conceived, and yet it is misperceived unless it is also conceived by and for our rational criticism, inadequate though such verbalizing is in expressing this primal spiritual perception.

This *participation* is *detachment* from the self, and thus it is not an opposite of detachment but its obverse side. We find a universal principle only by consenting to our own diminishment. The monist faith which is so implicating with its "That art thou" is, by implication from this, a faith most insistent on "detachment," everywhere reflected in the renunciation demanded in the *Upanishads*, and detailed in the *Gītā's* promise and injunction: "Do your duty, always, but without attachment. That is how a man reaches the Ultimate Truth." (*BhG* 3-19p) Even if this is initially still karmic, this noninterest can be preparatory for ensuing and more contemplative detachments, where what is significantly to be lost is the sense of egoistic agency. The prerequities of the Brahmanic quest—"renunciation" (*vairāgya*) of all desire for profit, "tranquility" (*śama*), "self-restraint" (*dama*), and "dispassion" (*uparati*)— have as their sum an ultimate detachment, which liberates us from all individuating and biasing illusions. "Through the company of the good, there arises nonattachment; through nonattachment, there arises freedom from delusion; through delusionlessness, there arises steadfastness; through steadfastness, there arises liberation in life." (Hy 66m)

This is borne out, if anything more sternly, by the entrance into *śūnyatā* which Madhyamika requires. "The perfection of wisdom is marked by nonattachment." (MP 440f,m) The very negativity of the Void is an indication of the depth of the detachment required, and Madhyamika's "nonclinging" is similar to the Advaitan "nonattachment." *Śūnyatā*, emptiness, when it comes around to destroying the self (*anātman*), even in the self's spiritual accomplishments, becomes the ultimate word for detachment. "A Bodhisattva is called a 'great being,' because he remains unattached even to this thought of enlightenment." (MP 126) The possessiveless life achieves a wisdom which comes by abandoning all clinging to it, and so Buddha is supremely the saint of nonattachment.

Ghazali's "passing away" (*fanā'*) uses a root which borders on death. The Sufi passes into God, and that is the positive pole, but there is a negative pole, a passing from self, a passing away of the self. Despite Ghazali's differences from the others in his affirmative meanings, *fanā'*, his category for ultimate detachment, is quite as cathartic of the ego as anything further East. "Self-mortification," we recall, is Ghazali's key to purity in thought and is the secret of illumination. The intensity involved in this death to self is indicated, perhaps not altogether happily, in Ghazali's celebrated image that the soul in the hands of God is like a corpse in the hands of a washer who prepares it for burial. That drives home with force how we die to self-impulse (*hawā*), before we are made ready for trusting unification with God. Again, the same term (*fanā'*) that intensifies participation in God also intensifies detachment from self.

We are given, advises Augustine, commandments to love three things: God, neighbor, and self. (CG 19-14) We will judge later on that there are ways in which the "passing away," the "emptiness," and the "renunciatory detachment" advocated by the others have no real counterpart in Augustine's mutual love of self and neighbor under God. But still we can notice here that Augustine has something like them. Any legitimate self-love is resurrected in Jerusalem only after the concupiscent self has died to and in Babylon, and we must lose the self in order to gain it. Jesus exemplified such an emptying (*kenōsis*), such a renunciation, or passing away and dying for God. Pride is the debilitating sin, humility is the facilitating virtue through which our reflection of God is restored. In that sense, Christ's life, and life in Christ, is one of disinterest in self owing to our interest in God.

Finite human beings, remarked C.S. Lewis, "wanted to be nouns, but they were, and eternally must be mere adjectives."[10] That adjectival being, which gives up vain self-substantiality, catches well the Augustinian truth that humility, more than rationality, is the intellectual condition of objectivity. When we further discover that God has first emptied himself for us, and that humility is the substance of this God we seek to know, we come to see that the meek find God because theirs is a blessed subjective detachment which corresponds with the objective nature of God. "My judgment is just, because I seek not my own will, but the will of him who sent me." (Jn. 5.30)

The saints unfailingly preach a frightful abandon of self, a great

---

[10]   C.S. Lewis, *The Problem of Pain* (New York: Macmillan, 1955), p. 68.

death. To put it bluntly, knowledge of the divine is by suicide, by a paradoxical death to self in which, beyond, one is resurrected and reaches enlightenment. The cost of knowing is always in proportion to the worth of what is known, and the cost of ultimate knowing is ultimate sacrifice. That is why the academic without the devotional quest is sure to fail; it lacks this sacrificial detachment.

But what of participation and detachment in the world? That question is almost too difficult for us here, and a larger answer must be deferred for chapter six. Our respondents slip between disinterest and uninterest in the world, and perhaps sometimes they even fall into world contempt, a very different thing from detachment. *Śūnya* and *māyā* have an eviscerating effect on our participation in the *saṃsāra* world, an effect which continues even after the world has been returned as *nirvāṇa* and redescribed as Brahman. And, although the perishing (*fanā'*) of things in Allah's countenance permits, with much equivocation, their pantheistic recovery, that is never so convincingly done as it is with the biblical promise that the meek will inherit the Earth. Nevertheless for all, whatever their truth about the world and our placement in it, that truth is only known as it is superintended by detachment. With the transfer of centeredness from the self to the real, we are free from and in the world to see things without bias, as they truly are.

"A *bodhisattva* comprehends the entire world as *śūnya* and remains completely nonclinging at heart. Being firmly established in the true nature of things, he does not any more cling to the world with passion." (MPCv 299m) "When one fares by clinging, then the world would be a mass of perversion; but when one fares free from seizing, free from clinging, then is *nirvāṇa*." (MPCv 97m) "A Bodhisattva should therefore be trained in nonattachment to all realities (*dharmas*), and in their unreality." (MP 120m) He loves "compassionate detachment" in the world. (AP 233f) Much is cloudy, but this is clear: only in detachment does *saṃsāra* return as *nirvāṇa*, known in emptiness as it truly is.

But, *mutatis mutandis*, this goes for all. Sankara's One without a second hardly leaves us a world in which to participate; but we may twist this round to see a separate self in a plural world replaced by integral nonduality, so that we see worldly things as they truly are by resolving them into the Eternal, by becoming "characterized by extreme detachment towards the world." (BhG int.) In Augustine, with our conversion from life in Babylon to life in Jerusalem, the world is not voided but validated by God. To those who seek first God's kingdom, all earthly things are added as well. "The man of faith, to whom this entire and wealthy world belongs by cleaving to You whom all things serve, is as one having nothing, yet possessing all things." (Co 5-7) We inherit the Earth for rightful participation only when we become detached from self-love, which permits disinterestedness and objectivity.

The capacity to be disinterested is, almost analytically, a function of our capacity to be selfless. In routine life, we can approximate that by finding an appraiser who is without personal stake in his judgments. The judge stands neither to lose nor gain in the lawsuit he presides over; the scholar's pursuit, if neutral, must be removed from his private life. The counsels of ethicists are dependably moral, not prudent, only if they are released from their own interests enough to see issues impersonally. Such counselors and judges are objective, but not necessarily selfless, for they typically operate where self-interest does not enter. But at ultimacy, in world scope, none are uninvolved and detachment comes only to the deeply religious mind. "Here the Bodhisattva, who wants to know full enlightenment, should behave towards all beings with an even mind. Towards all beings he should produce the great friendliness and the great compassion. He should towards all beings produce a thought which has slain pride and he should be honest towards all of them." (MP 385a)

Much of what we have been saying in this chapter will seem all too private and remote from daily culture and commerce. We here have dealt deliberately with the saint's inner life. But, if we should wish to turn religion outward for ethical guidance in the world, any who would rush into social contracts and reformations, trying to repair *saṃsāra* or redeem Babylon, ought first to note that the socializing process too is very largely a matter of chastening egoism, at worst by mutual checking of self-interests, but at best by inculcating the even-minded sense of living in a larger community of worth, transcending the self, and perhaps too a sense of this community as being a divine commonwealth.

We have with increasing intensity been exploring participation and detachment in religious inquiry, using the collective witness of these four giants in faith whom we have chosen as companions. We have now behind us more than half of our route and have reached a turning point at which we may pause for a glance backward and forward. The performative and personal character of religious truth, with which we began in chapter one, led us in chapter two to examine how the participant epistemic virtues, love, faith, purity, and humility, open us out, detach us for truth. We have more recently, in chapters three and four, sought to encompass two crucial areas in spiritual inquiry, that of language and its relation to experience and to reality, and that of subjectivity and objectivity in religious knowing. We hope to have shown how the spiritual inquiry uses but exceeds expression in language, subtending conception with perception, and how it reaches through the categories of subjectivity and objectivity, reforming and transforming them, seeking to know how things ultimately are by a blending of participation and detachment.

We have kept our saints together, comparatively; but we are from here onward increasingly going to have to make place for incommensurable religious differences. We will begin to work into that in chapter five, still consulting these witnesses, using an inquiry into various levels of *meaning* as these may be accessible to the participant and to the detached. From here onward these terms that entitle our study will bear rather different meanings, as the *participant* and the *detached* are now considered as the *insider* and the *outsider*. We will also ask about the *point*, that is, the impact, of understanding in its intermixture with undergoing. With that done, we will be ready in chapter six to address the question of why we adhere to some beliefs and not to others. This will put the saints whom we have so long kept in concert into eventual conflict. At that point, we will have to judge between those whom, in the first half of this study, we have kept in a moderated colloquy of faiths.

Chapter 5. Understanding and Undergoing

We now broaden our inquiry, distinguishing three levels of understanding: (1) *religious*, of one's real, at the level of faith in an ontic reality, (2) *intrareligious*, within one's domestic religion, believing in a system of faith, and (3) *interreligious*, outward across the foreign, historic religious communities. Our doctors say much about the first and second, but less about the third. It is the third, however, in which we are now increasingly interested, so we extrapolate there, mixing—injudiciously, some might think— multiple themes. But we judge that these three aspects of understanding are allied, for the first and the second operate so as to provide and to govern the possibilities for the third. And we further judge that an account such as we next undertake is sorely needed in a world that struggles for understanding, whether religious, intrareligious, or interreligious.

Afterward, taking an unexpected turn, although it is consistent with the logic of participation and detachment which we have been unfolding, we are driven in the following chapter to a principle of indeterminacy. Past their similar modes, when we press particular content from general form, there will be less togetherness among our saints. We find heartlands into which we cannot go. Unless we are Muslims, Mecca is forbidden to us.

The word *understand* is not fully synonymous with our current use of the word *know*, though it is sometimes a near synonym. The latter is often comfortable with a distancing "about," while the former is etymologically a "standing under." We describe wild hawks or mineral structures, and "know about" them. If that yields any understanding past knowledge, our minds stretch out to dwell in them, so that the integrity of the hawk or the mineral's beauty enlarges us; we enter into and share their worth. Unequivocally, we "understand" at the levels of human sentience—life, learning, and personal intelligence. Downward on the scale of being from this we may ask whether a virus is "alive" or a rat "learns." Upward, we consider whether God is a "person" or Brahman is "intelligent." We grade levels of being by a projected indwelling deemed to fit that rank. *Knowledge* is typically of what we stand over, though often it also is rewarded by a sort of understanding which enters into even subordinate being. *Understanding*, when it exceeds *knowing* in its meaning, is of coordinate or superordinate levels of being; its true home is *meaning*, of which the root is "mind," always near religion. Recalling Augustine, *knowing* tends to go with science, *scientia*, while *understanding* moves, later if not sooner, in the realm of wisdom, *sapientia*.

Further, the scope of understanding is across both what we call *meaning* and *point*. "Don't you understand?" "Yes, I understand." But does your reply mean that you see the sense of what I say, or further that you endorse that as appropriate for the actual setting? The one has to do with intension, the other also with extension. The former is what we call the *intelligibility* use, the latter the *viability* use of "understand." The one connects etymologically with *mind*, thinking, the other with a sharpened piercing of *life*, an impact. We shall find that in religiously "making sense" significance collapses unless reference can be found. To show how this is so, we weave now an argument of double-knit fabric, whose warp is *meaning* and whose woof is *point*.

I. Meaning: Intelligibility and Viability

Understanding is both by conversion and by growth. Dramatic

coherences can come rather suddenly under a novel perceptual set, qualitatively new, yet these are built up toward, and onward from, by quantitative growth. Understanding inches along and fills out, as well as flashes and explodes. Sometimes we either understand or not; at other times we partly understand. We will next construct an account of various levels of understanding, using the witnesses of these African, Persian, and Indian saints.

1. Unmeaning and negative meaning

To those far enough from a certain caliber of life, that life will make no sense, have no meaning and *a fortiori* no point. We call this *unmeaning*. Ghazali explains, "It is as difficult to believe in the reality of states of which one has no personal experience as it is for a blind man to understand the pleasure of looking at green grass and running water, or for a child to comprehend the pleasure of exercising sovereignty." (A1 68) "The knowledge of God Most High... demands...a power of perceiving. Then, in the case of him whose power of perception is imperfect, that he should have pleasure through it is not to be imagined. How can he perceive the pleasure of things to eat who lacks the sense of taste, and how can he perceive the pleasure of melodies who lacks ear, and the pleasure that lies in the conclusion of the reason who lacks reason?" (Ih II, 2, 230) "Likewise it is difficult for one to understand the state of saintliness and prophethood while still only in the stage of reason." (NN 95) Ghazali is careful to note that the spiritual level exceeds but includes rationality and, more problematically, sensation. His appeal to a transrational order is better understood if we recall Augustine's persuasion that the unsaintly reason is untrustworthy for religious judgment. Must Ghazali not be right that distance from experience produces unmeaning?

Similarly, listen to Augustine in a sharp exchange with unregenerate persons who expect understanding prior to faith. A citizen of Babylon says to Augustine as a citizen of Jerusalem: " 'Give me a reason why you ask me to believe.' To him I answer, 'Man, you don't want me to ask you to believe. You are full of evil desires. If I tell you of those good things of Jerusalem, you do not understand them. You must be emptied of that of which you are full, that you may be filled with that of which you are empty.' But he will say, 'Tell me, sing to me, give me the reason. Don't you wish me to learn?' 'But you do not hear with a right spirit; you do not so knock as to deserve that it be opened you.... Babylon bears you; Babylon contains you; Babylon nourishes you; Babylon speaks through you; you can take in nothing except what temporally glitters. You are ignorant how to meditate on eternal things. You do not understand what you ask.' " (NP 136-10f) Whoever lives in and loves Babylon cannot know the meaning of life in Jerusalem, nor receive communication from there, but rather must emigrate for understanding. "The natural man does not perceive the things that are of the Spirit of God, for these are foolishness to him, and he is not able to understand them because they are spiritually discerned." (CG 14-4; 1 Cor. 2.14) The meaning of an act of faith is not available to the faithless life. Literally profane, unfaith is outside the temple.

Nagarjuna's *Ratnāvalī* is full of parallel claims. "The law of salvation consisting in the subtle and deep vision of reality was said by the Victorious Ones to be terrific to foolish men who have not ears prepared to hear it." "It remains a secret for the ordinary people." "The ascetic (Buddha), after having realized this doctrine, declined, at the first moment, to preach it; he knew in fact that this very doctrine is very difficult to be understood by common people." "He did not preach this deep doctrine to those who are unfit to hear it and cannot, therefore, rightly understand it." (Rv 1-25m; 2-9, 18; 1-7m) Nagarjuna is lamenting, not bragging, recapitulating Buddha's frustration about teaching the ignorant, and Nagarjuna's career too is an attack on the common, worldwide failure of understanding. But Buddha is right; the secular do not understand.

We can at this point translate the Advaitan word *avidyā* by "nonunderstanding." "Brahman is intelligible only to a highly purified divine intellect and unintelligible to an ordinary intellect." (BrU 2-1-1) "To all beings who are ignorant and who correspond to the night-wanderers, the Supreme Reality is dark, is like night; for it is not accessible to those whose minds are not in It." (BhG 2-69) True knowledge makes that night day, and, conversely, what seemed light (*saṃsāra*) is found to be dark and unreal. In the blind earthly swirl, fools pass Brahman by, "all their understanding is but bewilderment." (*BhG* 9-12*p*)

Meanings rest on experiences, quite simply so in the cases of "red" and "pain." They still rest so, however much meanings enter into a conceptual web, as with "water," sometimes to become largely conceptual, as with "neutrino," which has a highly tenuous experiential meaning. "God," "Brahman," and "*śūnyatā*" are not sensory percepts, of course, but nevertheless their meanings root in spiritual percepts which underlie the belief systems they terminate, as the reference points on which sacred language must eventually come to rest. In the extreme, there is no meaning devoid of such experiences, although fortunately, as we soon develop, most persons can know some intermediate, linking analogues. Given some sort of parallels, any persons who are short on experience may defer to those who allege higher levels of entrance into that domain of experience, as we often do with those of much talent in art or music, or even rationally, as in mathematics. Algebra is an activity that one cannot watch with any notion of what is going on unless he himself knows how to do it. All those parts which one cannot do, one cannot understand.

Religion is like this. Unless one can do it, what he or she observes makes no sense. Failing this, we may reduce religion to that to which we do have existential access, as for example to the level of dreams, projections, or moral, emotional, and psychological truth, while dismissing the balance as unmeaning. Beyond such reduction and deference, every nonparticipant who makes a judgment will find the sacred to be opaque, a surd, absurd. Further details, including the interreligious import of this, lie ahead of us. But, for the moment, is it altogether amiss to claim that, so far as there is any truth to spirituality, only spirituality can judge it?

Here is Buddha speaking to his disciples with boldness: "A jackal does not enjoy the lion's roar. But the whelps of the lion enjoy his roar. Even so, like jackals, all the foolish common people are incapable of enjoying the great lion's roar of the Tathāgata, the fully enlightened Buddha." (SP 31a)

Unmeaning may first begin to break up with an experience that yields what we call *negative meaning*, although sheerly negative meaning carries the seeds of its own resorption back into unmeaning. Religion often describes its ultimate by negation, by felt otherness, as when *śūnya* erases the conditioned world of its form, plurality, and flux, and then goes on to sense the emptied remainder as the unconditioned ultimate. Brahman is *nirguṇa*, attributeless, having no ordinary predicates, though described with mixed falsity and truth by improper predication (*neti-neti*) as *saguṇa*, by the negation of apparent attributes drawn from the world. All the illusory world (*māyā*) is vaporized as we break beneath to Brahman. Allah is finally unique and unknowable, incomparably transcendent (*akbar*), and Augustine's God is immutable, contrasting with the mutable world. Before him, there is silence.

But pure negation is difficult to sustain. To a complaint that his description of Brahman is too negative, Sankara replies that Brahman is affirmatively *being*, *consciousness*, and *bliss*. "How can that Brahman which has been indicated as 'Not this, not this' by the elimination of everything else, be positively indicated?" The Upanishadic seer, on whom Sankara is commenting, then "gives the words that directly describe Brahman: knowledge, or pure intelligence, which is also bliss, (consciousness, and being) serene, beneficient, matchless, spontaneous, ever content and homogeneous." (BrU 3-9-26ff,m) So Brahman is "indicated, but not denoted." (TaU 2-1-1) Nagarjuna's linguistic negation is total, and we may complain about it; but when he sings his "Hymn to the Supreme Reality" we feel more. "For Thee there is no birth, no coming, no going.... Thou art neither existence nor nonexistence, neither eternal nor noneternal,... Thou art neither big nor small, neither long nor globular. Thou hast reached the stage of the limitless. Homage unto Thee, the unlimited One." (CS 4-3ff,m) The spoken negations somehow add up to a felt plus, not only to a zero but to infinity. The very negation of samsaric experience manages to bring him to touch his *śūnyatā-tattva*, supreme emptiness, as he goes out to what outgoes him. If this were pure transcendence, the sacred and the person would pass without contact, but here Nagarjuna salutes the supreme reality he has encountered.

Apparent moves from "some" to "none" take their meaning

under the background move from "some" to "all." Humans are finite; God is infinite, both "not-finite" and "all-finite," no thing, yet encompassing every thing. Infinity is the sum of numbers, but it is neither yet another number nor the absence of number. That is why Brahman, the Absolute, often seems to come round so closely to *śūnyatā*, emptiness. By a sheer impoverishment of mundane experience, and all words descriptive of it, unmeaning does begin to break away, but no actual meaning replaces it, until there is some experience of the transmundane within the mundane, however inexpressible or difficultly expressible this may be. And it must be obvious that no negative meaning of this kind can be conveyed to the nonparticipant. Religious experience may be described as of the wholly other, only if this has already been qualified to an undergoing in some measure of an immeasurable ultimate.

All the great predicates of the *via negativa* come *in via*. The great lion's roar is heard by his whelps with joy, and the Buddha's limitless life and his call toward it excite the novice *bodhisattva*.

2. Circumstantial and circumferential meaning

By *circumstantial meaning* we designate a bordering while yet remaining at the circumference of meaning. Standing on the edge of meaning, this is yet peripheral, and thus we shall use, less often, a synonym, *circumferential* meaning. If there is *no* contact, there is only what we have just called unmeaning. But with *bare* contact, one "stands about" (circumstands) the experiential area, and that in two ways: (i) At the sacred-to-secular boundary, we recognize a *vertical* bordering of meaning; (ii) At the sacred-to-sacred boundary, by *horizontal* bordering there are parallel, contacting senses of the holy, not (or not yet known to be) overlapping. Ghazali distinguishes between two epistemic levels. The first is *superficial* (*ẓāhir*), exoteric, public, shallow, what we are here calling *circumstantial* meaning. The second is *inner* (*bāṭin*), esoteric, a penetrant understanding which we shall presently find to reach across both comparative and convivial understandings. These levels apply intrareligiously and interreligiously as well. (Ih I, 2, 37ff)

(i) Muhammad remarked that he loved prayer more than perfumes or women, though these also were pleasant to him. Ghazali ponders what the non-Muslim might make of this remark. Pleasure is a general category, inclusive of sensuous and of spiritual things, else analogy fails, yet the unbeliever so knows about spiritual "pleasure" that all particular content fails. "If a child asks us to explain to him the pleasure which exists in wielding sovereignty, we may say it is like the pleasure he feels in playing bat and ball, though in reality the two have nothing in common except that they both come under a kind of pleasure." (Al 38f, 101f) To the sexually impotent man, we explain that intercourse is as pleasurable as eating, or to the deaf person we liken hearing to sight, an allied sense. But in such comparisons conveyed meanings are hollow, unlike the case of saying to one who has not tasted sugar that it is similar to the known sweetness of honey. (DP 56) By this model Ghazali sometimes offers his developmental tiers of knowledge, progressively the *sensational, discriminatory, rational,* and *spiritual* levels, hoping that those at the third level can glimpse advance to a fourth, already knowing three in their experience. That is *vertically* to border the sacred, to have its "words and terms" but by an analogous contact so generic as to be merely tangential and without any specific penetration into what the sacred means.

Augustine posits a knowledge of the genus despite ignorance of the species, as when we are alerted to understand that a thing is beautiful without having encountered it to know specifically how it is beautiful. (Tr 10-1-1) Such an alert prompts the Babylonian to ask about the beauties of Jerusalem, and circumferentially helps him even to understand what the vain Babylonian cannot be told, that there is a sacred form of beauty beyond their present experiential capacity. Even the secular in their own way know the category of faith, and, if they recognize this, they are at a boundary which touches understanding of the Christian faith. Sankara uses this same generic though nonspecific sort of appreciation, as when we know that someone is in pain but not its type. (VS 4-1-2) Nagarjuna insists that relative knowledge is empty, though nevertheless it is sometimes effective in its contacting of absolute truth. We may interpret this as a circumferential contact, that is, that phenomenal knowledge at its limits touches although it does not actually penetrate the noumenal dimension.

At this level of meaning we may qualify somewhat the rather severe treatment given to religious unmeaning in our previous section. "God is love." If I project the meaning of love wholly from nonsacred sources, I have only a circumstantial sense of what love in God may be like, but I have at least that. Are these human and divine loves as diverse as *erōs* and *agapē*, or as intimate as the biblical love of God and of neighbor? I cannot tell, since initially I stand at nearly equivocal specific senses of love, although I have some notion of the genus *love*. If these are quite equivocal senses, we revert eventually to unmeaning, sacred love being transcendently different from the secular love. But nearly equivocal meaning is not yet wholly unmeaning, for loves have formal features in common even where their material characteristics diverge. So far as one sense of attraction can locate another, we escape complete equivocation, but so far as the senses of love differ, there can be—at the sacred-to-secular boundary—a vertical, superficial bordering of meaning, at least that, but nothing more.

(ii) Further, one sense of the sacred can locate another, yet with virtually no entrance, a *horizontal* bordering at the sacred-to-sacred boundary. "There is no God but Allah, and Muhammad is his prophet." "The *Qur'an* is the Word of God." At the earliest encounter of this Islamic witness, without any experiential reach into the character of Allah, or the career of Muhammad, or the content of the *Qur'an*, the Christian can hear only, "There is no God but *x*, and *y* is his prophet." "Z is the Word of God." By his or her indwelling from *Christian* faith in God, prophets, and Bible, an alien religious confession is located, but there is as yet no penetration into the area of *Muslim* experience. Any eventual filling out is by comparative exposure to Allah, Muhammad, *Qur'an*, and prophet (*rasūl*). If, when he or she is only at a peripheral encounter, the Christian maintains that Allah is not God, nor Muhammad his prophet, nor the *Qur'an* the Word of God, that simply cannot have any *Islamic* meaning, devoid of all the peculiarly Islamic experiences that support the confession.

All its meaning comes out of a tangential *Christian* experience. Yet the denial does contact the witness it rejects and is not vacuous, while, at the same time, a circumferential denial by Christians cannot have the same meaning as a central, Islamic affirmation.

For what the one means by his or her denial is without penetration into the experience which another affirms. The sort of gap we encounter between the Christian and the Muslim only widens when we shift to the superficial contact of Brahman, and the gap becomes a sheer void at *śūnyatā*. In religious contacts, in the competition between world views, there is no simple negation.

It is at this horizontal bordering that comparative religion begins. The historian of religion will sometimes chide a theologian for being parochial, urging that the theologian consider the myriad spiritualities of others. This is well enough, except that only a *domestic* sense of the sacred can locate a *foreign* one. Those who would teach about religion, and yet have no religious dimensions in their own lives—by what means beyond hearsay will they locate the religions about which they propose to teach us? Have they sensibility enough even to contact, much less to compare them? While standing only at the borders, we call this, provocatively and pejoratively, an *objective* understanding, that is, merely external. "He whose insight is not keen will grasp nothing of religion except its husks and outward forms rather than its pith and truth." (Ih I, 1, 231) To circumscribe the husk is to know religion objectively enough, but the pith is opaque without some subjective entrance. The meaning here, laments Ghazali, is only silhouetted. (Ih I, 2, 46)

3. Comparative and consanguine meaning

"How can a man understand anything, if he does not carry the germ of it within himself?" asked Novalis. To sense or make sense of a thing, it must reach us, which happens when we are or become like it. Even in ordinary empirical knowledge, the mind hopes by the mental structures it forms to correspond with the world. Religiously, the saint seeks the personal impression of the sacred; he hopes to bring similars together (*comparo*) by making his life similiar to the divine life. Interreligiously and intrareligiously, understanding is ever by *comparative meaning*, that is, by the pairing together (*comparo*) of one spirituality with another spirituality. As with psychological apperception, understanding is always by a relation which modifies existing preunderstandings. By a synonym here, *consanguine meaning*, we refer to that common humanity under which we are all "of one blood." In every person all forms of human character are potentially present, asserts Joachim Wach, and if one cannot endorse this, then there is no basis for understanding religion.[1] But each is kin to every other because all stand under the divinity we understand; we understand each other interreligiously in our common God-likeness, as we understand ourselves religiously in God. "Were not the eye akin to the sun, it could never perceive the sun."[2] "Never did eye see the sun unless it had first become sunlike, and never can the Soul have vision of the First Beauty unless itself be beautiful."[3]

There are two elements here. One is a comparative *likeness* and the other is a comparative *reduction*, and we mix them for a sort of kindred or consanguine understanding. This requires a comparative fit of truth to the hearer, what Buddhism fondly calls "skill-in-means" (*upāya-kauśalya*), recognizing advancing meanings as we stretch to higher levels. *Upāya* is insisted on throughout the *Great Sūtra*, but is never better put in brief than in the *Lotus Sūtra*, chapter on "Tactfulness" (*Upāya-kauśalya*). Buddha says, "The *tathāgata* is able to discriminate everything, preach the laws skillfully, and use gentle words. Essentially speaking, the law which the Buddha has perfected is difficult to understand. Only a buddha together with a buddha can fathom the reality of all existence. If I explained this, men would be startled and perplexed. This is why, Sariputra, knowing that all living beings have many kinds of desires deeply attached in their minds, I have, according to their capacity, expounded the laws by various reasonings, parabolic expressions, and tactful powers."[4]

---

[1] See Joachim Wach, who quotes Novalis (Friedrich von Hardenberg) in "On Understanding," in A. A. Roback, *The Albert Schweitzer Jubilee Book* (Cambridge, Mass.: Sci-Art Publishers, 1945), pp. 133-146, citation on p. 134.

[2] Goethe, *Zahme Xenien, Werke* (Weimar, 1887-1918), Bk. 3, 1805; cf. Plato, *Republic*, VI, 508a.

[3] Plotinus, *The Enneads*, trans. Stephen MacKenna, 2nd ed. (London: Faber and Faber Limited, 1956), I, 6, 9 (p.64).

[4] The *Saddharma-Puṇḍarīka* in *The Threefold Lotus Sutra*, trans. B. Katō, Y. Tamura, and K. Miyasaka (New York: Weatherhill, 1975), pp. 52ff,a.

Nagarjuna remembers what Buddha said: "Just as a master of grammar teaches even the alphabet to disciples, even so the Buddha teaches the law as it may be accessible to those to be converted." (Rv 4-94) Indeed, we are here at the quick of the Madhyamika process. Short of consummation, all meaning is by approximate translation, "relative" not only because this lies in a fluxing realm but because there is some, but only relative, correspondence to the absolute. Even in his negation, Nagarjuna has recourse to analogy, and we hear of peace, greatness, space, nonduality, purity, compassion, of passing beyond permanence and impermanence, of being and nonbeing, of freedom from hunger, thirst, and pain, of going out to and in *nirvāṇa*, all by contrast to the *saṃsāra* described by so many similes—a mirage, a magic play, a trick, a bubble. The single word that best couples the mundane with the transmundane is the model *śūnya*, so wealthy in comparative meanings: empty, hollow, swollen, unreal, but also indeterminate, spacious, formless, unconditioned, desireless, nonpossessive, selfless, and silent. As propositional comparisons, these will fade literally to the point of becoming unintelligible, but not without some remaining consanguine point. All this deepens our earlier understanding of the Buddhist "recourse to two truths, the world-ensconced truth and the truth which is the highest sense." (Ka 24-9)

The Advaitan saint finds that there is a lower understanding (*aparā vidyā*) between higher understanding (*parā vidyā*) and unmeaning (*avidyā*). "This is the instruction about Brahman through analogy. The need for this teaching about Brahman through analogy is that It becomes easily comprehensible to people of dull intellect when instruction is thus imparted. For the unconditioned Brahman, as such, cannot be comprehended by people of dull intellect." (KeU 4-5) "Nor can the scriptures speak about an unknown thing without having recourse to conventional words and their meanings." (BrU 2-1-20) At one extreme, there is only unmeaning in an experiential void. Mediately, there is this range of consanguine meanings; this is the *neti-neti* zone. Sankara much dwells on these various "cognitions (*vidyās*) conducive to the springing up of perfect knowledge by successive steps." (cf. VS 3-3-1ff) For the many disciples, indeed for all who are short of *jñāna*, Advaita Vedanta offers *saguṇa* Brahman on any of multiple levels, Brahman in empirical dress, elaborated for limited experience. Intermediately, we may rest in the theism, pantheism, even the polytheism and animism of comparative Brahman. At the other extreme, immediately, there is the consummate truth in the oceanic *nirguṇa* Brahman.

All the positive Augustinian knowledge of God is derived from the creation's limited kinship with God, reached especially as that kinship approaches a resemblance in regenerated persons. *Comparatio* is Augustine's term for what was later and by others worked into the technical doctrine of *analogia*, claiming analogy as the way we know God. As the creature participates in God, the creature signifies God. Taken at the pitch, this is the burden of the *Trinity*, that God is known only by his analogues, whether in the historical incarnation or in psychological experience, however enigmatic and asymmetric these places of his proportionate presence may be. (Tr 15-19-5) The *imago Dei* is the comparative presence of the immutable Father God, known in the mutable life of his sons. Only faith can find understanding, since only trusting can introduce into the Babylonian's life enough taste of life in Jerusalem for comparison to begin.

If we wish to mark out a lower understanding (*ratio inferior*) short of a higher understanding (*ratio superior*), we could say that wisdom is proper understanding, by contrast with which knowledge, however necessary and pedagogical, is yet inferior. Beyond sheerly scientific knowledge (*scientia*) in religion, which is only circumstantial, we advance by entrance into understanding (*sapientia*), which occurs in the pairing together (*comparo*) of the saint with God, as biblical knowledge about a historical Christ is deepened and stretched into intellection of the living God.

"God created Adam after his own likeness." Muhammad's traditional saying (hadīth) prompts Ghazali to reflect how the human intelligence is like the divine reality. "Now the sample must be commensurate with the original, even though it does not rise to the degree of equality with it." "For the thing compared is in some sort parallel, and bears resemblance, to the thing compared therewith, whether that resemblance be remote or near." (Ni 48, 55) Ghazali finds this likeness especially troubling as he puzzles over the absolutely incomparable Allah, but relatively he makes a steady use of it. "Man does not comprehend except himself and his own attributes.... By comparison and analogy with these he understands the attributes of others." "If the Apostle had mentioned some of the attributes of God to which men have nothing akin and which do not resemble, even remotely, anything they possess, they would not have understood." (Ih I, 2, 40) We understand God by finding our comparative "portion" of each of the ninety-nine divine names, that is, by the reception and application of each attribute in life. (NN 12)

Thus we can say in this sense that all religion is comparative religion, if not at its ending, absolutely, at least en route, relatively, for we can solve encountered ultimates and religions only by having or receiving something comparable that they are soluble in, by some likeness which makes us comparatively kin to that which we understand. The perceptive, comparable life keeps the notion of analogy viable even when the conceptual expression of this analogy is not quite so intelligible as we could wish.

From this point we may extrapolate in order to license and to appreciate interreligious understanding. Idiosyncratic faiths never touch, but correlative beliefs permit fellowship. Only by this means have the preceding pages of this book been intelligible, speaking of collective virtues such as love, faith, purity, humility, or of similar educations from conception to perception. Comparatively, we brought around one axis the Madhyamika criticism of the ego, the Vedantan illusion of individuality, the proud and impulsive selves found to be so misguided by Augustine and by Ghazali. We saw how they prescribed rectification by a common thrust toward self-emptying. Whatever their antipathies and apathies to each other, our saints have great sympathies for each other, and we with them.

Nor has any reader understood them, us, or religion, except by remaining open, however wistfully or reluctantly, to the possibility of sainthood and to a stirring of the germinal numinous or mystical presence within. Further, in order to soften an exclusivism ahead of us, it would be facile to suppose that any Hindu knows Hinduism better than any Christian, for the latter may penetrate more deeply, while the former only very narrowly lives within his or her faith. That is a source of frequent confusion, beyond a mere mastery of religious histories and data. More than can the casual adherent, a nonadherent's empathetic powers rising from parallel spiritual experiences can make a deeply sympathetic, existential connection with a comparable, second faith. But this is nowhere nonparticipatory; rather, we might call it coparticipatory.

Finally however, we have to lament this level of understanding which we have so far praised, and to anticipate an indeterminacy to come. Meanings are integral to our forms of life. Though interreligiously these considerably intersect, in different faiths they do not coincide. Kindredship may be more or less distant, and family resemblances fade out through ethnic and racial traits into weaker although basic human conventions. Resonance is not identity, and we must not confuse two faiths which can appreciate each other with the same faith. When comparative truths go into their respective systems, they begin to turn around different axes.

The Hindu finds, for instance, that *māyā* and Brahman will hardly support the Christian meanings of incarnation. His effort to import the doctrine of incarnation slips between docetism and pantheism, and he can never quite place it in his system. The Christian stumbles over whether his Christianity should be called, in Hindu terms, *advaitan* or *dvaitan*, nondual or dual, over whether the soul, spirit, and resurrected body are most like the *ātman* or the *jīva*, the ultimate self or the individual self, whether God is most like Brahman or Ishvara, the impersonal absolute or a personal God. Some approximate answer is possible, and it may be refined with difficulty, as a tortured vocabulary lapses into meanings better felt than voiced, better perceived than conceived. But determinate, absolute understanding is not possible except with an impossible simultaneous standing under both systems, perceptually and conceptually. Since God is neither Brahman nor Ishvara, the Lord (*Yahweh*) and Father of Jesus Christ cannot be calibrated anywhere in the Hindu system without distortion.

Particular meanings, torn from the living matrix, cannot be delivered to an alien spirituality. Comparatively, but only comparatively, do we understand each other. There may be knowledge (*scientia*) of relative faith, but we do not there find wisdom (*sapientia*), except as we share the faith that produces that understanding, which then ceases to be interreligious and becomes immediately religious, in common worship. Inner (*baṭin*) meaning is inexactly and proportionately had, says Ghazali. Past any features of a religion that are nomothetic, lawlike enough over all religions to provide comparative descriptions, there are private meanings, idiographic to that form of faith, which provides Ghazali with a third and final level of meaning.

4. Compassionate and convivial meaning

At its flood we must recognize how religious meaning is *convivial* and *compassionate*. At the full flow of this increasing tide of meaning we prefer the strongest terms. Infeeling, as when we are at a drama, is by an imaginative transfer of our own passionate life into the enacted novel circumstances. If, as "empathy" suggests, feeling is only supposed and not in fact shared, understanding remains pretended, if not pretentious. Certain feelings we can comparatively but never absolutely pretend: those of pain, ignorance, humility, love, beauty, and the sacred. "Sympathy" is a stronger term than "empathy," and it does have the root idea of togetherness which we need. But in English use it suggests an analogical proportion, a like feeling and yet a with-ness short of the compassion which is actually there. But a full *compassion*, a shared passion, is what noble faith is oftenest concerned with, registering in the saint the passion (*agapē*) of God, or in the *bodhisattva* the passion (*karuṇa*) of the Buddha. For an alternate term, we can speak of *convivial* meaning, meaning that arises in the "common life" of the *ātman* as Brahman, of the Sufi passing away (*fanā'*) into God.

Only by compassion does the *bodhisattva* understand reality, and only by compassion is the Buddhist religion understood. Words alone are empty, and hence only a Buddha understands another Buddha in their shared common life. That "God is love" has myriads of believer-instanced meanings, which have enough in common to permit congruent usage. From these we may abstract *the* meaning, but this must always be keyed to that convivial community of *agapē*, which has been gathered around the atoning, forgiving Christ. So only in the loving life can God be understood. Highest understanding (*aparā vidyā*), Sankara warns us, is not found in the *Vedas* and *Upanishads* merely as texts comprehended, but lies in the apprehension of their "secret meaning" (*upanishad*) by a "sitting near" (*upanishad*) that elevates the textual "assemblage of words" into a convivial "higher knowledge" which is "the realization of the thing to be known." (MuU 1-1-5) To understand is to live in Brahman.

In the Sufi love of God, there is private meaning, and downward from this, hidden (*bāṭin*) meanings can be shared only with other lives which are secluded in God. As for "comprehending the inner meanings which the words of this (Muslim) creed signify, there is no way to attain any of them except through self-mortification.... They are a mercy from God which comes to those who expose themselves to its beneficence." (Ih I, 2, 35m) In a sense, this means that a plenary understanding of God is blocked for even the most saintly theist, for we never reach an identical life with God. God is both *Aẓ-Ẓāhir* and *Al-Bāṭin*, manifest and hidden, and "no one has truly known God except God himself." (Ih I, 2, 41) We do not univocally or literally understand love in God, but are restricted, says Augustine, to its analogues in human life, to Jesus and the incarnation. The East too is quite deferential about our attaining any absolute understanding of the real. Its seers often teach that enlightenment is long postponed and they offer only relative truth for all but the very few. But nevertheless all our faiths hold that we travel toward and into this range of meaning. Religions of love and identity are only understood with shared pathos and the communicant life.

Meaning is always a function of penetration. The believed theorem, says Augustine, is progressively understood with its further study. A child learns arithmetic rather simply. The student resurveys those truths in the fuller light of mathematics, and the formal mathematician with number theory exacts levels of meaning not reached by most of us. Esoteric meanings, says Ghazali, complete rather than conflict with exoteric ones; they deepen and broaden them. (Ih I, 2, 53) Two complementary components are operating in this enlargement of meaning. (i) Extensively, religious meanings run large, more like the meanings of novels and of careers than of words or sentences. To ask about "God is love" is more like asking about *Gone with the Wind*, or the place of Lincoln in American history, than it is like asking about "Sara is angry." Religious meanings are not available superficially, but haunt paradigms such as "City of God," "Middle Path," "One without a second," "Jesus Christ," "Nonduality," or "*Nirvāṇa*," words which serve as titles to a faith. Set in a gestalt, like the couplet in the poem or the episode in the novel, the creedal phrase stretches out into and is intersubsidiary with others. The part lives by the organic circulation of the whole. The meaning of the seemingly simple proposition really extends out into the widest horizons of the system of meaning. When its meaning is sought variously by disarticulation, comparative entrance, or by intimate embrace, each attempt shifts the relevant environment and thus the contextual meaning.

(ii) Intensively, every sincere spiritual utterance is a kind of love affair. I say, "God is love." Can you reply, "I understand that, but it doesn't seem to me to make sense in life, to make sense of life, so it isn't true"? Comparatively you may; but compassionately you may not. Any denial reveals a lack of the perceptive *agapē* under which it is true, a comparative rejection because of a compassionate failure. You cannot be rejecting the sense proposed to be understood, for you have whatever concept of love you have over a deviant existential field, not having felt life to be in *agapē*. You are forced to say, "I don't see it," as when my esteem for a work of art is unshared. To judge another's passion unfit for reality is to have a variant passion. She goes to her knees before the crucifixion narratives; he does not. They do not share a common passion before the Passion of Christ.

Here all understanding is emotional, and none can have this *in intellectu* who do not have it *in via*. To say that some encountered meaning is inappropriate is *prima facie* to reject what is found to be intelligble. But, more intimately, it is a confession that one has not been able to appropriate it, but has some other passion than that which is appropriate for its meaning. What touches the mind as truest is what touches life as being most real, actual. Along the boundaries, though, there will be those coming into faith who believe what they do not yet understand.

We are now before a puzzling quality of spiritual beliefs. Systems of the sophistication of those here examined gain a relative irrefutability, about which we have to be very circumspect. Though they are synthetic systems, which make claims about the world, their core statements are very like analytic ones in the necessity of their truth under the perceptions through which they are fully meaningful. Conventionally, we can distinguish between the meaning of and the evidence for a proposition. But spiritually all positive evidence tends to enlarge the understanding of the claim which it verifies. With more and more entrance which deepens the meaning, there is an increasing "mustness," and in due course settled conviction cannot see it any other way.

Oppositely, what of that which is judged to be false because of evidence which negates it? The idea is overcome while it is still incompletely understood, because it cannot be any further understood in the light of our evidence. It misfits, fails to "make sense," and is abandoned as we fail to find its "force."

This is why for Augustine religious truths are suprisingly close to mathematical ones. Remembering the exchange of Plato with the slave boy about geometry, we need only to be introduced to such truths, and, if and when they are well understood, they carry their own conviction. Thus the two areas of life so often taken as opposites, for the certainty in mathematics, the uncertainty in religion, move closer to each other. In both, the mind gains truth that is immutable, abiding, that is, intellected universally out of the world influences. But the forceful truth of religious statements is synthetic and comes under a certain experiential perceptual set, which may not be immutable, while the truth of mathematical statements is nonexperiential.

Some simple statements are experienced as true as soon as they are understood: "I exist." "One ought to keep promises." "Humans are the highest animals." Others take reflection: "I could not possibly say that it is ever bad to understand anything." (Lb 1-3) "Who can doubt that the soul lives, remembers, understands, wills, thinks, knows, and judges?" (Tr 10-14) "There can be no intellect without life and no life without existence." (Tr 10-13) Though they are much more complex than such statements, religious creeds are often such that when we have completely understood them, we know whether they are true. Even scientific theories are sometimes like this. To appreciate the meaning of "Electrons exist," or of "Gold is element number 79," is very much to become acquainted with the phenomena that constitute their truth. Such propositions are verified while they are being understood, not after they have been understood.

In "God is love," the predicate operates out of the subject to mix both analytic and synthetic elements. *Agapē* in life, felt to be divine and having an increasing impact, shapes the meaning of "God." The statement convicts because it impresses its meaning under that spiritual perspective. "All things work together for good to those who love him, who are called according to his purpose." (Rom. 8.28) That "working together," its "goodness," "love," "call," "purpose"—by the time one detects in existential struggle all that these mean in faith, past their routine, everyday senses, one sees whether the claim is so. Unless believed, the promise cannot be entered, since the working together in love, the working out of love is only to the called. Unbelievers will find that the claim does not make much sense, and be stumped by it. For believers it will be progressively understood as it is verified, until, with Paul, it becomes the nonnegotiable conviction that nothing can separate us from the love of God.

The meaning of the Hebrew divine name is hinged to history, and, comparatively, the linguists and exegetes can greatly help us. But, compassionately, the meaning eventually resides in the mystical sensing of a God who, in and over history, can say, "I am that I am." Yahweh is the one who is always there, and the Hebrew God-talk begins to make real sense only after the latter-day believer has his or her own Exodus and flaming bush which is not consumed. Such a numinous sensing of God moves us closer to saying that to understand "Yahweh" is to meet him, to know that he is present, present here in the believing heart, and so to believe that he was present there, in the Exodus, in his steadfast love of Israel, and in the Christ. Otherwise, one circumstantially or comparatively understands, and the balance of meaning collapses.

Those who reside in other faiths find their claims similarly impressive. Surveying the incoherences of Advaita Vedanta's competitors, Sankara concludes his *Commentary on the Gītā*: "Brahman appears to the unenlightened—to those whose reason is carried away by the differentiated phenomena of names and forms created by *avidyā*—as unknown, difficult to know, very remote. But to those who have attained the serenity of the self, there is nothing else so blissful, so well-known, so easily knowable, and quite so near as Brahman. For those initiates, differently situated, it is quite impossible to believe in the reality of the dual, the perceiver and the perceived, of our external perceptions, because they perceive no reality other than the Self." (BhG 18-50a)

"That art thou," Sankara tells us, like wheat that is threshed, is to be beaten until it gives its grain. What is meant by "thou," by "that," by "art"—to see this is eventually to see that it is so, and where there is no yield there has been insufficient threshing. (VS 4-1-1) The inebriation of monism is irreversible. But so also is that of Madhyamika's Void, when the *bodhisattva* reaches the treasured "irreversible stage." (MP 47; and passim; MPC1 1800ff) As we ponder "*Nirvāṇa* is *saṃsāra*" and "All is *śūnya*," one comes increasingly to feel what is meant by each crucial term. The absolute truth draws nearer, until, in the end, enlightenment comes with the irreversible realization of what they mean.

We have not yet finished with this compulsive power of conviction under an incumbent perceptual set. It is, in some sense, a dangerous aspect of religious inquiry, and needs careful criticism. But what it means for us at this point in our study is that, if meanings are analytic within because of their synthesis within a system that is only existentially appreciated, then we eventually surpass the reaches of a comparative understanding and come to this level that we call convivial meaning. Idiosyncratic meanings cannot be had in the public forum but only in the inner sanctum.

It is but half true that the nearer we get to their cores, the more the variant faiths become alike; the complementary truth is that there is a turning about incommensurable centers. Now we must say, curiously, that all real religion is ultimately understood out of a common passion, or is compassionate, and that comparative religion can never coincide with it. The *Qur'an* both is and is not in translatable Arabic.

II. Point: Understanding and Undergoing

Withstood belief is always cloudy, it confuses us. We do not *see* it; we cannot see *with* it. But there is also cloudiness within belief as well, for the believer too is struggling into meanings. Believers suffer a counterplay of feeling yet groping for point, of forceful apprehensions which they cannot get comprehended to suit themselves, much less others. We have just worked our way through levels of advancing meanings, accounting for how we gain the intensions of words by *circumstantial*, or *comparative*, or *compassionate* means. We will next resurvey that terrain, especially that of the participant's growth in his faith, under the theme of the "point" of understanding, its piercing impact in life. We are interested in how this develops and deepens, how the believer gains the extensions of his words, that to which they point, through an interplay of understanding and undergoing. Understanding resides in undergoing, and has its point there; but undergoing also makes sense or has its point only with reflective understanding.

1. Understanding versus undergoing

Consider at some length, though we abridge it, a provocative passage from Ghazali, in which he begins with perception in law, poetry, and music as these illuminate the sensitivities of spiritual understanding. Ghazali conflates and has not himself fully digested all his diverse cases. Still, the passage is remarkably fertile. Think how often we trouble over the unknown, which, when undergone, becomes at first brokenly known, and then increasingly understood, yet so as to remain only partially expressible! That is true alike of cognitive yet incompletely verbal judgments, which he calls "knowledge," and also of experience, which he calls psychic "states."

"Perhaps you will find strange a condition or knowledge the real nature of which you do not know and the expression of which is impossible; but you will find witnesses for this in your ordinary states. As for the *knowledge*, how many a lawyer there is whom two questions confront, similar in form, but the lawyer gets so far by his natural faculty as to perceive that between them there is a difference as to the decision, yet whenever he tries to state (conceive) the thrust of the difference his tongue does not help him to express it, although he may be the most eloquent of men. He perceives the difference, but the expressing of it is impossible, not on account of any falling short in his tongue, but because the idea is too fine in itself for expression. This belongs to what has been thought out by those who look into complicated things. Thus some people are distinguished above others by a natural faculty of taste in metrical poetry and a power of distinguishing what is and is not metrical. The possessor of this faculty so attains this condition as to perceive that he is not in doubt of distinguishing between good meter or bad. Yet he is not able to express the condition by anything which will make clear his meaning to one who has not a natural faculty of taste.

"As for the *states*, how many a man perceives in his heart, on some occasion, a contraction or expansion (a pang), yet he does not know its cause! Sometimes that is a strange condition, which a word expressing joy or sorrow does not indicate clearly, and for which he cannot come upon a suitable expression. (Music, especially that without a text, has this evocative, often religious power.) In the soul are strange states. The well-recognized ideas of fear, grief, and joy occur with the hearing of singing that has meaning. But as for vibrating strings and other musical tones which have no meaning, they make on the soul a wonderful impression, which it is not possible to express. Sometimes it is expressed as a longing, but a felt longing which does not know what it longs for is wonderful. He finds in his heart a state which demands he does not know what.

"Then, given the quality of the longing and the appearance of the thing longed for, the matter is clear. But if the knowledge of the thing longed for is not given, and the heart flames up, that without fail entails bewilderment. If a man grew up alone so that he never saw the form of woman and knew not what sexual intercourse was, and thereafter approached puberty and desire overcame him, he would feel in himself the fire of desire, but would not know that he was longing for intercourse, because he did not know what intercourse was and had no experience of women. There is a relationship like this of the soul with the upper world and the pleasures which he is promised there. Only he cannot imagine these things except as names, like him who has heard the expression 'sexual intercourse' and the name 'woman,' but has not even seen the form of a woman. So hearing moves him to longing, but abounding ignorance and being occupied with this world have made him forget his Lord and his abiding-place. His heart demands from him he does not know what, and he is confused and disturbed. This, and things like it, belong to the states, a perception of the completeness of the verities of which is not to be attained, and he who is affected by them is not able to give them expression." (Ih II, 8, 728ff,a)

To order these cases for the counterplay of understanding and undergoing let us begin with minimums and move to maximums.

A. The isolated youth, prior to sexual desire, neither understands nor undergoes. If he obtains terms such as "woman" or "intercourse," they are unmeaning, idle words for which he has no experiences. He is intellectually because physically impotent. The words he superficially has make no sense. The analogue is the soul who, short of identified or unidentified sacred experiences, finds religion pointless.

B. Later, experiencing sexuality, this youth ignorantly undergoes what he does not understand. He can neither name his longing nor what it is of. It makes sense in that he undergoes it, yet it makes no sense in that he does not understand. It is viable but unintelligible. In first awakening to God, the soul longs without understanding the quality or the object of its longing. Augustine notices how the carnal self, roused by grace, is wandering and hungry. (NP 106-4ff) Music may so stimulate us. Such nonconceptual perceptions are nontransferable.

C. The youth and the soul may identify their perceptions by reaching conceptions of them, by name understand what they undergo, and thus express both the object of their knowledge and the quality of their states more clearly. But this comprehension yields clarity only as it underruns apprehended experience; others see neither meaning nor point. This legitimates the theological enterprise, religious conceptions which clarify religious perceptions. The earlier undergoing was short of understanding, but later there is understanding by linguistic identification, but even then this is only semistatable to those of like experiences.

D. The maturely informed and experienced youth and soul both understand and participate. But Ghazali warns us even at this level that matters do not, after all, become wholly conceptually clear. We pass to the cases of the lawyer and the metrical critic. Both (presuming the latter is a poet) are amply eloquent. Now focusing more on "knowledge," and less on "states," subjective experience is elevated into objective knowledge, what the undergoing is *of*. "States" which are accordant with the real are "knowledge." The lawyer and the critic find themselves with semicognitive claims whose warrants are perceptual. Each can make the claim explicit in its outline, but neither can logically detail the tacit rationale that supports it.

The claim can be circumferentially stated, but even those standing within its meaning cannot deliver that into words. Here we can recall from chapter three Augustine's "inner word," and Ghazali's professors of music vainly seeking to make the tone-deaf understand. The lawyer affirms: "Case A is not like case B because its pattern differs, despite the similarities." The poet says: "This is good meter, that is bad meter." But neither is able to verbalize to himself, nor, *a fortiori*, to anyone who lacks his faculty of taste, how he knows. That is notoriously true of pattern envisaging, so necessary in law and metrical arts, where the particulars gain their significance when placed under a governing gestalt. That sort of synoptic scanning capacity is much a part of the religious genius.

E. Before the verbal level was reached, there was only a confused undergoing. But at the level of verbal criticism, which is the trade of the lawyer and the poet, our talk is ever, as it were, in search of taste. Neither in jurisprudence, nor literature, nor music, nor religion, can we trust uncritical intuition. Still, the pattern of a legal case, the just sense of fairness, the good meter of a poem, the quality of an art piece, the richness of a person's character—these are things one sees and feels. We are helped by argument from parallels, but only by parallel perceptions do we admit the parallels, which themselves must be felt, or else we cannot be argued into them. The case of incompetent intuitions is not sufficiently examined here, but a competent intuition will stand even though we are not able entirely to rationalize it. The freshman English teacher may insist that you do not know until you can say what you mean, but poets know better. Any who think they can say exactly what they mean are insensitive to these fuller sweeps of understanding.

A distinguished psychiatrist showed students a patient having a mild fit. Later, the class discussed whether this was an epileptic or a hystero-epileptic seizure. "Gentlemen," affirmed the psychiatrist, "you have seen a true epileptic seizure. I cannot tell you how to recognize it; you will learn this by more extensive experience."[5] That skill of art over science is present even in simple things, as when we say, "This is not the bark of spruce but of fir." "There is much richness in the subtle cast of those shadows across the lichens and mosses on that granite boulder." But especially the perception of life's most "complicated things"—of justice, beauty, and character, of harmony, of metaphysical or religious adequacy—is like that. " 'Tis not solely in poetry and music we must follow our taste and sentiment, but likewise in philosophy. When I am convinc'd of any principle, 'tis only an idea, which strikes more strongly upon me. When I give the preference to one set of arguments above another I do nothing but decide from my feeling concerning the superiority of their influence."[6] Polanyi's psychiatrist and Hume's philosopher are anticipated here by Ghazali's saint, as our deepest convictions finally prove "too fine for expression" even "to the most eloquent." Religion too is an art and not a science.

F. Lastly, we have to project the interreligious application of all this. What do we say of the peculiar flavor of Advaita Vedanta, or

---

[5] Michael Polanyi, "Knowing and Being," *Mind* 70(1961): 458-470, citation on p. 458.

[6] David Hume, *A Treatise of Human Nature* (Oxford: Clarendon Press, 1888, 1965), p. 103.

of Madhyamika, or of the Islamic in religion? Might not their idiosyncratic textures be too fine for expression? Perhaps, if we run this point out to an almost bizarre extreme, we can glimpse how Nagarjuna has reached a perceptual state for which his conceptual vocabulary is hopelessly empty.

2. Understanding underruns undergoing

We may use Nagarjuna to continue, though we shall shortly criticize him, as he notices how words are pointers, especially so with spiritual words. He cautions that we must not mistake the word for its convincing "point." "Look on to the meaning.... Words are pointers to meanings, but the meaning is not the word. Suppose a person pointed with his finger to the moon to help the confused find it, but the doubting stared only at the finger and did not look at the moon. That person would ask, 'I point to the moon with my finger that you may see it. Why do you look at my finger instead of the moon?' So it is here. The word is the finger which points to meaning, but the word is not the meaning. That is why one should not stand on words." (MPC1 538)

Religions are sets of "pointer words," and, like finger and moon, they succeed with their meaning only if they have point, and if they are "without point" then their true meaning collapses. Ghazali's naive youth found the word "woman" without point, and analogously the insensitive person finds that "*śūnya*," "*anitya*," "*anātman*," or "*duḥkha*" do not signify anything much at all. Disappointed in the failure of his understanding, Narada, a student in the *Upanishads*, complains to his guru, "Thus do I know, Sir, the mantras or words only, and not the spirit thereof." The verbal token is empty; he has only "nominal understanding." (*ChU* 7-1-3) Here language is symbolic, and so far as its sacramental or signifying power fails, there is no connotation without denotation.

Ghazali's complaint against the religious scholars (*'ulamā'*) is that they seek an understanding without any undergoing, *'ilm* without *islām*. He knew that error too much from his own youth. The result is superficiality, at best a comparative and at worst a circumstantial meaning, empty "names and forms." Such scholars cannot "travel the road to the hereafter," that is, see the ultimate, supernal point of

Islam and walk its straight path there, despite their loquacious jurisprudence. Though they are familiar with the history of Islamic religion, they cannot be active religiously. Their religious capacities are retroactive, not active. "Knowledge is not the prolific retention of a tradition but a light which floods the heart." Without that light, they cannot advance, or advance with, theology. (Ih I, 1, 126ff) With a vast but simultaneously vacuous understanding, they cannot, in more contemporary idiom, "do theology."

Who can teach Islamic theology? We might allow that it can be "taught," that is, reported with comparative discernment, by non-Muslims, but it cannot be "done" outside Islam. En route across a continuum of teaching, thinking, feeling, and enacting, to "do theology" is always to "go theology," to form and reform it, to mine and refine it by living steadily further into it. Any theology we might think to *learn* and still be unable to *do* suggests that we do not really see its "point." We are, in Ghazali's phrase, unable "to travel with it," and, past what we have called kindred and consanguine meanings, anything peculiarly Islamic in religion is judged to be insignificant. Like those who cannot practice law, hear rhythm, or perform music, we rightly wonder whether any really do understand who find theology so pointless for traveling. The map of a terrain is understood in an actual beyond an analogical way only by journeying there.

We can see the signifying character of religious language intimately in its Eucharistic use. "This is my body, which is broken for you." "This is my blood, shed for many for the remission of sins." "Do this for my recalling." Those are simple words, and any sympathetic observer may approximate their meanings. But their dynamic, ostensive "this" stretches out into the felt presence of the Christ continuing his atoning work. The denotation connoted by "this" has a "point" far beyond the bread and the wine. The peculiarly Christian force is achieved, to adapt Ghazali's term, as one "travels beyond" with them. Recalling Nagarjuna, they are like fingers indicating the moon, and only in this gestural power do they have any "point." Meanings are almost literally "communicant," and fail if the communicated reconciliation fails. Before this mystery, communicants too flounder for meanings, both perceptual and conceptual. Still, past circumstantial and comparative ones, no convivial meanings are had in the mind until these words become viable in life.

Rudolf Otto writes of *The Idea of the Holy*: "This book had its origin in efforts to provide in my lectures for myself and my pupils an approach to the profoundest of all Christian intuitions which I perceived to be both indicated and concealed in the orthodox constructions of the doctrines of 'reconciliation....' I came to the result that 'expiation' will not admit of a *theory* which shall express its profoundest reasons in the formal *concepts* of logic. But what I 'conceived' was that we often in the depths of our souls 'understand' what we do not 'conceive' (*begreifen*), and about which we have no theory. As Luther says, 'No one can *comprehend* God, but one *feels* him nevertheless.' And it seemed to me that the biblical story of passion and the great passion, the tentative terms of the Gospels, Paul, John, and the Epistle to the Hebrews...are quite enough to bring to the 'feeling' what cannot be put in logical form (*Begriff*). And I should expect of a cautious and acute 'historian of religion' that he would confess that he could neither 'comprehend' (*begreifen*) nor 'understand through the feeling' what the importance is which people attach to this 'fantastic' value of 'propitiation,' but that certainly the Christians imagined that they experienced it, and that, of all the 'fantastic' goods conferred in their salvation, this seemed to them the most important."[7] Every good doctrine is always sacramental, that is, its full, inner meaning is lodged in its point undergone.

A frequent objection to Augustine's requiring of faith in order to understand is that one cannot believe what is not yet understood, and faced with this criticism, Augustine grants that sheer ignorance prevents any belief. We cannot believe *x*. "Who cannot see that we must think before we believe. No one believes a thing until he has first thought what it is that is to be believed." (PS 5) But the complementary and the dominant truth in religion is that we cannot think in absence of relevant experience, which is had only by

[7] Rudolf Otto, *India's Religion of Grace and Christianity Compared and Contrasted* (London: Student Christian Movement Press, 1930), p. 105f.

communicant trusting. We move by faith from pre-understanding to understanding, from some initial significance to a deeper significant point. The understanding of a biblical passage, for instance, says Augustine, demands an initial analysis, but increasingly after that the sensitivities of faith. "To describe its beauty and show how it inspires the intelligent reader is impossible to communicate to anyone who does not himself feel it." "An intelligent reader is instructed here more by reading it with feeling, than by subjecting it to careful analysis." (CD 4-21) Truth is in this sense *dramatic*, that is, found by participatory reenactment.

In our context, we can catch this mood by replacing *believing* or *trusting* with *undergoing* in a passage from Augustine: "If a person says to me, 'I would understand in order that I may undergo,' I answer, 'Undergo that you may understand....' Certainly, what I am now saying, I say with the object that those may undergo it who do not yet do so. And yet until they understand what I am saying, they cannot undergo it. Hence what he says is partly true, 'I would understand in order that I may undergo it.' And I too am right when I say,... 'No, undergo that you may understand it.' Understand that you may undergo my words; undergo that you may understand the Word of God." (Sm 43-7, 9) "The mysteries and secrets of the kingdom of God first seek out believing men that they may make them understand. For faith is understanding's step, and understanding is faith's reward." (Sm 126-1) Enlightenment is the end of practice.

3. Understanding by ongoing undergoing

Next we consult Sankara, whom we have been neglecting, about the progressive nature of coming to religious understanding through what we call an ongoing undergoing. "That art thou," he warns us, is no simple, immediately available sentence. Rather the "thou," the "that," (and even their joining "art") have much "to be heard, thought, reflected on," recalling how the *Brihadāraṇyaka Upanishad* urges us to those three states of formation we have earlier examined.[8] For the vast majority of persons, the phrase

---

[8] See p. 74ff.

requires "repeated instruction," displaying its meaning in its inter-connections with the whole Vedantan literature. "Now in the case of those persons for whom the meaning of these two terms is obstructed by ignorance, doubt, and misconception, the sentence 'That art thou' cannot produce a right knowledge of its sense, since the knowledge of the sense of the sentence presupposes the knowledge of the sense of the words; for them therefore the repetition of the scriptural text and of reasoning must be assumed to have a purpose, viz., the discernment of the true sense of the words." The clearing up of ignorance is a matter of progressively erasing many wrongly superimposed meanings, each of them partial *avidyās* and *aparā vidyās*. "Now by one act of attention we may discard one of these parts (of unmeaning); and by another act of cognition another part; so that a successively progressing cognition may very well take place." (VS 4-1-2)

When a critic alleges that the repeated meditation is superfluous, Sankara replies that this is not so. "For we observe that men by again and again repeating a sentence which they, on first hearing, had understood only imperfectly, gradually rid themselves of all misconceptions and arrive at a full understanding of the true sense." If any should worry whether mantric repetitions tend to dry up the intelligible sense of the words, Sankara warns that such repetitions as of "That art thou" must rather increase their sense by a sustained sort of trenching into meaning. (VS 4-1-2) Like the meditation on OM, this remarkable phrase is a pointer to many meanings. If we would hear the teaching of any scripture, we have to remember that "its meaning is hidden deep, as within an aphorism." (VC 44)

But whoever puts meaning into aphorisms (*sūtras*) expects a progressive unfolding of much meaning compacted into a few words. Bhrigu's teaching by his father, or Indra's puzzlements, or the students of Pippalada are examples of *Upanishadic* dialogues going onward by an incremental spiraling around and around one truth, often over long periods of time. (TaU 3-1-1ff; ChU 8-7ff; PrU 1-1ff, 5-6f) Eventually, the *Upanishads* have their point only as the self recovers the Self, and "none but a knower of the Self can understand the purport of the *Vedas*." (GaK 2-30) Like a long-burning lamp, the understanding reaches Brahman only by "dwelling a long time steadily in the current of the same thought continuously, like a thread of descending oil." (BhG 12-3m)

The *Great Sūtra*, developing a similar thought, tells us that "the Bodhisattvas who teach the perfection of wisdom will understand it only after a long time." (AP 162) There are five deepening stages in working into *śūnyatā*, a "working in" that the *Sūtra* repeatedly refers to as "the gradual activity, training, and method of the Bodhisattva who courses in perfect wisdom." (MP 554) (1) We begin with phenomenal emptiness, learning that all the elements (*dharmas*), the plural things of the world, are void. *Saṃsāra* is *śūnya*. (2) Later, we ponder the distinction between conditioned and unconditioned things (*dharmas*), using the latter to measure the former and to find them to be wanting, the emptiness of conditioned things made all the greater by the contrast with the resplendence of the unconditioned. *Saṃsāra* is not *nirvāṇa*. (3) Still later, we begin to understand how the unconditioned too is empty, formless, undifferentiated, and, having abandoned possessiveness, we are increasingly drawn to the noumenal Void. *Nirvāṇa* too is *śūnya*.

(4) Now, reaching the threshold of the emptiness with which Nagarjuna is most concerned, when we advance from wisdom to perfect wisdom, we undo the preceding distinctions to contemplate the identity of the conditioned and the unconditioned. Here a realm of paradoxes opens up before us, making meaningful all those treasured claims that seem so incoherent to the outsider. All things are unborn, and if they are born, still they are undistinguished from the original Void. All things are inactive, still their exertions are not different from the calm of *nirvāṇa*. When joined by the highest understanding of *śūnya*, *nirvāṇa* is *saṃsāra*, there is no difference between them. (5) But even this has to be transcended, and lastly we are hushed. Beyond all thought, the meaning of *śūnya* is silence.[9]

---

[9] The *Great Sūtra* lists eighteen, or twenty, kinds of emptiness (MP 144ff) and Nagarjuna's *Śāstra* spends chapter 48 (MPC1 1995ff) in commentary about how they are progressively discovered. See Venkata Ramanan, 405, 338; Conze, *Buddhist Thought in India*, pp. 242-249.

At each level, to see its meaning is to undergo its point. Edward Conze comments on the understanding of these levels: "It will be seen that the word 'emptiness' in each case derives its meaning from the context created by a spiritual attitude. Outside that context it has no meaning at all.... Emptiness is not a theory, but a ladder that reaches out into the infinite. A ladder is not there to be discussed, but to be climbed. If one does not even take the first steps on it, the farther rungs seem, I admit, rather remote. They come nearer only as one goes up there. 'Emptiness'...has not only one meaning, but several, which can unfold themselves on the successive stages of the actual process of transcending the world through wisdom. Not everyone, of course, is meant to understand what emptiness means." (SP 24)

"There is no God but God, and Muhammad is his prophet." The claim seems simple enough, but, serving more like the title of a novel, Ghazali finds that the *shahādah* stretches over a whole Islamic career. Introduced to a child, "its meaning will continue to be unfolded to him little by little as he grows." (Ih I, 2, 13 & 55) Even with considerable Qur'anic exegesis, "no one is able to have a thorough knowledge of the prophet's teaching, except by training himself to the imitation of the Lawgiver." (Ri 356) By this imitation of Muhammad and the exploration of his teaching we validate prophecy, finding how this Prophet is a doctor of the heart, a theme underlying the *Book on the Conduct of the Prophet.* (Ih II, 10) "If you understand what it is to be a prophet and have devoted much time to the study of the *Qur'an* and the *Traditions,* you will arrive at a necessary knowledge of the fact that Muhammad is in the highest grades of the prophetic calling. Convince yourself of that by trying out what he said about the influence of devotional practices on the purification of the heart.... When you have made trial of these in a thousand or several thousand instances, you will arrive at a necessary knowledge beyond all doubt." (Dl 67m)

The "point" of the Muslim creed increases by so much awakening (*ilhām*) to and by that prophetic system, and such tasting-testing carries with it, Ghazali reports, the "necessity" of prophetic truth. At this reach, the more one understands the *shahādah* in the widening impact on his life of the prophet's teaching and of the divine oneness, the more one gathers all of Islam into this single sentence, and finds its daily repetition to provide a continuing profit, and increasingly sees that it is true. Finally the Muslim arrives at a certainty (*yaqīn*) based on experience, and which cannot entertain any other possibility, a certainty which Ghazali carefully distinguishes from an overconfident certainty lacking experiential basis. (Ih I, 1, 193f) But what does Ghazali say of those persons who reject it? "They denied that, the knowledge of which they could not compass, and whose interpretation had not yet come to them." (S 10.40*p*,m)

The Christ calls, "Learn of me, because I am meek of heart." We have already found humility to be an epistemic virtue, but need now to consider how this learning is by a lifelong incremental undergoing, during which the putting on, through trusting, of steadily more humility brings increasing comprehension. Jesus teaches, "Blessed are the meek, for they shall inherit the earth." We find that every word—"blessed," "meek," "inherit," "earth," even the "shall"—is laden with struggle for meaning. The beatitude is insane nonsense to the vain; oppositely, the more one comes within it the more we see its sense. As the Eucharist does not mean anything we take it to mean, so too must the beatitude's meaning accord with history, and so we need the interpreter to unfold its original setting. But the scholar cannot locate, much less translate and preach this meaning, except, by any of the routes here catalogued, there is some tasting of this blessed meekness.

These subtle qualities are gained only by a lifetime of entrance into a fertile aphorism that, detecting its expression in the incarnate Christ, understands in convivial discipleship this conquering perfection of God. But so too with what it means to be "pure in heart" and to "see God," to "hunger and thirst after righteousness," to "be satisfied," to "suffer persecution for righteousness' sake," to "be God's peacemaker," to "mourn" and to "be comforted." How these must be suffered and enjoyed to become significant! These beatitudes point us to a Christian career, a life in his steps.[10] We do not

---

[10] This incremental and participatory character of understanding through meekness the teaching of Christ is continually Augustine's exegesis in his *Commentary on the Sermon on the Mount.* Or see *Sermon 53* on the beatitudes, or the *Sermon 117* quoted earlier, p. 62f.

understand "baptism," "forgiveness," "incarnation," "Eucharist," or "Christianity" by consulting a dictionary.

Augustine offers us the maxim "Love and do what you will" as finely embracing the whole Christian ethos. (LJ 7-8) We may take this as exemplified in the parable of the prodigal son, a story which is too near the human condition to be wholly unmeaning for any person. Yet the deepest parabolic significance of this story is by no means easy and public. Rather, why that father's prodigal love is appropriate and divine takes much discernment. Only the life which is lived out in the same compassion will see God in the parable or in the maker of the parable, while to others the father will seem eccentric, too soft, unable to temper love with righteousness, just as the older brother was unable to temper righteousness with love. Or, worse, the foolish father will seem discordant with the rough and tumble world.

But to reject in this way its accuracy or relevance is not to see the point in this suffering love that does what it wills, because that sort of love is insufficiently incumbent in the rejecter's life. Only the faithful person who, like the father, loves and does what he or she then wills can taste the sweetness of this great commandment to love, as it summarizes all the rest, summarizes everything we seek to understand. "The sweeter the commands of him who aids us are, the more do we who love him search them out, that we may do them as far as known, and learn them by doing them. For the more they are done, the more perfectly they are understood." (NP 118-17-7) The kingdom of God is difficultly searched for, at once hidden and at hand, a seed growing, a pearl of great price, a leaven spreading, a ripening harvest, and all of this so much within. That is the "secret of the kingdom" which only the disciples know. (Mk. 4.11f) Jerusalem has a peace of its own.

Once more we should soften the exclusivisms here. "Whoever would lose his life shall gain it, and whoever gains his life shall lose it." Because the noblest of religious truths always lie on the far side of such experience, however variantly this is put, interreligiously this saying may be comparatively understood. But, extrareligiously, any who run short of this loss and gain of life are not going to find it meaningful but false. Rather its paradox will baffle them.

They will find it unmeaning, because they are unaware of how the theological and psychological facts run deeper. And there cannot be any undoing of the paradox without the humbling of *superbia* (Augustine), without knowing *anātman* and *śūnya* (Nagarjuna), without surgery on the individualizing *ahaṃkāra* (Sankara), without supression of the impulsive *hawā* by the unitarian *fanā'* (Ghazali). We must say, as Augustine said to the hesitant but interested Babylonian, "You must be emptied of that of which you are full, that you may be filled with that of which you are empty."[11] Then, if any critics still reject the ecumenical claim in all its forms, it is tempting to say that they never gain the essential spiritual experience that underruns the saying, which, unreached, remains unintelligible.

4. Understanding overruns undergoing

Understanding is not by any undergoing, but only by that undergoing which stands back to analyze and synthesize this into advanced undergoing. So far as it can be, that is conceptual and meditative, for that is what it means to reflect—to turn the mind on the self's ongoing. In part, this increases participation, adding a comprehension of undergoing for furthering apprehension; in part, this returns us to detachment, since criticism requires enough distance for review and overview. Our saints are intellectuals, and their systematic treatises from the *City of God* to the *Fundamentals of the Middle Way* are ample proof of that. They all of them seek knowledge (*jñāna, 'ilm*), wisdom (*prajñā, sapientia*), skill-in-means (*upāya*), discrimination (*vinaya*), and *science* (Ghazali, Augustine). But even so, differing gestalts control intellection, and we have in conclusion in this chapter to ask about whether they all know enough detachment cognitively to understand that in which they existentially participate.

We have watched how Augustine finds his intellectual desires nonnegotiable, finding an apodictic certainty not only that he is, but that he loves to understand, and that understanding is never bad. He is "deeply in love with intellection," and his great hope is

---

[11] See p. 163f.

"to perceive by pure intelligence the immutable substance of God." In the mind we most image God. That is not just academically, and yet the person is truncated except as his head does become joined with his heart, his knowing with his being. It is not any faith that suffices. The great doctor cannot too often remind us that the only adequate faith must seek understanding; it must think with its trusting. The grace which he finds that he undergoes sets him to work going round his life, his scriptures, his world to order these so that he might understand them, and the discursive result is his library. That too is "doing theology." After the trusting plunge we reflectively reap its benefits. For Augustine, to criticize may be to doubt, but not necessarily; we may doubt without criticizing, and criticize without doubting. To criticize is to understand by thinking through what we undergo. "Our intellect therefore increases the understanding comprehension of that which it believes, and faith increases our believing in that which is understood. So the mind itself, proportionately as these things are more and more understood, is intellectually advanced." (NP 118-17-3) At the summit of knowing there is intellection, an intellectual vision judiciously comprehending what it apprehends.

Ghazali concludes his *Book of Knowledge* by describing and praising the Muslim savant. Once, when some Muslims praised a pious man, Muhammad surprised them by asking about his intellect, and then warned that a pious fool does more harm than do even the wicked, and that "men will not advance to higher proximity to God except in proportion to their intellect." That *tradition* from Muhammad excites Ghazali to an extended praise of intellectual Islam. "Man gains nothing like a worthy intellect which leads him to righteousness and dissuades him from sin, nor does his belief become complete until his intellect matures. For everything there is a support and shelter, and the support and shelter of the believer is his intellect; in proportion to his intellect will his worship be." (Ih I, 1, 223f,a) So Ghazali agrees with Augustine in teaching that faith's maturity is in intelligent understanding. This can be used to defend Ghazali in other passages that might worry us, where the spiritual level supersedes the intellectual level and almost seems to disparage it. It reminds us how everywhere Sufism consummates but is reflectively controlled by Sunni religious science.

But if we travel eastward, even Sankara complains that the end state which is alleged by Madhyamika is meaningless in its denial of cognitive knowledge. (PrU 6-2) Sankara advertises his ultimate, about whose intellectual vitality we might otherwise be troubled, positively as *being, consciousness, bliss*. There must be something like *thought* in the superconsciousness in Brahman.

Alone, Nagarjuna is creedless, and this bodes ill for intellection. " 'Our bliss consists in the cessation of all thought....' Since all the objects of knowledge have died away, knowledge itself has also died." "O Reverends, you must enter that mystic condition where all concepts and feelings are extinct!" (Ca 208f, citing Ka 25-24; Ca 130) "One comprehends that in the universal reality there is nothing that is determinable and one abandons even these comprehensions. In the ultimate realization, all such modes of intellection come to an end. This is the universal reality, the same as *Nirvāṇa*. Water, for example, is cold by nature and it becomes hot only when fire is added to it. With the extinction of fire, the heat of the water also becomes extinct and the water returns to its original nature and remains cold as before. The mind using all the diverse modes of intellection is like the water getting fire. The extinction of all intellection is like the extinction of fire. The original nature of mind, the *tathatā*, is like coldness of water. It eternally remains in its fundamental nature." (MPCv 254a) Does any meaning remain in *prajñā*, this original mind, so perceptually gnostic, so conceptually agnostic? After this Buddhist extinguishing of intellection, only the enlightened can know.

Dualism, not mentality, offends Nagarjuna the most; still in the end he dislikes activity of mind. But it is one thing to hold that ultimate reality is described by our common language under a *neti-neti* caveat, warning that what we say is not quite so. It is another thing to say that speech is altogether void and useless. It is one thing to say that we have no literal account of the sacred, another that all our accounts are literally, rationally empty. It is one thing to note that perception goes *ill* into words, another that it goes *nill* into words. Silence is not profound in lieu of speech, it is only more profound than any speech when it exceeds the best that speech can do. Without language there is no religion, for there is no reflection, and without language there is no critical discussion. If it is true that we cannot say what we see; it is also true that we can only see, in any intellectual sense, what we can to some extent say. In mapless being there, in music without lyrics, or in unnamed longings, we do not understand what we undergo. The Madhyamika thesislessness affords us no distance for intellection.

Whether we like it or not, the characteristic of words is not, as with fingers, barely to point. But words have intension as well as extension. To be sure, with Nagarjuna, we do not confuse the finger with the moon. But words do not point like fingers; they point by describing, however analogously and comparatively, to name and to index an experience. They symbolize, as fingers cannot. Even those nondescriptive indicator words with such attenuated intension which are preferred by Nagarjuna—"thatness," "suchness," "emptiness"—do not point anywhere or to anything except as they are fitted into a supporting, significant conceptuality. Pointing to nothing, or everything, is the same as not pointing. Words cannot be understood as naked pointers, but only as reflective pointers. For this reason Nagarjuna always slips back into using the logic he later despises, into a preaching of emptiness. Else, with his thought gone limp, he indeed worships an unknown God.

In the Madhyamika ecstasies, thought drops away with the evils of *saṃsāra* and we are left silent before an impervious emptiness. In the Augustinian intellectual vision, speech fails of the inner word, which fails of the divine intelligence, but we are left before the *Logos*. If wordiness can be a vice in religion, so also is unrelieved silence. Intellection is not our samsaric curse, but rather it is when we are nearest God. Thinking to do us a favor by sublating every view, Madhyamika rather overkills with its thesislessness, for it so shears away understanding in excess of undergoing that we slip back from this lofty human intellectual genius into the preconscious oceanic emptiness, which is but doubtfully understood. There is no theory, there is no faith; there is only the illusion of belief overlaid on ineffable experience.

Socrates complained against the Athenian poets that, though they claimed a divine inspiration, they could not tell what they meant. Philosophy, he hoped, could draw out that meaning into sober prose. Yet Plato comes round at the end again to myth. The spiritual adventure begins in an intuition less clear than we could wish, then moves to conception which elevates our understanding, and finally returns to symbolic meaning with point. "The artist is ever less and more wise than he is," we say, for, without reflection, he knows things that he does not know he knows. Only the critic can bring to awareness what is there, and this is best done at reflective distance from the artistry itself. Yet if that veers into separation, our critical powers are lost. It is not only by being a saint that the saint understands, he or she also understands by becoming a scholar. Primitively, we may participate without reflection. Later, past that, thought detaches us for intellectual participation. Then, further still, in secondary naiveté, we return in piety to undergo an ultimate reality that, brokenly understood, we cannot forgo.

Chapter 6. Adherence and Nonadherence

Each of our saintly zealots rejects more belief than he holds. The *Commentary on the Vedāta Sūtras*, the *Kārikās*, the *Incoherence*, and the *City of God* are strewn with withstood and abandoned beliefs. Every affirmation in them carries a hundred negations, and from this we may draw out a doctrine of error, of supposed truth we withstand. Here our abandoning of formerly supposed truth is especially puzzling in its logical and psychological workings. Then, reflexively from this, we consider an account of believed truth, after that of error, and use our saints' marks of truth to specify the forces that bring us to conviction. Increasingly at partings of the ways, we must release in flood controversies we have long stemmed. If we here too often use the attacks of the West on the East, this is because we have not the skill to pose the counter-attacks. Doubtless, others can.

I. Nonadherence: The Failure of Understanding

Nonadherence arises from the incoherence, the falling apart, of a belief when we do not see the point, finding ourselves unable to gain the experience which makes sense of the creed we reject.

Circumferentially, comparatively, we may understand. But past these ranges, compassionately, we fail; and, before the intimacies of alien faith, we are unsure what it is like to be there. Our counter-experience makes the competing truths false, but in a way that swiftly opens further into their meaninglessness. We now develop these complex events of rejection with what we term *nonunderstanding, counterstanding, misunderstanding,* and *reunderstanding.*

1. Rejection by nonunderstanding

Our doctors find that their faiths are steadily rejected by the holders of variant creeds. Their claims bewilder others. But these doctors just as regularly do their own rejecting on account of failure to appropriate meaning. Faith is refused unless it yields understanding. If those are Augustine's words, the principle is present in Ghazali's incoherences of all the non-Muslim philosophies, in Nagarjuna's emptiness of all the *dharma*-doctrines, and in Sankara's sublatability of every non-Advaitan position. Though we do not forget the span of faith across nascent understanding, afterward, with adequate exposure, where understanding fails to mature there is warranted rejection because of *nonunderstanding.* Now we must put this principle to work interreligiously in the process where alien faith suffers rejection. We do this by offering both as an example of this rejection and as a conclusion to our own inquiries the case of what happens to the Christian who confronts the quite variant Hindu and Buddhist witnesses, or even the Muslim witness, which is more closely kin to his own.

A. Take Brahman or *śūnyatā.* Any who seriously share the theism of Augustine or Ghazali listen to Advaitan and to Madhyamika teachings politely, but all the while asking with disquieting pangs, beneath nodding agreements, whether these Eastern ultimates are, after all, so very desirable. What do we say of Sankara's homogeneous Absolute? Since neither of our Western saints was in touch with Sankara, let Ramanuja be their spokesman. "Rigid, motionless, and totally lacking in initiative or influence, (it) cannot call forth our worship. Like the Taj Mahal, which is unconscious of the admiration it arouses, the Absolute remains indifferent to the fear and love of its worshippers, and...Sankara's view seems to be a finished example of learned error.... The world is said to be an appearance and God a bloodless Absolute dark with excess of light.... He declares that to save oneself is to lose oneself in the sea of the unknown."[1] The Lord, Ishvara, *saguṇa* Brahman, does have theistic color, but this we are also told is mere name and form, reality only dressed up "as if" it were God, reality appearing as God in the *māyā*-world; and all the while the *māyā*-world is inaccurate illusion, somehow not up to the real God, in contrast to the sacramental capacity which the theistic creation does carry.

"That very Brahman is a terror to the learned man who lacks the unitive outlook," alleges Sankara of the theist who cannot relax into monism. (TaU 2-7-1m) It is theistic duality that Sankara fears; but it is nonduality that the theist fears, unable to appreciate an undistinguished monolithic absolute. The oceanic deep is rarely for Augustine the symbol of God; it is closer to the formless chaos from which in God we are rescued. (Co 12-3f) With Brahman as *being*, *consciousness*, *bliss*, we gain a comparative understanding. But beyond this severe economy in concepts, the nondescript "homogeneity of Brahman" (BrU 5-1-1) is a pinchbeck deity too bleak and undeveloped for address as the Eternal Thou. True, Sankara tirelessly urges a sweeping "Verily, all this is Brahman." (*ChU* 2-25-1m) But in this plural all-ness, any specific this-ness, any form, structure, or particularity is all overlay of ignorance; and the "all this" slips incoherently into a "not this." Can there be any diversity in Brahman? None whatsoever! "Therefore we must give up all such conceptions and know Brahman to be undifferentiated like the sky." (BrU 2-1-20) We begin to worry that all this is pseudo-understanding, and that in the blankness of *nirguṇa* Brahman there is nothing to understand.

Or consider sheer *śūnyatā*. Before this barren void, there are gnawing feelings of emptiness too, as much as with all the other *dharmas* which Madhyamika has emptied of content. For *śūnyatā* does, after all, root in *śūnya*, which means "hollow," "swollen," "turgid," and that paradigmatic symbol-word kept nearest their

---

[1] Paraphrased by Radhakrishnan, *Indian Philosophy*, vol. 2, p. 659f,m.

ultimate is a rough word to rid of all its negativity. Although it is supposed to mean something else when applied to the unconditioned than it does when applied to the conditioned, we are scarcely given sacred meanings in lieu of the secular ones. In its earliest use, *śūnya* means "without own-being," and hence "moved and destroyed" as applied to world things, but later it means "neither unmoved nor destroyed," neither absolute nor perishing, a refrain through the twenty kinds of emptiness. (MP 144ff) But it is hard coherently to couple these denials of both absolutism and of nihilism, especially when we are denied any theses, begrudged positing even a blank "thatness." And so? Is that peaceful Void resplendent? Or gray? "No Reality was preached at all, nowhere and none by Buddha." There is only the great "quiescence of plurality." (Ka 25-24s,m)

Charitably, we should respect Nagarjuna's final word. But frankly, this "emptiness" sounds not so much like the "fullness" promised in the Father of Jesus Christ, or even "the 'perishing' of all save Allah's face," as does it sound like the universal heat death of the distant future predicted by thermodynamics. Nagarjuna is delighted with the terminal "sameness of everything." (CS 1-4; MPCv 271) There *nirvāṇa* is neither unmoved, as Brahman is unmoved, nor destroyed, as *saṃsāra* is destroyed. But is this a consummation or a collapse of the real? Nagarjuna's later interpreters may reply that this is inexpressible positivity; but the great dialectician himself would not say so. He gives us nothing. Only the *śūnya* predicate is allowed, relatively, of *tattva*-reality, then that is absolutely erased too. Like Brahman, *śūnyatā* dissipates God into the blue sky. God zeroed hovers too near to nihilism. God the Void is a void God.

B. What of this environing *world*? How the energies of Advaita and of Madhyamika are given to depreciating it! "This (phenomenal) state has no beginning and no end; it has to be eradicated wholly and individually by each embodied being, because it consists of sorrow; and it flows unbroken like the current of a river." (MuU 1-2, int.) The regnant paradigm, *māyā*, means in its ordinary *Upanishadic* uses "crooked," "deceitful," and "false." "Therefore creation, which has been imagined as a help to the comprehension of nonduality, is unreal, referred to by the word *māyā*, indicative of unreal things. The idea of heterogeneity, implied by creation, is condemned." (GaK 3-24a) "The water on the lotus leaf is very unstable; so also is life extremely unstable. Know that the entire world is devoured by disease and conceit, and smitten with sorrow." (Hy 57) "There is no good to be attained by the knowledge of the narrative of the creation." (AiU 2-1) "Those whose ideal is the attainment of the highest good do not entertain any respect for creation in its diversity because it can lead to no purpose." (MaU 1-7)[2]

Śūnya is a virtual synonym with *māyā*, at least through part of its uses. The *Great Sūtra* world metaphors begin with *māyā*, and move through mirage, magical illusion, dream, mock show, airy castle in the sky, a bubble on the water, a passing stir in the wind. (cf. MP 38, 193) Nagarjuna elaborately comments on these (MPC1 375ff) and much dwells on the horrible unloveliness of, and our distrust for, everything in the world. World unsatisfactoriness, *duḥkha*, and world unreality, *anitya*, are the first of the noble truths. (MPC1 1311ff, 1431ff; SL 57-106) The world is " a disease, a boil, a thorn, a misfortune." (MP 204) It is literally blasted. "In antagonism to the entire world is the enlightenment of the *Tathā-gatas*, by which the *Tathāgatas* are able to expound this so deep a perfection of wisdom." (MP 376m)

After the Buddha has "hit the absolute reality," Candrakirti tells us unguardedly, Buddha exclaims, "There is here in this world neither reality, nor absence of illusion, it is surreptitious reality, it is cancelled reality, it is a lie, a childish babble, an illusion." (Ca 125m) Perfect wisdom, as Conze characterizes it, is "complete unworldliness." "The central idea is the total denial of, the complete emancipation from, the world around us in all its aspects and along its entire breadth." (SP 11, 24) Once again, for any whose world is a creation and gift of God, what is there in the *māyā-śūnya*-world to be understood? This lie, trick, and bubble is to be seen through, not seen into. All is a negative misunderstanding to

2 The last two translations are by Singh, *The Vedānta of Śaṅkara*, p. 277f,m.

be dissipated; positively no residue remains which can intelligently be evaluated. The world is but froth and foam on a deep, incomprehensible sea.

But earth is heaven, the conditioned is the unconditioned, and so, replies Madhyamika, we are given back the world now to be reunderstood as the ultimate real. That holds great promise, except that such a predication of the two as being identical is made again and entirely through that nonunderstandable *śūnya*. *Saṃsāra* = *śūnya* = *nirvāṇa*. The curiously plastic word that is used pejoratively of the world is spun round and used in praise of *nirvāṇa*. That is well enough if we equivocate, *śūnya* formerly meaning "hollow" and "unreal," latterly meaning "inarticulate" and "real." But then the world remains vacuous. If we predicate unequivocally or even analogically, allowing *śūnya* positive meanings for both world and *nirvāṇa*, it is hard to find what those meanings are in the face of Nagarjuna's avowed thesislessness.

If we try to find them and let *nirvāṇa* resuscitate *saṃsāra*, in some crossovers of meanings via *śūnya*, its erosive acids are still too dissolvent. *Saṃsāra* zeroed is *nirvāṇa*. But equation through zero is contentless. What is there to be understood? The Madhyamika world is washed out as it flows into *nirvāṇa*, and then *nirvāṇa* too is overcome with the power of *śūnya*. "Even *Nirvāṇa* , I say, is like a dream, like an illusion. If I could cognize any dharma more distinguished than *Nirvāṇa*, of that also I should say that it is like a dream, like an illusion. And why? Because dream and illusion, on the one side, and *Nirvāṇa*, on the other, are not two nor divided." (MP 211m) If, past *saṃsāra*, even *nirvāṇa* is found to be a dream and an illusion, what remains to be studied? Magnificent nothingness! The theistic world is vain when it falls out of God, and so there is in Augustine's model of it as Babylon a comparative understanding of *saṃsāra*. But the theistic world, Jerusalem, is not zeroed in God. What could that mean?

C. Have we not in the colloquy of these faiths found them to prescribe a common emptying of *self*? Yes, comparatively. But this is not without unresolved conflicts. The same *śūnya*-word spread through real, through world, and through *nirvāṇa* is urged also against the self. As in *nirguṇa* Brahman, so too in *nirvāṇa*, our consciousness literally "goes out" into emptiness. But such annihilation is the perennial stumbling block which the Buddhist can never quite explain to others, even other saints. Candrakirti tells us that in *nirvāṇa* there will be "no existence, no ego, no living creature, no individual soul, no personality, and no Lord." "There is in it no individual life whatever." (Ca 127m, 182m) "No entity corresponding to a Bodhisattva who courses in perfect wisdom does exist, or can be got at, just as in space the track of a bird does not exist, just as the track of a dream, an illusion, a mirage, an echo, or a magical creation cannot be apprehended." (MP 118a) "A Bodhisattva does not seize on a self, or a being, or a soul, or a person, because, absolutely, they do not exist." (MP 173m) We may be helped by reminders that our desires and cravings are put out in *nirvāṇa*. There are metaphors of peace, and we may be a little comforted but more mystified by counterdenials of *nirvāṇic* nonexistence or annihilation. Still, too much is extinguished. Exhausting the *śūnya*-self, whatever is left of us in the end seems too near to nothing to be intelligible. *Śūnyatā* makes everything vain. Vanity of vanities, all is vanity.

There is more promise in the Advaitan claim to gather everything into the *being, consciousness,* and *bliss* of Brahman—until we notice how this is achieved at the cost of the personal dissolutions of all the saints. Then we are no longer so sure we understand. "Having thus attained identity with the supreme Immortality, they discard individuality, like a lamp blown out or the space in a pot when broken; they become freed on every side." "Just as the footprints of birds cannot be traced in space and of aquatics in water, similar is the movement of the men of knowledge." (MuU 3-2-6m) In this queasy dropping off into Brahman, so commended as "flowing into" it, we are not able to distinguish salvation from suicide. We are like the comet drawn to the sun, and vaporized before its arrival. If *nirvāṇa* seems too much like the quiescent heat death of the universe, Brahman seems too much like an astronomical black hole into which detailed things may be drawn, but from which nothing can return, and in which there is crushed all particular content.

This religion which takes the Self as the Ultimate seems to end, equivocating at Self and self, by devaluing that same self. Ramanuja protests against Sankara and the Advaitans that, if Sankara is right, "the whole doctrine of salvation—which our opponents seek as much as we—would become meaningless."[3] Augustine would concur; this liberation is so near to lostness. Alas, the theistic mind is not subtle enough to catch the difference between being saved and being sunk in Brahman or in *śūnyatā*, between their infinity and a cipher. Unable to couple "thou" and "that," "*saṃsāra*" and "*nirvāṇa*," their paradigms do not clarify our understanding, but only confuse us.

2. Rejection by counterstanding

Already we are ranging beyond a mere vacuum in meaning. There has here appeared the pressure of opposing meanings, and we find that we withstand proffered meaning, lest it rupture our own. It would be simplest, but too simple, to say that we understand and judge to be false the alien faith we confront, or that we wholly fail to understand and judge it to be meaningless. Actually, what happens is that our meaning presses away this competitive, alien meaning, preventing our reception of it. So we are denied access to, and yet must deny, these variant significances which we find to be incommensurable with ours, as one form of life prevents a multiformity of meanings. We wrench their "truth" to find it will not turn round our axes, never quite understanding because we must negate apparent, threatening meaning when it is still only partly understood. We *counterstand* and are set in contrast (Latin: *contra-stare*). This is why, beyond comparative understanding, interreligious dialogue most often ends in a stand-off.

"But now, my years are wasted in sighs, and you, O Lord, my comfort, my Father, are eternal. But I am distracted amid times, whose order I do not know, and my thoughts, the inmost bowels of my soul, are mangled by tumult and change, until being purged and melted in the fire of your love, I may flow altogether into you." (Co 11-39) "I beheld other things below you, and I saw that they

---

[3] Cited in Otto, *India's Religion of Grace and Christianity Compared and Contrasted*, p. 37.

are not absolutely existent nor absolutely nonexistent; they are indeed, because they are from you; they are not, since they are not what you are. What truly exists immutably remains." (Co 7-17) Casually, we might think that Augustine is not far from Sankara. "He sees truly who sees the immortal Principle in the midst of things perishable." (BrU 4-4-6m; *BhG* 13-29) Ghazali writes: "Being is itself divided into that which has being-in-itself, and that which derives being from not-itself. The being of this latter is borrowed, having no existence by itself. Nay, if it is regarded in and by itself, it is pure not-being. Whatever being it has is due to its relation to a not-itself; and this is not real being at all." (Ni 58) Is this not rather close to Nagarjuna's claim that the world is "without own-being"? Before this relative being which is borrowed from the absolute being-in-itself, even Nagarjuna's transmundane in the midst of the mundane may seem in comparative agreement.

But more critically, it is almost axiomatic in all the classical religions that the world and the self "have no self-being," no final autonomy and are so far empty. Nagarjuna, if he is only saying this, is not saying anything different from the creeds he thinks he has demolished. But if we ask what value the contingent world derives from the ultimate real, counterstandings will swiftly arise. After a common fugitive element ascribed to the world and self, there are incommensurable perceptual sets. Nondualisms dispel the things of the world and of the self as delusory phenomena. Theism elevates the sacramental presence in nature and in history to its source in God. God prevents what would otherwise be the *māyā* of the *śūnya*-world; Brahman and *śūnyata* prescribe what God proscribes. In God, I myself abide, with all things. "It is good for me to adhere to my God, for if I do not abide in him, neither will I be able to abide in myself. But he abides in himself, and he renews all things." (Co 7-17) But in Brahman, in *śūnyatā*, where am I, where are they? Brahman is a lion's den in which every foot is seen entering, but none coming out. *Śūnyatā* does not renew things; it stills them. There nothing abides.

"All things which he has made are indeed good because made by him, but they are mutable because they were made, not out of him, but out of nothing. Although they are not the supreme good, since

God is a greater good than they are, these mutable things are, nonetheless, highly good because they can be united with him and be blessed in the immutable good." (CG 12-1) "If you find pleasure in material things, praise God for them, and direct your love to their maker.... In themselves they are mutable; in him they are fixed and established; else they would pass and perish. In him, therefore, let them be loved, and with you carry up to him as many of them as you can." (Co 4-18) "All these beautiful things which you seek, which you love, he made. If these are beautiful, what is he himself? If these are great, how much greater is he! Therefore from those things which we love here, let us the more long for him." (NP 84-9) How Augustine can sing about that creation, repeatedly expounding *Genesis*, even doing so midway through the *City of God* and concluding the *Confessions*! In his favorite epigram, God gives *form*, *order*, and *disposition*, or *measure, type*, and *number*. So Augustine's Platonism blends with the Hebraic creation.

There is no positive evil either in nature or in society, only a privation of the good. The Doctor of Grace reproves Origen for judging the world to be a prison, and he left the Manicheans because they held matter to be ungodly. (CG 11-23; Co 13-30) We are pilgrims here, but never mendicants. Yes, there is Babylon, but only when Jerusalem falls because of the sins of Adam and his progeny. "In the torrential river of human history, two currents mix and flow along together, that of evil which flows from our progenitor and that of good issuing from our Creator." (CG 22-24) In this tale of two cities the latter, Babylon, is only the loss of the former, Jerusalem.

But while God *saves*, Brahman *sublates*. We lose name and form in the return to the divine sea, where attributes (*guṇas*) and adjuncts are stilled. The West embraces plurality; the Indian East here despises it. Shifting things stand firm in God, and we carry as many of them up to him as we can. In Brahman they perish, and "nobody who knows their worthlessness will hanker after them." (KaU 1-1-28) Here, the world is a *gift*; there, it is a *disease*. Augustine's beatitude lies in the Earth inherited in the Heavenly City, the Eden City restored and watered by God. Augustine prays, "Thy kingdom come on earth as it is in heaven." Sankara prays for "the total eradication of worldly existence." (IsU 7) Brahman is the One without a second, the One who dissolves every other; but God the Father is the One who wills a second, the creatures to be with him in community.

Śūnyatā teases us with more and seems to want to infuse the divine through the earthly. We are first told: "That the conditioned as such is not unconditioned is the deeper significance of the teaching of *śūnyatā*." But then we are told that "the unconditioned again is not anything apart from the conditioned. The ultimate truth about the conditioned is that it is itself the unconditioned reality." (VR 210, 329; cf MP 641) But in this latter phase, when we turn back to embrace *saṃsāra* as *nirvāṇa*, what survives? The conditioned gets reduced to the unconditioned by erasing its form, order, and structure. "That state which is the rushing in and out of existence when dependent or conditioned—this state, when not dependent or not conditioned, is seen to be *nirvāṇa*." (Ka 25-9m) Only with the "cessation of phenomenal development" is *saṃsāra* seen to be *nirvāṇa*. (Ka 25-24)

The beauty of Madhyamika, thinks Candrakirti, is that "it saves us from misery and from phenomenal existence altogether." "There is in this plurality not the slightest bit of what is absolutely real,...nothing at all to justify the claim that a phenomenal reality has been established by us." (Ca 84m, 111m) But it is hard to see how the voided conditioned, this exhausted *saṃsāra*, with all its phenomenality gone, when returned as the resplendent unconditioned, has been validated in any of the senses in which Augustine's God validates his creation. God fills; but *śūnyatā* empties.

Edward Conze locates the orienting mood here. "The teachings of the *Prajñāpāramitā* have little significance for the present age. To be quite truthful, they are equally irrelevant to any other age. They are meant for people who have withdrawn from society.... Leaving worldings to get on with their worldly problems, these Sutras assume that the whole sense-linked, or conditioned, world is unsatisfactory, and that preoccupation with it is unworthy of our true mission in life. To make anything of them, one must take this for granted." (SP 16f,m) But that is just what Augustine cannot take for granted; he wrote the *City of God* to show how Christ redeems the historical process. The Lamb of God takes away not the world, but the sins of the world. There is for Augustine a suffering Babylon, and Christ's comfort is to those who mourn; and this permits a comparative understanding with the world of *duḥkha*. But Madhyamika knows only a fluid tableau through and through. When it is gutted to gain *nirvāṇa*, it is more deconditioned than reconditioned, and the resulting unconditioned world is not Yahweh's creation.

He who *forms* the heavens and the Earth *names* his creatures in Eden. History, His story, preserves that dignity until the consummation. Christ loves the world and gives his life to establish here the City of God. True, standing before Pilate and the politics of Babylon, he says, "My kingdom is not of *this* world," but that remark is not made of God's created world. Augustine zealously defends the resurrection of the earthly body against the dominantly Greek idea of the immortality of the soul, showing how he treasures natural personality. When it is said of God, "He gives his beloved sleep," this does not mean that they are extinguished for their rest. We hope for more, and the beatific vision involves no desertion, but rather the intensifying, of the personality. The highest unity we know is not elemental or homogeneous, but social and compound, with all items "making their particular contributions to the beauty of the universal commonwealth." (CG 11-22) The theist fears neither plurality nor contingency, he discriminates the *versus* in the *universus*, and finds in personality and in plurality a showing of the "fullness of him who fills all in all." (Eph. 1.23)

India's mood is destructively simpler, and here we must use pejoratively their praise-words: indiscriminate, nondiscriminate. Brahman and *śūnyatā* fearfully uncomplicate things by a departicularizing and an unnaming regression into a primitive adualism, into what things must have been like before individual consciousnesses arose. Life undoubtedly evolved out of the maternal ocean, but to return there is not to be saved. Rather, the oceanic feeling is retrograde and infantile. Though many have been led to the divine by them, *māyā* and *śūnya* are the two most tragic metaphors in the history of religion, for by their overkill half the world has been lost to creation and to the kingdom of God. In the end, what we might call the creative divine determinism of Christianity can only oppose these undifferentiated nondeterminisms of India. They permit their Absolutes to determine, to fix and warrant nothing relative.

Who fears what? Sankara and Nagarjuna fear mutable dualism, and solve it by the plenum and by silence. Augustine fears mutable chaos and posits the catholic ingathering of multiplicity. Were he to try to use their perceptual sets, there would return by the back door a retaliating duality of *māyā* versus Brahman, of the conditioned versus the unconditioned, of the temporal so incommensurate with the eternal. Their outlooks, while promising nonduality, actually worsen his unity, since they only pronounce plurality to be unreal and empty. They make no integral sense of it.   Religions are best classed as the evaporative or the collective kinds. Our Christian is of one mind; these Indians are of another, and there is really no congruence between them. What is denied here is never identical in perspective with what is affirmed, yet still it must be counterstood. To choose to travel on one path is to be unable to travel on another. We both cannot and do not want to exchange places and get into their story. What delights one, damns another.

Ghazali is not wholly sure whether his pantheistic tendencies solve or dissolve the secular pluralities. His misfortune, which others might consider his genius, is to live halfway between the West and the East. Intensely theistic, he struggles to legitimate plurality in God. But if this is sometimes gained by him, it hardly survives in his ecstasies, and at the end he is too close to God to have much use for the world. In Allah, all things "pass away," and Ghazali sees nothing but God. But Augustine's God wills to the contrary, envisions something besides God, creates it, and, lest it perish, redeems his created Earth. The vision finishes with a new heavens and a new Earth. By contrast and unfortunately, Ghazali can bring himself to analyze "the reality of the present world" only under the rubric of a book "on the blameworthiness of the world." (Ih III, 6; B259ff) What, asks Ghazali, is "the truest verse the Arabs spoke?" "Everything except God is worthless." (NN 12)

The Sufism that revives Islam also infects it with the "passing away" of all into God. "All things are singing His praise." (Ni 67; S 17.44) But before long they have "perished in his countenance." (Ni 97; S 28.88) And then do they still sing? As he grows older, Ghazali hears their music less and less. If he does not drop over the pantheistic abyss, he very much likes to look into it. His head stays with the West; he will not allow our identification (*ittiḥād*) with God, which he finds to be the characteristic Sufi error. Still, his heart is tugged eastward and in his raptures the "mystics are themselves blotted out, annihilated. For self-contemplation there is no more found a place, because with the self they no longer have anything to do. Nothing remains any more save the One, the Real." (Ni 97)[4]

Beyond any shared faith with Christians, Ghazali finds their distinctive Christian experience to be "pure blunder," committing the error of *ittiḥād* in uniting God with Christ. As our account predicts he should, Ghazali finds Christianity an incoherent muddle, and is unable to make sense of incarnation and atonement. (RD, 25ff and passim) But what Ghazali calls blunder Augustine finds the distinctive meaning in Christianity, the more excellent way of Christ's *agapē*, self-emptying love, past Muhammad's prophetic powers. What Augustine does not read in the books of the Platonists is what he would not have read in the Muslim's *Qur'an*, how God became a suffering servant, the divine capacity for kenotic passion. God's blessed meekness, his blood shed, his body broken, is inevitably eroded in meaning when the Christian attempts to understand the peculiarly Islamic claim about Muhammad's finality. If the Indian world is a cross, that is only in the sense of meaningless suffering; their world is not worth a cross, seen as redemptive suffering for the creation. By contrast, the Islamic world is worth a cross, but the Islamic God shows no interest in it.

Islam knows our self-emptying into God but not that of God on our behalf. All *islām* is to God; there is no *islām* in God. Allah must rule. Though Allah knows how to love, he does not stoop to suffer; in him there is no meekness. He requires, but does not exemplify kenotic love. Allah does not know how to wash feet, nor walk the

---

[4] According to R.C. Zaehner, Ghazali moved, later in life, from monotheism to monism. Ghazali's Sufism at the end is very close to Sankara's Advaita Vedanta. R.C. Zaehner, *Hindu and Muslim Mysticism* (London: University of London, Athlone Press, 1960), pp. 162-174.

via dolorosa, nor be crucified. But what does love mean in God, if not in him too that *agapē* by which we imitate him? If we stand by Christ, Islam too must be counterstood. Falling back from the Father of Christ to Allah and his messenger would diminish both Christian meaning and point.

We are more locked out of each other's intimacies than the ecumenically inclined interpreters among us like to admit. The experience of *saṃsāra* precludes that of creation, and vice versa. Muhammad as the seal of the prophets precludes Jesus as the Christ, and vice versa. Everything we learn is at the cost of something unlearned; every route taken leaves others untraveled. Every form of sensitizing leaves us otherwise less sensitive. To be male is to preclude being female; we must remember this when we marry East and West and seek androgynous offspring. The attempt to be universally religious without being particularly so is like trying to think without using any particular language. We must be black or white, Jew or Gentile, Occidental or Oriental; our particularities humanize us as well as do our generalities. But the same idiosyncrasy subtracts from our powers of compassionate understanding, not at first but in the end. The truth in belief as absurd is that alien belief is ever a surd to the nonparticipant. The wisdom of Jerusalem is foolishness to those in Athens, or in Benares, or in Damascus. For those who gain that wisdom in Christ, the senses in which Brahman, or *nirvāṇa*, or Muhammad and his Allah can be so final are, and must remain, enigmatic.

3. Rejection of and by misunderstanding

Difficult as it is to obtain interreligious agreement, it is yet more difficult to specify the differences. Seldom when another states what he or she considers to be wrong with our faith do we find that he or she has rejected what we consider to be an adequate witness. Very likely, no Madhyamika or Advaitan adherent will be comfortable with what has been ascribed to them in the section just concluded. Even formulas of concord written to bring religious agreement are imprecise and rough enough to hide diverse meanings and rejections. The Hindu accomodates Yahweh, only to sublate this Hebrew Ishvara to Brahman, or he charitably accepts

Jesus as an avatar, unaware that his doctrine of *māyā* hardly permits room enough for a true incarnation in the Christian sense. There is what we call now a miss of understanding, a *misunderstanding*. *Prima facie*, we can lay this to ignorance. It is true that, if we become more attentive, we can eliminate a level of adventitious or *contingent* misunderstanding. This calls for comparative religion, for the phenomenology of religion, for scientific study, the history of religions, for exegesis, hermeneutics, apologetics, and ecumenical colloquy. But our concern is now beyond this. It lies in the inescapable limits in the confrontation of counterfaiths, where we now find that rejection is of and by indeterminate meaning. Without prejudice to whose it is, this is "the misunderstanding." From the perspective of nonadherence, it is an *external necessity of misunderstanding*; from that of adherence, it is an *internal necessity of misunderstanding*. The adherent, inside, necessarily finds that nonadherents reject because of "their" misunderstanding.

A. *The external necessity of misunderstanding.* The person who rejects another faith must reunderstand it by bringing alien faith over to some domestic idiom. What a text brings to us mingles reciprocally with what we bring to the text. Any who have not undergone atonement, *śūnyatā*, Brahman, or the finality of the *Qur'an* will of necessity subordinate each of these to local experiences. This may be by considered judgments. These are not prejudices which prevent our understanding but are our preferred judgments which dispose us to understand. Then, after having made of it all the meaning we can by translation into our experiential idiom, we find no more sense to the rest, and we judge that those who think they there further understand in fact misunderstand. Our rejection is by finding in the adherent some miss of understanding, some understanding amiss.

The sensitive rejecter concedes that this is by translation across a significant void, when imported meaning is exported from its home soil. Here one exacts meaning, which is perforce inexact, since it lacks indwelling. But that conceded indeterminacy is also defended, for to determine, as does the adherent, that appropriate meaning lies there is an illusion. The adherent's passion is inappropriate; my variant passion allows no other course here than to remain dispassionate. Religious understanding is always of and with a certain *pathos*. If there is not *sym/pathy*, then by etymological and psychological necessity, there is *a/pathy* or *anti/pathy*. That is to confess that one does not have at this point the pathos which makes understanding possible.

It is not possible, after finding joy in the good earthy creation, finally to make sense of *saṃsāra*, for one cannot pretend *māyā* and *duḥkha*, as one may not pretend pain. Missing that passion, I miss understanding. Compassionately, *saṃsāra* has no point, though, comparatively, I retranslate it with my fallen world. Or, knowing the ultimacy of Almighty God, the theist can make no sense of the Advaitan *māyā* of God en route to Brahman, since in Brahman there is less to understand than there is in God. In reverse, the Advaitan may in some sense accept the theistic account, but not in the ultimate sense, since *māyā* already testifies to the nonultimacy of any personal and creative "God," determining that the Advaitan is unable to see this theistic point. And how much more will Madhyamika find theism finally empty!

"God is, and Muhammad is his prophet." The Christian will find this senseless in its exclusivistic range, missing understanding in the Muslim finality, losing meanings already secured in incarnation. In reverse, through Allah's experienced finality, Ghazali finds every theism "incomplete" unless the second word of the *shahādah* is added, the witness that only Muhammad is his final prophet. (Ih I, 2, 8) Meanwhile, he judges that Christians blunder, because he is prohibited by his Islamic perception from the compassionate experience that would make sense of atonement.

Even our Indian respondents mutually dismiss each other. Sankara finds Madhyamika hardly worthy of counterargument. What meaning he can make of it, something like nihilism, he dismisses, beyond to find no meaning. (VS 2-2-21; BrU 4-3-7) Nagarjuna will have nothing to do with eternalism or absolutism, finding the notion of eternal being beneath the phenomena (Brahman) quite incoherent. Past their comparative overlap, the four faiths are variant geometries in which, though each faith succeeds in measuring the world, what is axiomatic in one is absurd in the other.

Misunderstanding is especially crucial for those who stand outside Madhyamika. Candrakirti comments, "Those who see being even in *śūnyatā* are not such as we talk with. He who in reply to the remark, 'I shall give you no money,' says, 'Well, let me have the no-money,' cannot by any means be convinced of the nonexistence of money." (Ca 49f,m)[5] After such a remark, how may the nonadherent react?

(i) Taking the obvious interpretation (*money* = *being*), many, with Sankara, bring Madhyamika over as "complete and pure nihilism" (H. Kern) and "absolute nothingness" (B. Keith). The Madhyamikas were "the most radical nihilists that ever existed." (J. Wach)[6] So we import the Madhyamikas with rejection. Emptiness is too thin for meaning; to think it has any is a misunderstanding. But Nagarjuna says that nihilism is the worst misunderstanding one can have of *śūnyavāda*. "If this doctrine is not well understood it causes the ruin of the unintelligent man, since he sinks into the impurity of nihilism." (Rv 2-19)

(ii) Others apply *money* rather to *theses*. The denial is not of *being* in *śūnyatā*, but of *talk* about this being. Such talkers "are not such as we talk with." The point is semantic, not ontological, and Madhyamika is brought over as "a very consistent form of absolutism." "The Madhyamika does not deny the real; he only denies *doctrines* about the real."[7] Stcherbatsky expounds Nagarjuna as "emphatically monistic," finds "pantheism" and even "cosmotheism" in Nagarjuna and, despite Sankara, an "almost absolute identity with Vedanta." "The universe viewed as a whole is the Absolute, viewed as a process it is the Phenomenal."[8] But to give us back the undivided whole as an Absolute, while rejecting the divided parts, goes against a steady Buddhist insistence, using a famous metaphor, that *neither* the chariot *nor* its parts are real.

Meanwhile, Nagarjuna denies that he teaches any absolutism, and states that this is the second worst misunderstanding one can have of his teaching. "There nothing appears, nor anything disap-

[5] Translation by Narain, "*Śūnyavāda: A Reinterpretation*," p. 331.
[6] Cited in Stcherbatsky, *Conception of Buddhist Nirvāna*, p. 37.
[7] Murti, *Central Philosophy of Buddhism*, p. 218, 234.
[8] Stcherbatsky, p. 61, 48, 52.

pears; nothing has an end, nor is there anything eternal." (Ka preface, Stcherbatsky, 69m, Ka 15-1ff; 25-1ff) Any who look for an Absolute in the undoubted writings of Nagarjuna must wrench it out of a single verse (18-9) in the *Kārikās*, "*Tattva* is indeterminate." If this verse can be strongly interpreted, "There is an undifferentiated reality," it can better be read more weakly, "About what really is, we can say nothing."

Here questions of authorship entangle those of understanding. Venkata Ramanan laments that the undoubted *Kārikās* are "all too abstract and overwhelmingly negative in emphasis and character" and that "on the basis of the *Kārikās* alone it is difficult to get a clear picture of the Madhyamika philosophy." (VR 16m, 42f) The more positive *Śāstra* complements this by the quest for "the undivided being" (*advaya-dharma*) and "the indeterminate ground," and Venkata Ramanan finishes by comparing Madhyamika with Advaita Vedanta to find "there is hardly any difference between the two." (VR 320; ch. 9)

But the differences of attitude in the undoubted *Kārikās* and in the infrequent passages in the disputed *Śāstra* are quite as likely to mean two hands, some later revisions in the *Śāstra* making over Nagarjuna's thesislessness into something more, supplying enough positivity to make sense of what cannot otherwise be understood. The world "has for its ground the unconditioned reality which is eternal being." (VR 178) But such an eternal, undivided being does not occur in the *Kārikās*; indeed it but obscurely occurs in the *Śāstra*. This absolutizes and reifies *śūnyatā*. Now, regardless of whether the interpreter hopes to reject or to accept Nagarjuna, the deeper question is whether Nagarjuna has been understood, brought over so into an alien idiom. To make *śūnyatā* the same as Brahman, to trip emptiness over to absolutism is to cast it in a new color; and even when apparently accepted, the authentic Nagarjuna has been rejected because he has been misunderstood.

(iii) Lastly, Candrakirti's "no-money" may mean sheer silence, forbidding either nihilism or absolutism, in "blank phenomenalism without a reality subjacent to phenomena."[9] "If I would make any

---

[9] Narain, p. 333.

proposition whatever, then by that I would have a logical error. But I do not make a proposition, therefore I am not in error." (VV 29m) Not surprisingly, the nonadherent then finds an indeterminacy of meaning. Nagarjuna is neither wrong, nor right, just silent. He refuses to point to any-thing or no-thing; and Madhyamika is, alas, pointless. There is nothing to be understood; they miss understanding. Emptiness, silence, is only a kind of confession of ignorance.

B. *The internal necessity of misunderstanding.* We have just seen how the nonadherent finds insignificant meaning in and rejects proposed belief, unable to cross that indeterminate area which the adherent has successfully crossed. By contrast, since he has determined meaning to be there, the adherent reckons that the nonadherent rather misses understanding. At this reach, any who reject a standpoint that I stand under, necessarily misunderstand owing to a variant perceptual base. Take, for instance, the Augustinian life in grace, in which evils are redemptively overcome and promised the more to be overcome by the atoning God. Here all things increasingly work together for good to those who love him. In the *agapē* career, I find myself placed in a field for fruitful life. The harvest ripens; the leaven spreads. I circulate within the divine embrace of "I, yet not I, but the grace of God," where grace is intelligible because it is viable, it has meaning because it has point. But what of those who reject this grace? They do not know it, for, in the Augustine formula, the experience of grace is irresistible. To have it is to know that it is true. Intermediately, it may be confusedly had, undergone but not understood. But immediately understood, it carries its own conviction. So the Father's love can be rejected only if missed, only if misunderstood by a Babylonian vainly trying to understand Jerusalem, by a Greek finding only foolishness at Calvary.

Jesus says to the Twelve: "To you has been given the secret of the kingdom of God, but for those outside everything is in parables; so that they may indeed see but not perceive, and may hear, but not understand." (Mk. 4.11f) Insiders know; outsiders misunderstand, getting no further than a parabolic, comparative understanding. When Augustine finally believes, he does not accept a Christianity which he had long understood and rejected, but rather finds that he for so many years had refused a caricatured Christianity which he did not in fact understand. When he reunderstands it, he embraces it. (Co 6-4) Circumstantially, comparatively, he rejected something else than grace; but, when he met that grace, he could only acquiesce. We have yet to consider cases of lost conviction after the rich experience of grace, but the number of such cases is rare. Except for these, rejection is always of a gospel that is not really understood. Where there is no faith, there is no understanding. "Father, forgive them, for they know not what they do." Said first at Golgotha by one who intimately understood what he underwent, that saying applies with changes of psychological scope to all who reject the cross they misunderstand.

Madhyamika finds to be still more severe this internal necessity of misunderstanding. When the gods are puzzled by Subhuti's dramatic announcement that *nirvāṇa* too is empty, they complain, " 'What Subhuti has just told us, that we do not understand!' Subhuti read their thoughts and said, 'There is nothing to understand, there is nothing to understand. For nothing in particular has been indicated, nothing in particular has been explained.' " (AP 98m, MP 208f) Candrakirti supplies us with the following dialogue: "Madhyamika: 'We absolutely deny the possibility of problematic judgments regarding transcendental reality.' Logician: 'You thus insist that you make no assertion whatsoever. But we hear from you a proposition which looks like a definite assertion. Do you really mean to say that these saints believe in no argument?' Madhyamika: 'Who can say whether they have or not any arguments? About the absolute reality (*paramārtha*), the saints remain silent! How is then a conversation possible? How can we decide whether there are arguments or not?' " (Ca 136f,a)

Not surprisingly, Nagarjuna worries that the nonparticipant inevitably misunderstands him. In a wholly perceptual and utterly nonconceptual religion, those who have, absolutely, nothing to say, do not expect to be understood by others, so long as they remain others. Even for the relative adherent, there is an indeterminacy of meaning; how much more so for any who reject it. They "do not know the profound 'point' (*tattva*) in the teaching of the

Buddha." (Ka 24-9) Given no public argument, outsiders cannot but reject something else than the highest truth, which goes unsensed and unsaid. They are jackals who do not enjoy the lion's roar.

Muslim theology, which Ghazali calls a husked fruit, reserves its inner meanings for those who come within. Only by going inside can one taste its pith. And if any reject it? Ghazali must say that they miss his understanding, otherwise they would join his witness. They refuse only a shell, a husk. Sankara also uses, a little differently, this simile of fruit when he notices that "That art thou" is like wheat to be threshed until it gives its grain. When nonduality is tasted, one will see that it is true, for such is the inebriation of monism. If the phrase gives no fruit, it has been insufficiently threshed. Those who reject it do so with nonunderstandings (*avidyās*) and misunderstandings (*aparā vidyās*), unable to beat these into final understanding (*vidyā*). As we earlier heard, "Brahman is intelligible only to a highly purified divine intellect and unintelligible to an ordinary intellect."[10] Hence the common person who rejects it does not understand it, and rejects something else than the highest understanding, rejects an *aparā vidyā* across an indeterminacy of meaning.

To put this boldly, before whatever, if any, religious "truth" is *true*, nonadherence is always in misunderstanding, missed understanding. We should somewhat soften that boldness by adding a symmetry, that all rejection of *false* religion is by understanding where and how it misses understanding. True religion is both intelligible and viable; false religion is neither. Whatever is *true* is not rightly understood until understood as true, but whatever is *false* is not rightly understood until understood as false because it cannot be fully understood. In the mind of God, that is, only the truth is rational and error is irrational. Augustine contends that, in the end, we either understand truly or we have no understanding at all. That is, there is no such thing as a *false understanding*, in something like the way he also holds there is no such thing as an *unjust law*, since an unjust law is no law at all. A false understanding

---

[10] See p. 164.

is no understanding at all. Error is only what we call a miss of understanding, apparent understanding. Meanwhile, humanly speaking, disagreement resolves into whether and in whom there is misunderstanding.

4. Rejection by reunderstanding

What of those who depart from a once-held faith? It might seem that, subsequently, they continue to understand their ex-faith, though now at a distance from it. In a satisfying faith, believing what we do not yet altogether discriminate, Augustine's trust launches undergoing, which is later confirmed in understanding. But what if things go ill? What if, as they so often did for Augustine, indiscriminate beliefs unfortunately fail progressively to increase our understanding? Ghazali, having become a savant, critically threshes out sound belief (*'ilm, dhawq*), but what of all the creedal authority and naive belief (*taqlīd, īmān*) which he discards? Nagarjuna begins with faith (*śraddhā*) and verifies this as wisdom (*prajñā*), but in the process he abandons by dialectic all belief in cognitive theses. Sankara hears, reflects, and rejects as false or imperfect whatever he finds that he can sublate. In all these cases, the attitude toward once-held, earlier faiths is one of what we call *reunderstanding*. We now observe what happens in rejection by such reunderstanding.

When we first believe, we are committed to an inevitable scope of that faith, of which we were earlier unaware. So long as we have made only partial explorations, like it or not, we also believe what we do not yet understand, that is, all the unfoldings of our belief, lying ahead of us, as these do in fact follow logically and psychologically from it. We believe over gaps which, we hope, the future will close with understanding. Projecting a universal faith beyond our regional experience, we trust in the capacity of this faith to handle later experience and better to incorporate present anomalies. As soon as we adopt the premises of a faith, these as yet indeterminate implications are inescapable.

Even the scientific materialist trusts that gaps which he or she admits to be now present will be filled in with the advance of science. He or she understands in part and believes that more understanding will come. Likewise for progressing believers too, who yet are outside portions of the meanings of their beliefs, meaning is indeterminate, not yet unfolded, although (unlike the nonadherent) they trust that it will be forthcoming there. In sound belief, we rejoice as these meanings unfold with further progress. But in unsound belief, miscarried, our understanding shipwrecks; what formerly floated sinks in foreign waters.

We superficially believe a theorem, Augustine notices, when its depth logic is not yet understood, and, while a good theorem can be later understood, a false theorem will later be found to be incoherent or to remain hopelessly indeterminate. When we subscribe to theories of heat involving the concept of phlogiston, or to the theory of the space-time relativity, we are committed to consequences by which we test theory. But more, by these consequences we understand the theory and its reach to the actual world. Theology, like a theory, falls when by incoherences and discordances in life these consequences become unsatisfactory enough.

Consider some examples of incoherence here. (i) A theist naively holds that God is omnipotent, all-loving, and omniscient, and that evil exists, but later comes to find here an inescapable dilemma, and is obliged to revise his former beliefs. (ii) A Christian has never joined "perfectly human, perfectly divine, one person," in significant reflection, and, doing so later on, comes to fear, alas, that they are an inconsistent set of claims. Then, before an indeterminate meaning stronger than any underlying experiential base, the would-be disciple rejects the incarnation once sincerely confessed. (iii) An Augustinian believes in irresistible grace but later comes to find that this cannot be joined with human accountability, and the latter prevails. Those others who repudiate paradigms once held, as for instance "Ātman is Brahman," "Nirvana is samsāra," or "God is, and Muhammad is his prophet," likewise will find incoherences of which they were earlier unaware.

Or consider some examples of discordances growing in experience. (iv) The youthful theist is later ravaged with increasing tragedy, so that the level of evil which he could earlier accommodate to God is exceeded, and belief in God becomes discordant with new suffering undergone. (v) The catechumen finds the creedal claim that Jesus was "perfectly divine and perfectly human" weakened by the critical portrait of the historical Jesus provided in modern biblical scholarship. (vi) The Augustinian comes to revised feelings about grace owing to a deepening awareness of human autonomy.

What happens in all these cases is that understanding has failed over a shifting reflective and experiential base. But, owing to newly discovered implications and experiences, the subsequent understanding is no longer the antecedent understanding. The ex-theist finds the concept of "God" not only false but meaningless, beset with logical and existential complications, and he or she cannot any longer find appropriate what he or she has not been able to appropriate in continuing thought and experience. Meanwhile, for the continuing theist, atheism never quite makes sense, since the believer cannot understand it, or, what is the same thing, he cannot understand with it. Pretending to that perceptual set, life is finally unintelligible, and those who have departed from theism have done so through misunderstanding.

When Nagarjuna abandons the Advaita Vedanta of his youth, and when he reunderstands the Theravada Buddhism in which he once stood, he forges the later Madhyamika. During this, he rejects, again and again, what he finds either incoherent in logic or discordant in life. The first is the trouble with all theses; they run logically aground short of contact with any ultimate. The second is the trouble with noisy pluralities; they will not collect into his envisioned nonduality. Similarly, Sankara comes to swear by monism as he sees through partial understandings (*aparā vidyās*) and ignorances (*avidyās*).

Ghazali first moves through, by finding the "incoherence" of, the prevailing philosophies of his day. He next fails in dozens of local theologies, being delivered from their discordant errors by reaching the Sufi union. Augustine later sees that he stayed in Manicheanism longer than he should have, more by expectation than by conviction, until finally it could not deliver what it had promised and it fell into incoherence. (Co 5-5ff) Similarly, his hope in the Academics was disappointed. In earlier religious inquiry, Paul failed to find satisfaction in pharisaical Judaism; much later, Luther lost his way in Medieval Catholicism.

All these persons who abandon a faith find altering understandings of that faith. If Manicheanism, Pharisaism, and Medieval Catholicism are unsound, that is the better understanding of them. But this is not because they are ill understood, but rather because they are understood to be ill. On the other hand, if they are sound, any who move out will no doubt do so by developing a misunderstanding; but, for all that, they move out also by a reunderstanding. It is courteous to say that Paul misunderstood Judaism, or Luther Catholicism, or Nagarjuna Advaita Vedanta, or Augustine Manicheanism, else they would not have repudiated them. Adherents must say so. But Augustine, Luther, Paul, and Nagarjuna thought rather that they saw their ex-faith's misunderstandings. Any who reject a former faith do so as they shift their understanding of its intelligibility and appropriateness, else there would be no cause for rejection.

Belief later denied is not belief once affirmed, but a variant version of it. This is revealed when, quite sure that we cannot recover a belief, we say that we could never again find it comprehensible. With every change of conception there goes a change of heart, and vice versa. The rejected creed no longer seems the same, just as a woman once loved but now rejected no longer seems the same as she was before. She does not even appear in the same gestalt. We have lost that passion by which we once understood. "This is a breakage which cannot be mended," sighs Ghazali resolutely of those naive beliefs which he has abandoned; he knows he cannot go back. (D1 27)

Augustine finds the supposition that the Earth is round "utterly incredible," "absurd." (CG 16-9) Roughly, he knows what it means, yet with his limited horizons, the claim cannot really make sense. We know better, but after centuries of struggle that conceal a creative maturing of the human spirit from which we cannot recede, as the adult cannot become a child again, or even exactly pretend to be one. We know too much. Something in us has grown too greatly and something perpetually perished in the aging. The paradigmatic phrase "round world" symbolizes the difference between the ancient and the modern worlds, and final understanding of this simple phrase includes all this background, which we may now take for granted. Fully to know what "round world" means is to have the intellectual back-up and scientific complementation, and to know that it is true. We have flowed on the river of no return.

Afterward, it is too late anymore to understand "flat world," for "world" has changed its meaning. With his constricted vision, Augustine did not repudiate the view we now have, for which view vast amounts of post-Augustinian experience are requisite. Linguistically, "flat" moves out and "round" moves into the meaning of "world." Environmentally, scientifically, we virtually move into a new world, which, with its heavens, turns on another axis. We find ourselves in a different world than we thought. Roughly, we can pretend to those ancestral views. But pretending that we do not know what we do know is never very authentic. Augustine did not notice this, but we see that the old, flat world is so oppressively small, even silly. Where are the borders of the flatlands? Where do moon and sun go? What holds the Earth up? Atlas? Some supporting turtles? God? The flat Earth always ran into troubling mythology.

Now the myth has been forever broken by Copernicus and by Magellan. Once we are released into the expanses of geological time, the six-day creation becomes permanently childish, as even Augustine had begun to see. The Borneo savage in New York City will see cars as demons and skyscrapers as canyons. To see what the New Yorker sees is permanently to leave savagery; and, though pretending at superstitions, the New Yorker who visits Borneo can never see there what the native sees. Consanguine we all are; the Stone Age native is a brother with Einstein. Nevertheless, a sound education is cognitively irreversible and the holding of one view precludes our making sense of another.

The human religious history is mostly one of abandoned beliefs. Must that be the fate of these noble, but medieval beliefs which we have been examining? Astrology was once consistent, perhaps, with what little was then known; but no more. Gathering up the gods as they do, Brahman, nonduality, and God make polytheism permanently incredible. They have disenchanted the world for us; but do we now become disenchanted with them in turn? Nagarjuna does close with silence. Does belief in no god, in lieu of one, lie ahead? Or would that bring us down to a one-dimensional, horizontal living, and ignore the experienced depths of multidimensional, vertical living? Would not such a move from one to none be qualitatively different from bringing many to one, in the way that collection is different from elimination? Zero is not better than unity; rather it would fragment us again, because of the lack of an axis of turning.

In the future, the now-contending religions may converge and their peculiarities may become incoherent. This would be rather like the way in which, looking past, one now has trouble seeing what the denominational fusses within Christianity were all about. Or, more like nations, the religions may continue long in coexistence. Or, one may make the others eventually incredible. Any which cannot give a positive account of the secular will fail, but so also will any which cannot sustain the timeless, the eternal, the sacred in such a way as to bring unity, intelligibility, and worth into the secular, not only for yesterday and today, but for tomorrow, and forever.

II. Adherence: The Compulsion of Understanding

We have already been tracing the forces of conviction by noticing what they negate, but we are now ready for a positive account of them. The mark of truth in Augustine is its immutable intelligibility; in Sankara it is truth's nonsublatability; in Ghazali it is its unitive divine taste, and in Nagarjuna it is its emptiness.[11] We will in

---

[11] Frankly, we are virtually unable to use the *Prajñā-pāramitā* mark: emptiness. When the gods ask, "Which, O Lord, are the marks of the deep perfection of wisdom?" Buddha replies, "Emptiness, Gods, is the mark of this deep perfection of wisdom.... This deep perfection of wisdom is marked like unto space. In this way, Gods, this deep perfection of wisdom is nonmarked.... Gods, those marks cannot possibly be altered by the world with its gods, men, and Asuras. And why? Because that world with its gods, men, and Asuras has also that very same mark. For a mark cannot alter a mark." (MP 351ff) "The Bodhisattva's development of perfect wisdom reaches its fulfillment, if he does not review 'dharma' or 'nondharma.' And why? On account of the essential marks of Dharma, on account of irreversibility, of nullity, of vanity, unsubstantiality, and voidness." (MP 325a) The mark of truth is almost bizarrely the same as that of untruth.

this section revert to the generic or formal marks of truth, since the specific or material content of truth is in dispute among our saints. Still these will help us to penetrate the participant religious mind, and to gather the many facets of our long argument into a summary of the impressive forces in truth. What is it that attracts us, that even compels us to an understanding? Then, in the section to follow, we will ask whether and how far we can bring our religious inquiry toward a conclusion, what kind of progress we can expect to make in religious truth. There we will notice some of the factors that put those of us who do religious inquiry in the modern world in a different position from any which these ancient saints occupied.

1. Inherent point

By *inherent point* we designate the sacramental power that a religion has to convict us of its successful correspondence to the real, recalling the combined etymology of "point" as an indicator beyond and of the Latin *inhaerere* with its "stick" and "cling". The appeal of both concept and percept is not resident in either *per se*, except as these have this capacity to make present by re-presenting the real. We adhere to concept and percept because they adhere to what actually is. We judge that they correspond to the divine reality; they have objective reference. They do in fact point, though we have made it clear that this inherent point never lies in any propositional set except as this is underrun by the personal backing we have called correspondent truthfulness. For although this inherent point is importantly conceptual, it is finally perceptual. By religion we gain a vision of such power that persuasive forces emanate from it and convince us that it is veridical, truly a vision, a map of what is and is not of value. By it something has come into our focus.

While such *point* is required of all objective truth, whether secular or sacred, the peculiar feature of religious truth, or of any truth as it nears religion, is that this point is not superficial, empirical, or public, but is a pointing not only beyond the words but beyond the immediate, ready-to-hand world. Although our representatives do not identically locate this ultimate resplendence, they all find that a superficial estimate of the world they see is inadequate, and look to religion for its supernal capacity to lead them to see inherent values lying beyond, within, beneath the present process. Daily data are circumstantial; any understanding of them requires further point, and this comes only by these religions to which our saints adhere because of religion's effective, penetrant, scenic capacity to light up, to see into, that overarching beyond.

Critics of epistemological theories have noted that we cannot check correspondence theories of truth since, imprisoned within the supposedly correspondent perceptual and conceptual set, there is no escape to some independent viewpoint from which we can adjudicate correspondence. True not only in *scientia*, but even more in *sapientia*, this fact indeed requires of us a critical rather than a naive realism, icons rather than pictures, soft rather than hard truths. But afterward we must yet hope that our beliefs bridge us over to reality. Otherwise they are pointless. Given no circumvention of them, we are reduced to this sense of point which invests some beliefs more than others when they seem to convey a forceful representation. We adhere to those truths best able to communicate this sense of touch with a deeper reality, with reality in its depths.

As we next see, religions know truth by coherences of meanings, by mediate validation through mutually supportive claims, but not simply so. When parts-in-whole are gathered for a verdict, they are validated by their collective inherent power, as that is felt to provide a vision of something beyond. One does not go around or outside the system, but through it for the appeal. The whole religion is not validated by an *para-systemic* or *extra-systemic* aid, but by a *super-systemic* and yet *per-systemic* significance. Something beyond the religious system nevertheless meets us by coming through it. A specific intuition is ever corrigible and yet any one intuition is corrected by a synoptic or gestaltic intuitional power which broadly authorizes understanding.

This inherent point underlies the self-certifying power of religion. "The knowledge of Brahman...requires no other witness than the testimony of one's own experience; so what can be better than this?" (BrU 4-4-8) Augustine's model for theology is the slave boy's education into geometry by Socrates. Whatever their differences in denotation, or in requisite epistemic virtues, good mathematics and true religion have this in common: To understand is to see that they are true by their own compulsive power. Ghazali's gnosis (*ma'rifa*), tasted, brings its own divine impact, a sense of receptive witnessing. Nagarjuna's self-evident *prajñā* comes with its own absolutely attractive force and is not established by any relative support. Through its coherence and attractiveness, a religion must be self-supporting and must carry its own weight.

The authority of the pointer-words, that is, never rests in the words, or elsewhere in the world, but comes only when they successfully point to a supernal realm, which then carries its own authority to empower the vision. The recurrent symbol of "illumination" is again relevant, involving the self-luminosity of God, Allah, and Brahman, all of which deliver their own illuminative power. Even the more reticent Madhyamika "suchness" is depicted relatively by the self-luminous Buddha radiating light to the corners of the Earth. By this sense of inherent point, religious truth is known to be not merely subjective vision, not *māyā*, but the receptive illumination of the divine reality, manifested to us by its own light. Here the epistemic virtues give us clairvoyant powers. By disregarding the blinding forces of self we see this inherent point.

2. Coherent meaning

Given this attractive power of a system of belief, we further understand by appreciating the intellectual beauty of its *coherent meaning*. But merely to add coherent meaning to inherent appeal would not reckon with their interdependence. What counts as logical coherence can only be judged under the inherent life impact of a truth set; and, in turn, part of its inherent appeal is its capacity to deliver this sense of coherence. Similarly to the way in which we can gain no neutral viewpoint from which to adjudicate the supposed correspondence of our truth to reality, we can escape to no objective coherence-faculty, such as the autonomous reason, with which to estimate the coherence of our system of truth. I am not rightly rational prior to my coming to the system I search. The system corrects this "I" to its own rationality; but if it cannot make that conversion, its intrinsic appeal collapses. Coherence theories of truth suffer the same imprisonment as do correspondence theories, although this is less often recognized. Reason approves but does not prove, or provide, the vision. We do not establish its conceptual integrity independently of perceptual backing; but belief which is of inherent appeal may also be found coherent.

Sankara is thus correct in locating the power of reason critically to unfold intuitional powers. Each of a series of debaters, he notices, can persuade us, demolishing opposing positions, so long as we come successively and empathetically under the sway of each mindset. The trouble is not a vacillating neutral reason, but that reason is ever in the service of a viewpoint. It cannot hang in midair. Mere reason fails "for want of foundation," a perceptually axiomatic set grounding subsequent conception. We agree, readily enough, to certain abstract formal logical principles, but so soon as we attempt to evaluate the worth of any concrete system of belief, we find that in the weighting and sifting of the interpenetrating experiences and doctrines, logic is integral to, not external to, that system. As the logician begins with premises, so reason must have its "foundation" in experience; but, more than that, what follows and what does not follow from these premises is not judged by abstract implication but by an existential testing that unfolds them to see where they lead. There is thus no "bare independent ratiocination" but rather only "reasoning as a subordinate auxiliary of intuitional knowing." (VS 2-1-6) This does not denigrate reason, for Sankara steadily tests his beliefs for consistency. But it only claims that consistency tests cannot be run in the abstract by sheer thought devoid of experience. "Noncontradiction" is a permissible translation of the "nonsublatability" (abādha) which is his paradigm of truth.

Augustine's account is in some respects preferable to Sankara's. At the level of sapientia past scientia, intellection depends on the capacity for spiritual vision. The lower reason calculates over empirical experience; the higher reason understands the intrinsic appeal of the divine, exceeding though not freed from the former, since the divine presence is incarnate in the empirical world. The mark of understanding is that one sees intellectually, as faith delivers its own convincing rationality. The unbelieving reason will never suffice, since trusting produces that gracious experience whose inherent appeal is to be understood. There is a danger here of forgetting the caution that all intellectual forcefulness rests on a perceptual base, which may shift over time. But there is a delightful insistence that faith must believe in and find *intellectual* satisfaction most of all in the divine *love*. It can finally be said, though not simply said, that to be religious is the supremely rational act.

Ghazali's science of religion *tests* what he has *tasted*, to see whether it has coherent meaning. We have seen him reticent before the Sufi claims until he has brought them "under the sway of the intelligence, which is Allah's balance scale upon earth." Truth lies beyond the capacity of the unaided intellect; but the mature saint becomes the savant who has clothed his piety with rational warrant. The mystic becomes intellectual. Nagarjuna is not less fond of coherence, only, alas, he can find none in all the myriad available theses. That reveals their emptiness, but we should not forget (what Nagarjuna does forget) that their inconsistencies are not so much out there, standing alone, nakedly visible to all who can think straight, as are these inconsistencies a derivation from his own *śūnyatā* vision. Precisely the appeal of this inarticulate emptiness, once it has been experienced, is how it demolishes (so he thinks) all the pretensions of doctrinal coherence. Each of our saints exemplifies Whitehead's observation that in religion "any cogency of argument entirely depends upon elucidation of somewhat exceptional elements in our conscious experience—those elements which may roughly be classed together as religious and moral intuitions."[12]

Charity and their noble histories bid us hold that each of these faiths are, though variant geometries, more or less rational within their axioms, subject perhaps to the Nagarjunan anomaly. They are consistent maps. But it does not follow, interreligiously, when each observes the others, that this intrareligious rationality can be fully appreciated, that we can internally check their maps without being there. Various acts of faith result in various rationalities; and our

---

[12] A.N. Whitehead, *Process and Reality* (New York: Harper and Row, 1960), p. 521.

taste for logical coherence is a function of our taste for, our perception of, the real. Our agreements are maximal where logic is materially empty; they become partial where logics overlap. They become minimal as soon as logic is pregnant with concrete content, when rationality begins to take its bearings from the orienting spiritual experiences.

From that point onward, intelligibility follows from viability. No apprehension or comprehension can be checked unless this is against some gestalt that digests experience. What makes sense is a function of the sense-making system. We can appreciate rationality across great stretches of other's arguments and charitably project it across their whole. But someone else's faith is always a fiction, a logical fiction. Ultimately, owing to their peculiar indeterminacies, we never really find another belief system equally as inherently and coherently appealing as our own, for then there would be no serious reason to prefer our own, except perhaps that it was handy. No one can serve two masters.

3. Nonsublatable understanding

Continuing past this perceptual inherent appeal and this conceptual coherent meaning, we reach next an allegedly abiding character of truth, for which Sankara's term will serve for all. Truth is *nonsublatable*. "Since the knowledge of the identity of the Self and Brahman, once it has emerged, is never sublated, its origination cannot be denied or pronounced erroneous." (AiU int.) "Perfect knowledge has the characteristic mark of uniformity (*abādha*, nonsublatability)...for whatever thing is permanently of one and the same nature is acknowledged to be a true or real thing, and knowledge conversant about such is called perfect knowledge." (VS 2-1-11) Thus he finds the appeal of monism incorrigible. Or, using a more dangerous phrase, it is irreformable.

Despite its thesislessness, Madhyamika craves irreversibility. Using a similar test, Nagarjuna rejects all the doctrines for the silence of nonsublatable emptiness. "The true Dharma, where the Buddhas abide, can neither be rent nor scattered. It is comprehensive. By comprehensive we mean free from all faults, immutable, and invincible. How so? Except for the absolute truth, all other teachings and points of view are subject to destruction." (MPC1 38f,a) This is the much celebrated "irreversibility" of *prajñā*. "Those will be irreversible from the supreme enlightenment to whom this perfection of wisdom appears on its own accord, and who then take it up, bear it in mind, recite and study it, and wisely attend to it." (MP 321, 388ff; AP ch 17; MPC1 1800ff)

"Immutable" is the Augustinian synonym for this. "When the human mind is forced to admit itself mutable because of its regress and progress in wisdom, it discovers above itself immutable truth, and, attaching itself to this truth,...it becomes blessed." (DQ 45) "This truth, mutable though I am, I so far drink in as I see nothing mutable." (Tr 4, preface, 1) "The mind's understanding should be proportionate to its capacity to approach closely and to adhere to immutable truth." (Lb 2-34) We change, but God does not. The genius of intellection, in which we are like God, is by the intellect to see into that permanent, intelligible presence in our otherwise fluid and senseless lives. The truth is what survives by proving itself so stable and compulsive that we can no longer entertain its possible corruption. Ghazali adds, "Sure and certain knowledge is that knowledge in which the object is disclosed in such fashion that no doubt remains along with it, that no possibility of error or illusion accompanies it, and that the mind cannot even entertain such a supposition." (D1 22) What one fears, and yet what one wants, is truth that can no longer be resisted.

Although all this is more absolute than modern, cautious critics can any longer accept, short of more compelling visions than most of us reach, the nonsublatability of truth, perhaps never quite real, remains as an ideal. No truth is final, while yet subject to change. Persons who forget that not one of our saints has allowed certainty to reside in inherited, traditional truth, or who bypass the rigors of submission to what we have called truth's inherent appeal and coherent meaning, or who are insensitive to the escape from propositional capture of personal perceptions, or who forgo the epistemic virtues, will soon slip into dogmatism and scriptural or ecclesiastical inerrancy. The blessing of the religious mind is very close to its curse. Not one of those whom we have consulted has offered us catholic infallibility. All of them have offered correspondent truthfulness in which conviction may become non-negotiably resident.

This is a subjective or personal certainty, not an objective or impersonal one. Only so far as the purified mind, with its faith matured in understanding, is able to see with such intellectual finality as to see to be true, may we say that intellectual vision does not err. (LG 12-24f, 51f) God is necessarily right because he is rational, and we are too, so far as, being like him, we see the intelligibility in things. Meanwhile, we remember that the immutable truth is scattered in the midst of our mutable forms. We always fear the opposition of vanity and verity, and we seek a judicious balance of certainty and of humility, "certain in the truth, yet seeing in a glass darkly." (Co 8-1)

The way we know whether the historic religions are right is to see whether we can sublate them, whether the passing years have brought their overthrow. Most of the religious speculations of humankind have been sublated, but there is in these four noble faiths a level of conviction that has proved resurgent enough to transcend much aging. Today, we must see whether these fathers' faiths can remain productive of present understanding. If so, good. The immutable truth stands across another generation. If not, when these old faiths become incoherent, we must pass to something else. Some truths do have impressive staying power: that love is universal, that there is permanence behind the flux, that things interrelate in a divine oneness, that Jesus' divine humility is revelatory of God, that Brahman is the ground of being, or that *śūnyatā* is the silent bosom of being. Compared with these claims, the secular sciences and cultures are much more in flux. Sacred truths are often wrong, but whatever is right in them should prove from here onward yet more nonsublatable. Still, these historical verdicts, which are but the aggregate of personal verdicts, can never impress us except by our own existential interiorizing of them. Any boasted nonsublatability of a classic faith should be intended to challenge our criticism before it can be expected to comfort us.

No one is long liberated who does not find enough conservative unity in his or her faith not be be upset tomorrow. Augustine knows how much we lisp when we speak of God, but he knows he is onto

God, in unfinished certainty. He does not arrive, but he knows where he is traveling. *Mutatis mutandis*, that is Nagarjuna's thesisless quest for *prajñā*, Ghazali's taste of and for *ma'rifa*, and Sankara's intoxication with and in *jñāna*. The mark of any still-greater religious genius who may supersede them is to be open-minded enough to erase whatever tragic deceits infect our saints, while being settled enough in conviction to preserve whatever ultimacy they may have achieved. The persevering saint comes to marvel how faith has been *semper reformanda, nec tamen consumebatur*. These old saints looked too much and too soon for immutability, irreversibility, nonsublatability, incorrigibility. We know better. But that is still the test. If any perfect truth is ever found, when it is found, no religious experience, world phenomena, or sound logic should be able to falsify it.

4. Ecstatic understanding

Religious understanding is marked by its joy, by its ecstasy. That has to be mixed also with a countercurrent, with the cooling of desires. But the tranquil self is vibrant; there is passion in dispassion. "Joy in the truth is the blessed life," confesses Augustine. (Co 10-33) "What else is the happy life, unless it consists in an intellectual grasp of what is eternal?" (DQ 35) The *bodhisattva's* wisdom is consummated in "jubilant rejoicing." "All other kinds of rejoicing are infinitely inferior to this one, and by comparison with them this rejoicing is called the most excellent." (MP 281) "Such indeed is Self-knowledge," eulogizes Sankara of Brahmanic knowledge, "it gives one the conviction that one is completely blessed." (BrU 4-4-8) Ghazali continues, "The ecstasy of him who is consumed in the love of God Most High is in proportion to his understanding." (Ih II, 8, 239)

Like poetry, art, music, or sexual intercourse, if religion does not elate, then one does not have it right. Either one enjoys it, or one does not understand it. If our understanding is of Christ's grace, then it must be with grace. If it is of being, consciousness, and bliss (*sat-cit-ānanda*), then it must be in consciousness of bliss. In *śūnyatā*, if it is of peaceful quiescence, then it must bring peace. If we pass away enwrapped in Allah, then there must be rapture. We thus add what we might call a saving ecstasy as the evidence of truth.

Exhilaration can be not only the result but also the evidence of truth. Every artist, author, and scientist has sometimes exclaimed, "Eureka! I have found it." The delight of such a breakthrough by the searching mind is a notice of its arrival. Supremely that is so in God. "The highest function of the soul of man is the perception of the truth; in this accordingly it finds its special delight. Even in trifling matters, such as learning chess, this holds good, and the higher the subject matter attained, the greater the delight.... Seeing then that nothing is higher than God, how great must be the delight which springs from the true knowledge of him." (Al 27f) That is Ghazali's *Chemistry of Happiness*; we test the truth by its precipitation of happiness. In a similar way Augustine joins intellection with beatitude. His inquiry, which begins with the restless soul lost from its God, concludes, "Behold, here is truth itself. Embrace it if you can, and enjoy it; delight in the Lord." (Lb 2-35) Participation is at once in wisdom (*sapientia*) and in blessedness (*beatitudo*). We are taken out of vain isolation by redirected love, by faith, by purity, and by humility, and we join the joyous divine intelligibility to find authentic enthusiasm in God (*en-theos*).

After Augustine's beatitude and Ghazali's delight in God, we may better appreciate Sankara's nondual bliss and Nagarjuna's peace in *śūnyatā*. Despite their seeming suppression of intellection, both indicate that the struggles of intellection are over when truth is achieved in this nondual union. The mark of this victorious insight is the exhilaration of an erased boundary between the knower and the known, wisdom without otherness. Hence the test of *jñāna* is bliss without differentiation (BrU 4-3-32), and there is no more characteristic mark of *prajñā* than its peace. While others may puzzle over the extinguishing of conception, the Buddhist perceives that the labor of understanding is gone. Perfect wisdom remains, joyous and calm, so that even inexpressible silence is an index of its beauty.

The Arabic term for ecstasy is *wajd*, literally a "finding." This joins with our sense of ecstasy, *ek-stasis*, a standing outside of the self. It follows that ecstasy is a delusion if there is no finding, if the ecstasy is only private and without cosmic content. But good religion intends precisely a standing out from the self which avoids delusion because it has righted the self by finding the universal real. The self is detached to participation and nonduality in the whole. We do not look for truth that suits us, as might lesser religions, but we look to suit the truth, to which we submit, and then find that this sacrificial expansion into the ultimate brings great joy. And we take this as a mark of ultimate truth. This ecstasy is, in its deepest reach, the result of a discovered unity, whatever allowance may be made for plurality. For so far as there is plurality without unity, there is not so much a variant understanding, but variant things but partly understood, and ultimately no understanding at all.

All this suggests that there can be no bad news in religion, not finally so, and in a way this is true. It is not true in limited perspectives, as when one is sorrowful over sins, or one dwells on the *duḥkha* of the world. Nor does it mean that religious inquiry does not frequently fail, and bring pain, when no truth is discovered. But our saints in the end maintain that successful religious inquiry is always good news. The world is either found to be intelligible, and we correspond to it in joy; or it is found impenetrable, and we suffer from the failure of our hoped-for education. To find the world absurd is to find that it cannot be understood. Release from that pain, by whatever enveloping ultimate—God, Brahman, *śūnyatā*, or some other—is to find understanding and to be saved. Nor should we forget that this unity is learned in a self-giving love which overcomes absurdity and suffering. That is why this ecstasy is finally hidden in the intelligibility of the cross, or in the Buddha's cryptic and compassionate smile.

III. Finality and Relativism in Understanding

More than we first envisioned, we have been driven toward relativism in religious understanding. Our portrait has finished with different persons each all but locked into a compelling religious perspective. Each gains understanding to his own satisfaction, this very satisfaction initially permitting but finally preventing an appreciation of other perspectives. The several perspectives are relatively commensurable but finally incommensurable. Even though we have stood with the Augustinian theism and protested incoherences in the others, we nevertheless have posited for them their own sense of authenticity and sanity, a sense which we allow to be there though we cannot reach it.

So where are we left? If each finds his own creed (or *pace* Nagarjuna, creedlessness) to be compelling, then perhaps one is as good as another, and none any nearer right than wrong. Are we at the end returned to that conditioning which we feared at the start of this study, a conditioning by which, according as various obediences are undertaken, truths will be of that color?

If we are accurately to describe these careers of spiritual inquiry, it seems necessary for us to recognize (and criticize) in them more of this relativism than we may care for. Our saints do become all but nonnegotiably resident in their convictions. In this they exemplify the conservative or nonsublatable power of religious belief. The four superior faiths they represent, Mahayana Buddhism, Advaita Vedanta, Christianity, and Islam, together with a rather few others, have historically had the sort of staying power which is predicted by our account. Before them, most of the myriad faiths of humankind have vanished, stalled, or retrenched, more or less because they were pressed by a stronger faith insisting on more coherence than they could supply. But these noble faiths remain, in a sort of competition in the finals of the advancing debate of faith. When in this century they have been brought into colloquy with each other, there has not really been much altering of their basic gestalts. There is greatly increased tolerance, but each faith in its deepest conviction desires, if not to sublate the others, then to hold them as a surd at an agreeable distance.

Further, it is a psychological, almost a biological truth that the aging of an individual into some selected form of life which proves fruitful makes radical conversion increasingly impossible. To travel on one road does prevent our returning to travel another. We may fairly observe that the senior Augustine could never have embraced *śūnyatā*, nor the patriarchial Nagarjuna have confessed Christ. All of us who have settled into some stable outlook with holding power can specify other positions which we can now never occupy. But do we approve of this situation which we are forced to recognize? Can we in any sense gather enough logic to stand astride these streams of faith, rather than merely in one of them, or merely alongside of them with yet one more, different but neither better nor worse?

We may straightway grant an element of relativism to all spiritual inquiry, one that we do endorse. No person can ever gain serious religious truth without plunging into a radical relationship with that which is taken to be ultimate. If there is any finality in understanding, this cannot come in the public and open debate that sorts out conventional kinds of objective truth. Religious truth is irremediably relative in this sense that it requires a participant junction, a private closing between the knower and the known. No one nears this absolute level of truth by standing off from it, by standing aside of it, but we only approach it by the existential plunge into that reflective subjectivity which is "up to" this objective real. An objective estimate of truth will be invariably linked with this subjective personal character which is appropriate for judgment. On reflection, we do not see how it could be, nor do we wish it to be, any other way. The place for God rightly to be known is in the righteous heart.

Nevertheless, we do wish to deny an unqualified relativism among the competing truths of faith, and rather to hope for a significant maturation toward finality in religious truth. This may later if not sooner separate out for us something which is nearer the truth among the incommensurable faiths which we have reviewed. The competing faiths are, we have said, like variant geometries which map the world. The best of them are well thought out within their axioms; they do conceptually unfold and refine the basic perceptual sets which support them. Each has universal intent. But it is very difficult to tell, though it is not impossible to tell, which one or which ones best map the real world. For good geometries may succeed, even in their errors, proving more or less adequate across great stretches of experience, relatively true even if they contain some absolute axiomatic error.

Indeed all geometries and religions may be like this, and the best we can then hope for will be some complementarity of them to compensate for the fact that none is wholly accurate. But it may nevertheless be the case that some one among them is considerably more accurate than the others, and that a recognition of this accuracy will in due course prevail, eroding the others. But that recognition will not come easily, for those who reside in the less accurate faiths have nevertheless found great success and joy in them, like those who apply the less adequate geometries, a success which tends to fix that perspective the more firmly. Just because the Newtonian axioms about an absolute space and time were so successful, they were so difficult to dislodge when challenged by Einstein. But they were for all that quite wrong, in some sense absolutely wrong, while yet relatively right. Einstein's relativity of space and time is more adequate to the real world than was Newton's view, and incommensurable with it, although it permits the relative incorporation of much of Newton's perspective.

In religion, we do hope for progress in the interfaith dialogue, for a maturing of the minds of religious scholars from which they do not recede, any more than we can recede to the flat world of the ancients. We have indicated our conviction that this irreversible progress happens to those who find sacred value and integrity in the plural creation, so far as they can gather it into a divine unity, so far as they can redeem it. It happens to those who perceive the ultimate divinity of suffering love, to those who perceive the connection of righteousness with truth, to those who out of this love and righteousness find the intelligibility of things both mutable and immutable. It happens to those who enjoy the abiding and supreme significance of personality and who insist on its projection into the divine center, into God.

Now if anyone objects that even the view which succeeds the others is still relatively true, an approximation which may later be altered, as some future science may supplant the Einstein who supplanted Newton, we do not object. Rather this is what our saints have often wished to say, that religion is not literally or absolutely true, but only comparatively or relatively true. We only partially comprehend the incomprehensible Absolute. Meanwhile, one faith may partially include and yet radically exclude another, and prove the superior to its competitors; and we may expect of the superior faith such a compulsive power that those who stand in it do not see how it could be any other way. Otherwise they would adopt that way.

But all ecumenical progress is deeply compounded by the participant character of the struggle for religious understanding. For when we say, as we often do say, that we understand a religious claim but do not find it convincing, that cannot mean that we know its significance as that is given to those who stand convinced within that perceptual set. It only means that we know its significance as that has been translated by us into some other perceptual set, which we find the more convincing. Since we do not have its native "convincing," but have some foreign "convincing," our other feeling, passion, and sense of appropriateness limits our capacity to understand it. We understand from a distance, limited to a remote understanding. It is not then true that we can know what a religion claims prior to our later assessment of that claim, except in outline or in silhouette. For it is in the attempted assessment of a half-understood or comparatively understood claim, by testing its match-up in our ongoing life, that we see whether it can be further and satisfactorily understood as appropriate in life. Such a probing of its capacity to be understood constitutes its assessment.

We cannot test our faith against another, competing faith by understanding that faith as those do, or think they do, who stand within. We can only point out what from the viewpoint of our own faith seem to be its incoherences, unmeanings, and experiential failures, and so confront the adherent of a foreign faith with our contention that his understanding, for all its seeming success to him, for all its relative adequacy, is built in part on an axiom that deceives him, absolutely. That may leave us only confronting each other, each steadfast in his own faith, each prevented from the other's inwardness. When both of us turn to preach to inquirers, differently as we do, we can only hope that such inquirers, initially outside both gestalts, can make their way into that gestalt which is the most adequate.

Although we cannot get out of our particular, owned systemic faiths, but must always conceive and perceive the world through these, it is not true that our systems enable us to catch only what they arrange for. Our systems can hit hard facts. We meet troublesome events, unexpected phenomena, new ranges of experience which prove anomalous. Perhaps the better way to say this is that, although we cannot get outside our systems, what is outside our systems can nevertheless hit us hard enough to make dents in our systems. We can be shaken, sometimes more, sometimes less, usually setting about to repair our systems, more rarely put on the alert for alternative paradigms. In our own century, this shakeup from the outside has come to the classical faiths in the main from two sources.

(i) The first lies in the encounter with competing faiths. It is this encounter which we have been trying to address in the second half of this study, cross-examining the classical faiths to draw them onward into this issue. Though we must view other faiths from within the perspective of our own faith, the witness and experience of such faiths can sometimes force revisions in our own systems, as when, for instance, Christianity has largely dropped its claim that outside the church there is no salvation, and done this because of an increasing familiarity with the other world faiths. We do need to look for the falsifications that other sectors of the religious world can bring to our own faiths. Reciprocally, we need to see whether our own witness and experience can falsify the systems of others. It may sometimes, and with great difficulty, result that my criticisms, *comparative though they are, and coming from without as they do*, nevertheless begin to erode areas of another's conceptual and perceptual gestalt. Enough critical dialogue may sometimes produce his or her conversion to my gestalt as a superior one. My comparative criticisms may trigger in another person new experiences, and bring that person to see what he or she could not see before.

(ii) The second main area of shakeup in contemporary religious inquiry lies in religion's encounter with the sciences, both the natural and human sciences, bringing as these do vastly altered perspectives of nature and history. This inquiry lies beyond the scope of our study; but contemporary religious inquiry has here a level and type of assignment which none of our four saintly doctors faced. We have only to mention the changed concept of nature given us by Darwin or the information we now have about the depths of historical change over millions and billions of years. Christianity, for instance, has to see whether it can make sense of the histories of the myriad non-Christian peoples, or to help them make sense of themselves, an assignment greatly expanded over anything Augustine attempted. Hinduism and Buddhism have to see whether their *saṃsāra*-world, their *māyā* and emptiness doctrines, can accomodate evolutionary development, both in biology and astrophysics. Islam and Christianity need to accommodate these to their concepts of creation. All the classical faiths have to see whether they can withstand the various psychological and sociological reductions of religion, exemplified for instance in Freud and Durkheim.

These classical theories—God the Father of Jesus Christ, Brahman, Emptiness, Allah—do commit us to consequences and expectations about what the world will prove to be like. These faiths are not just exhausted by inner experiences of grace, or of passing away into Allah, or absorption into Brahman, or silent emptiness. They have external implications for what the courses of nature and history must be, at least in outline and form. We who live with such greatly expanded awareness of the operations of the natural world and of the depths of historical change have to ask ourselves whether and how far these old faiths can survive these new experiences. What falsifications, if any, do the phenomena with which we have become familiar in the natural world bring to our experience of God, Brahman, *śūnyatā*?

In the light of what we now know about the operations of nature and history, can those experiences which our four saints undoubtedly underwent still be interpreted in the way in which they interpreted them? The unparalleled expansion of the human consciousness in knowing the worlds of nature and history which are the ambience of this consciousness means now that no religious experience can be trusted which is not double-checked against this environing world of nature and history out of which such a consciousness has evolved. The discovery that the cosmos has evolved our consciousness merges into one the problem of the intelligibility of the generative natural universe and any inner experiences of perceived meaning there.

At this point, how much of the classical faiths proves immutable, nonsublatable? Sometimes, this may be a matter of finding what kind of detachment from our religious experiences is provided by the objectivity of science. But it can just as often be a matter of seeing whether the alternative subjectivity of science (for science, just as much as religion, is a form of conceptually laden perceptual experience) can dissuade us from the classical paradigms. Perhaps the classical faiths can counterstand what science teaches, or revise themselves appropriately so as to reassert their essential perceptual and conceptual sets in a post-scientific era.

Having said this, it remains true that religious inquiry does not succeed merely by reckoning with other faiths, or with science and with history, but it must eventually advance to the saint's reckoning with God in his or her own life. If God is anywhere known, we can still suppose that this will be quite as fully in the subjectivity and intersubjectivity of human experience, as it will be in the objectivity of the natural processes. If this is true, God can well have been present to our four saints, under the limits of their time and place, even though they are hopelessly inadequate in their concepts of nature and history.

Religious conflicts are not merely and not finally bare rational conflicts. Nor are they matters of objective world description. They are personally intellectual. The saint, unlike the geometrician, must invest the whole of his or her life in the detection of this adequacy to the real and to the world. We cannot simply think our way out of our radical errors, since it is not a matter just of shifting our thoughts but of shifting ourselves, not of merely altering our concepts but of the struggle for a new perceptual and existential gestalt, a change of heart to support a change of head, which comes at cost both to our present selves and to our sets of mind. Here to know the relativities in which we are enmeshed is already partly to escape them. We can only bid each participant in religious inquiry to use as best he or she can these marks of truth, and to believe that, beyond the struggle, faith will find joyous understanding.

Whether our conclusions in religious inquiry end in relativism must be asked both with respect to the *real*, what ultimately is, and with respect to *religion*, the views of others. In regard to the first, we do conclude that there is a divine Absolute, called by many names, constituting objective truth, and that there is significant human access to this real, so that the real is known by us, albeit brokenly. Our sainted doctors did know this real, under the cloud and cover of their climates. This is a relativism in that we know this final truth only relatively, approximately, comparatively. Nor does it follow that all our estimates, being relative, are of equal value, for we hold that there is error, and sometimes great error, in our religions.

Secondly, regarding our access to the views of others, our conclusions in this study do not bring us to a relativism of isolation. For we do hold that there is genuine access to another's belief; it is indeed just by relation, by a relativism, that we can gain this access to foreign faith. But we do end with a relativism which limits our access to foreign faith. We can see it only from here and never from there. Foreign faith is never transparent, it is often translucent, and it is finally opaque. Remember, please, that there are great stretches of the territories of faith where we may work approximately and comparatively to evaluate each other, and this work is quite genuine. But remember too that in the final reaches of faiths—at their cores, in their ultimate axioms as these touch perceptual base, in their fundamental gestalts—there lies this indeterminacy of meaning that prevents our absolute knowledge, our exact calibration of each other. This condemns us to a relative knowledge of each other, as we are all of us condemned to a relative knowledge of the real.

Further, all our knowledge of any religious significance is relative in that we do not ever see by the naked analysis of particular items. We always see relative to an interpretive and presiding gestalt into which the elements of truth are fitted in holistic synthesis, and thus these units of truth are always interrelated to each other, always relative. This way that we work in our heads corresponds to the integrated structures of the world. There is no final relativism in the universe because we hold that reality is finally one—nondual. But it is just this final, absolute unity that demands that every specific thing, every local truth, be fitted into it, be related to it, yet so as to give us, in the end, a relativism, an interdependent plurality that survives within the embrace of the divine unity.

In holding all our knowledge to be relative to an interpretive framework, we grant that this very claim is to some extent an exception to the rule it states. But this exception is largely formal and not material. That is, we may know in principle the nonperspectival truth that none of us sees without perspective, and still be unable in practice to see without perspective. Still, the exception is a welcome one, for it to some extent alerts us to our inescapable perspective. Thereby it helps us, perhaps not to escape perspective, but the more readily to modify that perspective toward one nearer the truth. To know that we are finite, and to wonder beyond this finitude, is already to taste a little of the infinite. Or, as all our respondents would put it, each a little differently, if our perspective aspires to be and approaches that of the infinite, we do not lose perspective so much as do we move perspective out of ourselves and increasingly bring it to coincide with that of the transcendent center of things.

We believe that interfaith appreciation and criticism can and ought to operate effectively. We hope in this book to have made a contribution to that endeavor. Such labors will lead, slowly, to increased religious truth. But no one labors in this ecumenical effort without perspective. We come nearer the truth not by eliminating our perspective but by altering it. Our warning here is that this is done with great difficulty, increasingly so as we near the truth.

Chapter 7. Learning (about) Religion

"To do evil is simply to stray from education." (Lb 1-2) Understanding is our ecstatic goal, and to miss it is to suffer; we understand, or we perish. Each of our axial educators in his own way vigorously endorses Augustine here. Each so invests his life as to leave his magisterial mark across many centuries. Their curricula deliberately intended and subsequently shaped an ideational heritage. The great father of the church "has formed the intellect of Christian Europe."[1] The Reviver and Proof of Islam is in the Muslim world still more dominant. The Hindu *āchārya*, epitomizing Advaitan monastic education, has taught all religiously literate India. The patriarchial *bodhisattva*, fulfilling the prophecy of his consummate unveiling of the Buddha, launched Mahayana Buddhism, a "great vehicle" for its coursing of so many toward Suchness. We will conclude our study by placing the *bishop*, the *sheikh*, the *guru*, the *tathāgata* on the scene of learning methodology, and in so doing seek a rationale for the study and professing of religion in multiple contexts, that is, for religious inquiry at diverse levels.

These pages will reach no reader who is not learning (about)

---

[1] J.H. Newman, *Apologia Pro Vita Sua* (Oxford: Clarendon Press, 1967), p. 237.

religion, and few who do not often teach it, and none whose interest there is not, positively or negatively, to find and to show the significance, relevance, beauty, insight, and utility of religion Those so engaged will know the puzzlements of teaching and being taught spirituality. Our modern selves and societies are quite unclear about the linkage between religion and education, whether in seminary, church, school or university, sacred or secular. We will next let these faiths bear their witness for hermeneutics both to license and to limit learning (about) religion. With this we will conclude our search whether and how far the pastor and the pupil should be participant and/or observer, scholar and/or saint, conceivers and/or perceivers, scientific and/or humane, intellectual and/or spiritual.

Our doctors' labors were largely religious and intrareligious. We must extend them interreligiously and extrareligiously. Beginning with the contemporary and returning to the classic, we move by four steps from the outside in, becoming ever less public and more private. Religious inquiry may be *empirical*, or *ecumenical*, or *catechetical*, or *confessional*. These noetic levels cross a spectrum beginning with what we have called the *circumstantial* and move across the *comparative*, the *compassionate*, and the *convivial*.

I. The Empirical: Studying Extrareligiously

We here refer to two learning contexts. In the first, that of behavioral study, the student does not utilize any domestic faith, but externally assesses religious behavior. In the second, that of phenomenological study, the detached inquirer methodically uses a domestic faith for comparison and understanding, but does not desire to naturalize the alien faith. Rather he or she resolutely remains without it. The descriptive quest is literally profane toward the studied faith, and truth questions are only asked about the religious phenomena under study, asked phenomenally. What is true *about* this religion historically and currently? Religion can be studied as what it undoubtedly is, an *empirical* event. Such scientific study is first positively if later pejoratively interested in the phenomena on hand, in the religiosity evidently present in the cultural world. In this way it is interested in what is present in the world, this present age, and is so far secular. Those limits at once promise neutral objectivity and seem doubtfully subjectively responsible.

1. Behavioral study

Strictly maintained, an empirical study includes the behavioral observation of personalities and communities, the effects of scriptures, cults, and cultures, which, being public, are accessible to the psychologist and sociologist, the historian and the archaeologist. However much religions may exceed or be uninterested in the empirical order, it remains patent that we cannot understand our own or another religion aright if we are in significant error about relevant data. Accuracy of truth *about* their religion is indispensable for any further inquiry into truth *in* their religion, whether they are foreigners to, or fathers of, my faith. Augustine's *City of God* shows strong a factual awareness of religious history, and the others, though less historical, know well a heritage to learn and the necessity of accurate acquaintance with the pluralisms of religious diversity.

But none, Augustine included, is well enough disciplined for scientific study, and their genius in teaching at more inward levels is often marred by their outward inaccuracies, as with Madhyamika's fanciful ascription to Gautama of the Sermon on Vulture Peak, quite unworried about ordinary fact in its concern for extraordinary truth, or with Ghazali's indiscriminate use of Muhammad's *ḥadīth* and biography, or with Augustine's often naive acceptance of the biblical record. The less their investment in history, the more religions tend to drift untethered to their actual origins and operations, loose from and with empirical fact. But our saints are not without an antidote to their own illnesses here. Each advises us to be true to truth first and to denominations, including one's own, afterward, and we may direct that allegiance here. There is a surrender of pride, a spiritual detachment, necessary to achieve the "even mind" of empirical accuracy. Our analysts know that nonpartisan study cannot be presumed to come easily, but must be purchased by the reformation of one's loves.

Desirable so long as it stays with knowing facts and makes no pretensions of inner understanding, this sheerly empirical study afterward becomes as worrisome as it is rewarding. By its own resolve it is severed from both ends of the actual spiritual process, on the one hand from the real—God, Brahman, *śūnyatā*—and on the other from the self, whether the empirical self as proud, self-willed, and possessive, or the spiritual self as soul, or *ātman*, in divine union or in emptiness. Where there is neither the question "What is true *in* this religion?" nor "Am I true to its truth?" how can there be any inquiry *into* what one insists on staying *without*? The behaviorist will neither enter Jerusalem nor ask of his or her own unsuspected residence in Babylon. In nonconcern for religion's concern, we cannot presume that the distance kept is innocuous, since we lose meaning as we prohibit point. It is as though we sought the intensions of words without their extensions. Perhaps we can empirically understand "religion" as a phenomenon in history, but are we prepared for full-blooded inquiry about "true religion" or even about "religious inquiry"?

Every student is prone to hasty judgments, pupils more so than masters, and we must often defer the "noumenological" or ultimate truth question until the phenomenological or relative truth has been established. But anything more is not studious postponement but unstudious repudiation of the spiritual truth question. If our interest is not in *reality* but merely in *religion*, the deeply religious intent in truth has atrophied. Religion is an inner formation for outward information or it is nothing; its public words and works cannot inform unless they claim to point past the conventional and ordinary world. Refusing to taste the pith of religion, behavioral learning about religion's husks is circumstantial and circumferential, since religion itself is not available for external access, although its forms and effects are tangible. With this sort of detachment which resolves to remain *extra*, there is gained an objectivity that undermines the study of religion by condemning it to be merely superficial.

"Academic" is not a word that joins well with "merely," and this is seen here in how the empirical study of religion obtains its "academic" freedom and status only alongside a "merely" which it simultaneously acquires. It becomes "merely academic," but this banishes the passion that is the basis of understanding. The sort of truth we come by is a function of the scope of our focus, and if we inquire only empirically, the results will be only peripheral annals, only data. Such inquiry about religion may be scientific, philosophical, historical, or psychological, but it is still nonreligious inquiry.

2. Introspective study

But there is a subjective as well as an objective meaning to phenomenal experience. We put one, but only one, foot within religion when we reach that level of study which is frequently termed the phenomenology of religion. I am introspective, although I remain circumspect in that I do not address questions of noumenal truth. I interpret religion from within my own and its own stream of consciousness. When the science of religion becomes humane, when it earnestly seeks to appreciate what it does not appropriate, it regards this subjective experience as not less real than objective behavior. Here the study of religion becomes more an art than a science. But this kind of learning about religion is transitional and unstable, for it proves difficult to specify and to defend the limits of entrance.

We may call this level of learning parareligious, alongside the studied faith, inside one faith but outside another, no longer unreservedly extrareligious but now coordinately religious. But this is not yet interreligious study, owing to a curious kind of resolving that one will become sensitive to the religious phenomena, which are nonultimate and relative, by resolving to be (at least during the phenomenological study) insensitive to the ultimate truth questions. One asks what is true of their religion, but never whether their religion is true. One does not try to understand objectively, but only intersubjectively, remaining neutral in that we bracket the final truth questions, yet becoming participant in that we use a domestic faith to identify and to appreciate the foreign faith.

Rudolf Otto introduces *The Idea of the Holy* with a memorable caveat: "The reader is invited to direct his mind to a moment of deeply-felt religious experience, as little as possible qualified by other forms of consciousness. Whoever cannot do this, whoever knows no such moments in his experience, is requested to read no farther."[2] It takes religion to learn about religion, and Otto's notice endorses what each of our saints has said, that he can offer no ideational illumination about religion in a perceptual void of its experience. This requirement is initially minimal, since some germinal religious impulses are indigenous to all of us. But it is finally maximal, since spirituality is variantly developed in us each. The teacher's particular faith-words will fall on deaf ears, until meanings are divined by the student who becomes "up to" the master in existential resourcefulness.

Always participatory in this way, the study of religion does not at the comparative level require *adherence* but it does require *relation*. Some capacity to understand here is trivial, but much capacity to understand is taxing. Unless we have a comparable level of faith, meaning will be necessarily indeterminate. Meanings which are not already owned cannot be imported, except as we are modified. But in this case we have barred ourselves from growth by our sustained refusing to ask whether truth is really there. Thus we prevent the novel experiences which might make sense of now foreign meanings. The phenomenological quest both promises success and invites stagnation.

Every student, as we have done, is entitled to conclude that religious meanings are sometimes indeterminate, where a determination to enter has failed. But where no entrance has been sought, the indeterminacies may be a local product of our premised untesting of it, rather than intrinsic to the studied faith. When the phenomenologist does not ask about their *real* the better to ask about their *religion*, this can beneficially produce a patient listening and the avoidance of what we have called contingent misunderstanding. But do I, or do I not, set aside my faith to go inside that of my fellows? We at once meet the paradox that their putative truth can be understood as meaningful only if it is allowed point, and, if I have resolved not to stretch or reform my sense of

---

[2] Rudolf Otto, *The Idea of the Holy* (New York: Oxford University Press, 1958), p. 8.

point to understand theirs, any nonsignificance may be mine and not theirs. My *epochē*, suspension, which is intended to gain phenomenal or factual accuracy, in using ony my sympathies to domesticate their point, refuses to ask the very question that would better understand them, and keeps me tangential to precisely that performative area that I desire to inquire about.

It is fashionable to say that so far as viability and point are concerned, we can remain extrareligious, not asking whether a religion is appropriate or is true, but that so far as intelligibility and meaning are concerned, we can become interreligious, entering someone else's stream of consciousness. But our saints were unable to separate these two activities, since all understanding is steadily underrun by undergoing. Here there is an oddness introduced by the phenomenological limit: I understand my own faith domestically only by a struggle to find the ultimately real, by love, faith, purity, and humility. But this level of struggle and these epistemic virtues I will not export and let operate over the field of foreign faith, and so I use less participation there. I will not taste their faith but seek to understand only with the projected taste of my own. So the phenomenologist falls into a kind of nonresident understanding, a trap which was intended to be escaped and an insensitivity often alleged against the missionary advocate.

The "fair witness" optimistically intended by bracketing the noumenal truth question results rather, and pessimistically, in only a fair witness, i.e. only an approximate one. Not to ask whether a "truth" asked "about" is binding is for us to treat it differently from the way its holder does, to sidestep it by holding it at arm's length. Wanting information without inner formation, we have insulated out the live religion. That is to study with a distant and therefore variant because ungrave passion. We are prohibited from a fully sensitive understanding. *Indifference* makes a *difference*; it locks out the intellect from the will and its loves. But our passions, like our pains and pleasures, our knowledges and convictions, are not something that can be laid on or laid aside at will. Could they be, there would be no perceptual base remaining on which to erect conceptual understanding. We cannot bracket gravity, and if we could, we could not study it. Spiritual disinterest born of interest is one thing; spiritual uninterest is another. Not to ask whether a religion is true, if first a sign of patience with it, later becomes a sign of impatience toward it. If it is first a sign of courageous dispassion, it becomes subsequently a failure of passion, a failure of nerve.

Such a mandated neutrality leaves us phenomenally free but noumenally unfree, free to inquire about *experiences* but unfree to ask about ultimate *reality*, with a first delightful and then merely academic freedom. Its instability lies in the way in which toward the other faith we are phenomenally—relatively and penultimately—comparative, communicant, responsive, faithful, and disciplined, while remaining noumenally—absolutely and ultimately—circumstantial, incommunicant, nonresponsive, faithless, and undisciplined. This is not to say that critical distance is not often needed in religion; indeed it is needed there of all places. We have seen our respondents insist on the rational screening of their intuitions, on understanding past undergoing, and watched them reject as erroneous many of the beliefs which they were offered.

But this was a critical distance in the service of and the quest for ultimate truth, not a critical distance that had abandoned or ignored the quest for ultimate truth. This latter sort of distance prevents rather than permits critical testing. In doing theology, to understand what other persons are saying is the same as to understand what they are saying *to me*. If these levels are separable, then one is doing religious studies. If they are not, I am doing theology (although I may pretend this is religious studies, especially if I am resisting commitment for or against that which is being said to me).

We are forced here to invoke the Madhyamika grading of understanding into relative and absolute, the Vedantan *vidyās* lower and higher, and to recognize that comparative understanding is only comparative, and, if restricted to the short phenomenal focus, still the more halting in its competence. It degenerates with decreasing parareligious experience into the "empty" (Nagarjuna) and the "illusory" (Sankara). Comparative religion is always and only on the borders of faith, except as the comparer has an owned incomparable faith and finds similar dimensions comparatively in those other faiths estimated. From Madhyamika we can borrow the term *relative* for comparative religion, using it both to comfort and to warn. From Vedanta we can adopt the term *phenomenal* to permit and yet to test the phenomenology of religion. From Ghazali and Augustine we adapt the terms *scientific* and *historical*. Via Augustine's *scientia* or Ghazali's *science of religion*, one may know about other religions too, alike by inspection and by introspective penetration. But neither the *scientific study of religions*, nor the *history of religions* can savor their wisdom, feel their point, discern their enlightenment. That comes only with *advaitan*, nondual understanding. In every case the name of the method suggests where the teacher and those taught by it remain: phenomenal, historical, scientific, comparative, relative.

II. The Ecumenical: Studying Interreligiously

We become more gravely comparatively religious when the truth question is absolute and noumenal. We seek wisdom, *prajñā*; the brackets are gone that kept us "merely" academic. The "about" in learning (about) religion fades to translucency, though not yet to transparency. Our quest becomes vital, interparticipatory, and possessive. In the marketplace of religions, ever open to foreign faith, whether as a competitor or as a friend, we watch for point, trying to understand, trying to see whether we can stand under their preaching. There is real adventure, real venturing toward the other. *I* address their *real*. The phenomenon of their religion takes on its truly communicant religious scope. To call this an *ecumenical* study is perhaps to stretch that word's earliest usage, drawn as the word is from Christianity; but such a stretching is toward its fullest etymology, the study of religion in a colloquy of "the whole inhabited world of faiths."

1. Centered and uncentered inquiry

Here the instability over which we were puzzled doing the phenomenology of religion is gone, but we are now perplexed by diverse ecumenical postures. We first are inclined to say that the inquirer into religion is not serious until he or she is open, noncommitted, objective to all, subjective to none. But then we must notice that such an unimpressed inquirer proportionately yet lacks the positive spiritual formation at home which permits understanding abroad. To be altogether open is to be confused in the forum, to be extrareligious after all, empty of any answers if not of questions. To see merely an interesting puzzle is not to see any intelligent point. Or, possessing only a lost asking, one brings sympathetic stirrings, yet is apathetic in regard to all convictions. Aphoristically put, this would-be learner is pathetic, to be pitied, because he is so nonpathetic, passionless, in personally owned capacities for arriving at conviction.

Stumbling over this impossible openness, we may change our approach, going over to the other extreme. Inquirers into religion cannot be serious until they have already reached some more or less settled religious convictions. The ecumenical search is better when it takes place among persons of conviction. It must be interconvictional, since it is the having of these convictions that permits comparative understanding. But now the ultimate truth question, though formally opened, is perhaps materially closed because everyone in the dialogue has already some cherished or at least provisional content. So the truth question is only comparatively and not unreservedly entertained.

We prejudge the issue with the judgments which we bring to study the other. Our personal closures of conviction may, fortunately, dispose us to appreciate others we study where they are like us. These foreign meanings can be domesticated after all; these are similar meanings in another tongue. But such closures may also, unfortunately, reduce our capacity to appreciate those we study who are unlike us. These other meanings are truly foreign, of indeterminate translation. What we cannot appropriate, we find inappropriate, being indisposed to it by our variant understandings. So the commitments that *provide* comparative understanding seem also to *prevent* open inquiry.

But we must not infer that religious study is not serious if there are already achieved answers that govern our inquiry. Ecumenical inquiry may be (a) *uncentered* or (b) *centered*. In what we call an *uncentered ecumenical inquiry*, the pupil lacks the paradigmatic gestalt that characterizes maturing faith. His or her search is open but unperceptive, it is dis-integrated. Later, as the student begins to find point, his or her education comes under the centered superintendence of a vision, often gained from one faith, oftenest that of one's particular catechetical rearing, more rarely some generic or polyglot abstraction of several faiths. Other religions are estimated in the light of an owned faith, that one esteemed because it yields integration for one's own life, and this we call a *centered ecumenical inquiry.*

This centered inquiry may in turn be (1) *expansive* or (2) *inclusive,* or alternate between these according to the matter at hand. Inquiry which is centered and yet *expansive* is *unbounded.* In this case, the presiding center of an owned faith, from which we operate, keeps us from any immediate question of catechesis in, or conversion to, the studied faith; but still our paradigmatic picture has soft, nonspecific boundaries. In our interreligious searching we may extend these boundaries or we may resolve areas before unmapped. We appropriate other faiths to our own use; they enlarge us, but we do not convert to them. We stretch to new understandings, but we are not loosed from the pivotal center of previous, precedent faith. The Christian studies Buddhism not to become a Buddhist, but to become an enlarged Christian, to enrich his Christianity. It is sometimes held that only such unbounded, expansive inquiry is authentic, that we cannot study another way of life without extending ourselves into it. "Seriously to study another way of life is necessarily to seek to extend our own—not simply to bring the other way within the already existing boundaries of our own."[3]

By contrast, centered ecumenical inquiry can also be *inclusive* or *bounded,* and we find this posture also to be authentic. Such a search tends rather to dissolve and restructure a foreign faith, to resolve it into topography already mapped. We expropriate the other faith to our own use; and in this we are hardly further instructed, but we subsume it under our own centripetal paradigm. We see no further with it, but see into it as a preface, a parallel, a distortion, a mistake, or a struggling toward our own. We are

---

[3] Peter Winch, "Understanding a Primitive Society," *American Philosophical Quarterly,* 1(1964): 307-324, citation on p. 317f.

unstretched by it to any new understandings. We give the alien faith rather a reunderstanding, as we learn about it, though not from it. We find it mappable from within our system of coordinates, or judge it to be indeterminate therefrom. One here seeks a Christian appraisal of Islam, a Vedantan account of Christianity. Even the previous, seemingly more open, expansive posture of inquiry was still in its fashion also centered, not less than this more inclusive attitude. If we can sometimes extend the radius of our circle of understanding, we are not less serious when we find that we must rather include the other within, or exclude it from, a circumference of understanding which we have already drawn.

The charitable accommodation and respecting of other faiths is what we often hope for here, but we cannot disallow those inquirers who find that their own faith continues to preside and to govern, and overrules so as to subsume other faiths under it, if not to sublate them. Appealing for what some today term the "older" approach in comparative religion, Max Müller wrote, "But this is not the only advantage of a comparative study of religions. The Science of Religion will for the first time assign to Christianity its right place among the religions of the world; it will show for the first time what was meant by the fullness of time; it will restore to the whole history of the world, in its unconscious progress towards Christianity, its true and sacred character."[4] So long as, with Max Müller, this is a conclusion, or even so long as it is a premise by which faith finds understanding, this is not provincial, as "later" comparativists have judged. It is an ecumenical, but perspectival, interreligious appreciation from a perceptual set. There is no other kind of serious appreciation; there are only other perceptual sets. Islam treats other faiths as partial; Advaita Vedanta makes them *aparā vidyās*, lesser understandings; Madhyamika relativizes them before its perfect *prajñā*.

Other students may find pointless such exclusivism in particular faiths and repoint all of them toward one goal, thinking that all of

---

[4] Friedrich Max Müller, "Plea for a Science of Religion," in Jacques Waardenburg, *Classical Approaches to the Study of Religion* (The Hague: Mouton, 1973), vol. 1, pp. 85-95, citation on p. 86.

them are generally right and particularly wrong. But this diluting of the concrete paradigms of classical faiths by finding some nondescript common denominator of all faith is quite as perspectival as to think that only one is right. In the synoptic approach, thinking to be less provincial, we partly understand but are largely excluded from those distinctive provinces of faith. Every such seeming reception, being only a halfway reception, is reciprocally largely nonreceptive. It maintains a nonresidence; it reunderstands that faith from some broader perspective. The other religion proves impenetrable—not generally where comparisons broadly succeed—but at the specific core, where divergent paradigms turn sharply around incommensurable centers. We understand in principle (*love*), but not in particular (*agapē, karuṇā, mahabba, ahiṃśa*), and thus we only seem to share their paradigm, while actually we so re-view their conviction through ours as to reject more than we accept.

Note that throughout all this comparative accommodation— whether by our own composing out of the other an enlarged faith for ourselves, or by our recomposing of it through a reduction of it under our own faith, or by our decomposing its proffered meanings as indeterminate—we are steadily nonreceptive to it on its own terms. The pupil has been turned into a teacher and seeks rather to persuade the other how he or she should reform his or her faith. Serious colloquy is almost invariably concluded by apology, where we begin to say something to those to whom we have been listening.

2. The ecumenical forum

All our doctors were pupils before they became teachers in an ecumenical forum. If later in their careers they became confessional, earlier they interrogated multiple sources of faith. While none of them had our modern global knowledge of faiths, they still confronted options as radical as do we. Each saint was as cosmopolitan for his time as is likely to be any reader of these words; and they became great in our religious history for their ranging through these currents, arranging for themselves and posterity an integral vision. Much of the tedium of their works lies in their protracted engagement with now archaic viewpoints. The creeds of Palestine, Greece, Rome, Africa, and the barbarian north converge on Augustine. He stays long uncentered, but then gradually picks a Catholic way among the Platonists, the Academics, the Manicheans, the rhetoricians, the sophists, the poets, the Donatists and the Pelagians.

Ghazali reports how he "scrutinized the creed of every sect," (Dl 20) and, besides the Mediterranean melee that Augustine knew, Ghazali encountered the exotic views of Arabia, Syria, and Persia—not only the Sunnis, Sufis, and Shi'a, but also the *Bāṭinīyah*, *Zāhirīyah, Mu'aṭṭilah*, and dervishes. Every reader of the *Incoherence* is soon distressed in and by the diffracted philosophical spectrum across which Ghazali sought integration. The Indian scene is of unrelieved creedal confusion, Hindu and Buddhist, over which Sankara labors for Advaitan coherence, while Nagarjuna fends his way through Brahmanism and the intricate Hinayana debates before his breakthrough to Madhyamika. Their entrances to silent *prajñā* and *jñāna* do not come until after they have wrestled with the clamoring theses around them. All these masters first learned (about) religion in public colloquy, and, later becoming centered, they stayed on in the ecumenical debate both to learn and to preach.

This makes a place for the "representative" view of religious studies. True, the historical and scientific facts of religious life objectively are what they are, regardless of their representation in the subjectivity of any "representative" spokesman's faith. But beyond learning such data, which either insider or outsider can present, even the phenomenologist wants inwardness to consult, someone who can "see it from there," in whom there is the perceptual backing that sustains conceptual discourse. Whether a faith is contemporary, classic, bygone, or even fossil, we cannot contact it except through its representatives, or something residual from them. In ecumenical study, representation needs to be multiple and extensive. The difficulty is in getting, not in getting rid of, good representation.

From a vast scene of spokesmen, the pupil must choose judiciously, but such choosing is already to presume who represents what competently. Do we best listen to primary witnesses, enacted, spoken, or written? Or do we hear by secondary report, which is summary and swifter but lamentably comparative? How few teachers can we read and fewer still converse with! Shall we hear more of less, or less of more? How soon must the scholar make a responsible representation, a presentation, not only of his or her owned faith but on behalf of others under the scope of inquiry! How often the student must under our guidance be introduced to another faith through our relayed witness or through trustees whom we select! Ghazali, Augustine, Sankara, and Nagarjuna? Have we chosen each as, and given to each, a fair witness? Have we in this work created an ecumenical forum, and is this despite or because of an author's spiritual intent?

Does not intellectual integrity demand that the moderator, unless he or she is presiding over a forum as yet unjoined, be both detached and participant, able to select witnesses impartially, hear their evidence, and then judge it? Must not even the monitor-judge be "up to" those saints which he or she judges to be representative? Once again, save by hearsay, we cannot even recognize spirituality except by our resonance with it. The teacher who ventures to sponsor an ecumenical context must not hide his or her personal convictions, but see those placed in the midst of evident others, especially any who are denied an immediate witness by the strictures of the teaching environment.

John Stuart Mill wrote, "We are not so absurd as to propose that the teacher should not set forth his opinions as the true ones, and exert his utmost powers to exhibit their truth in the strongest light. To abstain from this would be to nourish the worst intellectual habit of all, that of not finding, and not looking for, certainty in anything. But the teacher himself should not be held to any creed; nor should the question be whether his own opinions are the true ones, but whether he is well instructed in those of other people, and, in enforcing his own, states the arguments for all conflicting opinions fairly."[5] More than did Mill, our saints have explored

---

[5] J.S. Mill, "Civilization," in *Mill's Essays on Literature and Society* (New York: Collier Books, 1965), pp. 148-182, citation on p. 179.

being tied to a creed. If this means servient allegiance to borrowed belief, faith disinclined to seek understanding, authority *(taqlīd)* in place of experience *(dhawq)*, extracurricula constraints, control other than by the subject matter, proud attachments, the mistaking of relative theses for absolute truth, then they much concur.

But our saints also know that finding is productive of faith, and faith of finding, that commitment yields truth, and truth commitment, that spiritual attachments can and ought to detach the ego for a better search, that a convivial understanding necessitates an adherence, while the nonadherent is reduced to a comparative understanding. Meanwhile, each of our educators as much as Mill enjoyed an instruction in the opinions of others, giving these fair witness, and then exhibiting the truth of his own opinions in the strongest light. What makes teaching genuinely academic is not whether advocacy is absent, but whether argument is present, and its caliber.

"Religious" is properly an adjective of persons, and derivatively from this applied to communities, and only obliquely applied to institutions. Though we cannot deal adequately here with the intricacies of corporate religious education, the teacher and the taught may seek the sustaining institutional representation of a heritage. Gathered students may, in schools and seminaries, *intensively* select catechetical intent, at a level we next examine, but they may also select, *extensively*, to be universities. If universities are to be true to their name, to represent and survey the "universe," they must within their resources provide this ecumenical forum. In this ecumenical context, plurality should not be confused with externality, nor nonrepresentation with multiple representation. An institutional neutrality is to be distinguished from neutrality on the part of professors or students there, and the former may be desirable where the latter is not. The university community may remain uncentered, nearer then a "multiversity," for the lack of a communal gestalt. Such a community, like the "teacher" who remains uncentered, must realize that it is ever inconclusive, ever pluralistic. Still, an institutional permissiveness may be designed which permits effective professorial advocacy.

An alternate university form is to be found in the gathering of teachers sharing and undergoing together a curricular control. This common gravity of intent makes such a university less public and more private, but this kind of university need not shrink because it centers its ecumenical scope. It need not be less catholic because it is, for instance, a Catholic university. Indeed, just such a gestalt is required to place the *uni-* before the *versus* to gain the synoptic *university*, the university that studies the diverse world but with a unitive vision. Scholars who elect to be there remain free to embrace their attracting, orienting faith. That freedom is finely academic and exceeds that of communities who are self-limited to the study of bare religious phenomena, barring themselves from ultimate truth questions.

Whatever the community or the colloquy, the religion resides ultimately in the singular student, where only its existential presence can finally re-present to a particular life some historic faith met in a cultural education. So we add to the celebrated exchange between Max Müller and Adolf Harnack, not that to know one religion is to know all, nor is it to know none, but that we can know genuinely only one religion, our very own, and from and after that some of all and all of none.

III. The Catechetical: Studying Intrareligiously

When we leave the forum to seek the sanctuary, the student becomes a disciple, and study becomes *catechetical*. Faith seeks understanding. Study is initiatory, though not yet confessional; we trust a system of faith to bring us to an ultimate real. Faith in Buddhism, in Christianity, Islam, or Advaita Vedanta is expected to make us Buddhas, to unite us to Christ, to make us Muslims, to uncover the *ātman*-Brahman nonduality. The context is an entrant one; it is presentational as this goes past the merely representational. The spokesman has become a master, beyond us in his disciplinary advance; and we hope to share his spirit, we search for his quality of life. In "ascent" (Ghazali), the teacher and the taught "do theology," where academic study has come to include a devotional love.

By outsiders, this catechetical study will be too readily disparaged as "biased." But to be cultured at all is to be catechized in some way, and the educational question is never whether we shall be catechized but what kind of catechizing shall it be. When it takes the form of focused inquiry this catechizing becomes seminal for life, and the student becomes what we have traditionally called a seminarian.

1. Advocatory teaching

The *guru, pastor, sheikh,* and *spiritual friend* "call toward" an embodied faith, in the root sense of "advocate." There is a fetching plainness to the *prajñā-pāramitā* term for teacher, "good spiritual friend," revealed in the following exchange: "Subhuti: 'How should a Bodhisattva who is only just beginning, stand in perfect wisdom, how train himself?' The Lord: 'Such a Bodhisattva should tend, love, and honor the good friends. His good friends are those who will instruct and admonish him in perfect wisdom, and who will expound to him its meaning.' " (AP 188m)[6] The Friend *par excellence* is Gautama and the *Sūtra* is one grand catechism with Sariputra and Subhuti. We can thus understand and tolerate its repetitiveness, and we can appreciate its routine dialogue under the grand opening symbol—the Buddha radiating light to the many gathered at his feet from the corners of the Earth. (MP 38ff; MPC1 431ff) Following him, Nagarjuna says to his pupil, "I set forth the teaching of the holy ones, in order to produce in you the happiness of religious merit, and to excite you towards the practice of it." (SL 1) Indeed, Madhyamika esteems him to be the veteran teacher who makes *dharma* for all time plainer than even Gautama could. The massive *Śāstra* ascribed to him is still another catechism on top of the Buddha's *Sūtra*.

The teacher is a *bodhisattva,* an enlightenment-being, equipped with compassion (*karuṇā*) and skill-in-means (*upāya*). The truth he teaches so sublimely not only *is with* but *is* the Buddha's compassion that stoops to bring all to *śūnyatā*, with tactfulness appropriate to each. The truth-finder has "gone thus" (*tathāgata*) to his end; he

---

[6] Consult Conze's MP index on "spiritual good friend," "teacher," and "skill-in-means." See Chapter 22 in the AP version; also SL 64f.

longs that we come there too, and can gently lead by his pedagogical wit. "Here the Bodhisattvas win full enlightenment and then take away all the darkness and gloom of the un-cognition from beings who for long are enveloped in the membrane of the eggshell of ignorance." (AP 189) The Madhyamika dislike of the Theravadin single-Buddha (*pratyeka-buddha*), which we might translate as a "nonteaching Buddha," is in prohibition of a self-defeating concern with one's own education at the neglect of others, drawn from Madhyamika's just appreciation of the *bodhisattva*-teacher who sees *nirvāṇa* but stays from it for advocacy, in whom devotion to truth is coincident with devotion to others, because truth *is* the nonduality of others. (MP 58ff; AP 163) The mediation of truth to others *is* the message, compassion *is* the truth, and for the Buddhist too to do evil is to stray from education.

"He who has a duly qualified teacher learns his way." (*ChU* 6-14-2m) The guru of the *Upanishads* is not less a catechist, where, by etymology, the student "sits near" his teacher. Sankara warns, "That knowledge alone which is imparted by those who have realized the truth—and no other knowledge—can prove effective." (BhG 4-34) "Right knowledge is unattainable to those who have not been properly initiated into the traditional knowledge by the gurus, who have not learned and studied the Vedanta, and who have not been trained in the right sources of knowledge." (BhG 18-5a) "Brahman can be known only through such a traditional instruction of preceptors, and not through argumentation, nor by study, intelligence, great learning, austerity, sacrifices, etc." (KeU 1-4) Sankara is embarassing both in his insistence that Brahman cannot otherwise be learned, and in his demand for almost fawning admiration of the guru, an admiration which he profusely gives to his own mentors. (KaU 1-2-7f; Hy 103; GaK 4-100) That insistence later degenerated into a sort of tight apostolic succession; but the concern was first generated by the conviction that only those could teach true religion who had been there, just as one torch must light another.

"Teachers offer themselves for imitation, and this is precisely what people call teaching." We are not really surprised to find Augustine speaking from the treatise *On Music* (1-6), since education, alike in music and in religion, is caught more than taught. For longer accounts of how religion is learned, we can turn to *Catechizing the Uninstructed*, *The Teacher*, and *Christian Education*. "Whatever may be the grandeur of his style, the life of the teacher will count for more in winning the learner's obedience.... They no longer listen attentively to a man who does not listen to himself, and, in despising the instructor, they learn to despise the word that is taught." (CD 4-59f) The words of a professor of religion are empty if they are without personal backing.

But beyond this, we are not concerned merely with the person of the teacher, except as his or her life has come into a correspondence with the ultimate truth. "Teachers do not claim, do they, that their own thoughts only are learned and grasped by the pupils, but rather the disciplines which they intend to transmit by speaking? For who would be so foolishly curious as to send his child to school to learn what the teacher thinks? But when the teacher has explained, by means of words, all those disciplines which he professes to teach, including the disciplines of virtue and of wisdom, then the pupils consider within themselves whether what has been said is true by looking to the inward truth, so far as they are able. In this way they learn." (Mg 45) We do want magisterial biography, and so we have turned here to Augustine, Sankara, Nagarjuna, and Ghazali as they embody faiths. But in the quest for education we never want to know what anybody else thinks, except to consider whether it is true.

"He who finds a *sheikh*—a gnostic, wise, realizing the faults of the self, compassionate, able to give counsel concerning the religious life, one who has accomplished the amendment of his own spiritual life, and is concerned with the amendment of God's servants—has found the physician for his ills. Let him cleave to that physician who will deliver him from the destruction with which he is threatened." (Ih III, 1)[7] "When souls are so weak that they do not follow the right road to the realization of their own true nature, they attach themselves and have recourse to a master who is compassionate and wise, and ask for his succor so that he may assist

---

[7] Cited and translated by Smith, *Al-Ghazali*, p. 152m.

them.'" (Ri 371) When Ghazali found himself to be a theologian who could not hear the music, a physician who could not heal himself, he resigned his professorship and became a disciple of such masters who could. Only then did he become vocal again, and the *Revivification of the Religious Sciences* results. The consummate Islamic teacher, which Ghazali sought to become, is much praised at the end of the *Book on Knowledge*, first for his effective piety of person and then for his maturity of mind. (Ih I, 1, sec. 6f)

But, lest this praise of the teacher should seem all too finished an ideal, an analogy given by Augustine suits all here. What the guide along the road says makes no sense unless the pupil is traveling too; and once seen, the guide's authority is soon past. But the guide, if he is a good one, will find that he is helped by the pupils' responses to see afresh and more deeply. (CI 17) Further, the guide must himself exemplify a continuing education, or else he will himself stray from the very education he advocates. "In my eagerness to answer those who inquire of me, I shall myself also find that for which I was inquiring." (Tr 1-8)

2. Evocative teaching

But the teacher-advocate can only evoke religion, calling it forth in willing and perceptive pupils. He cannot deliver it to anybody anywhere. When the *prajñā*-teacher begins to address nonentrant pupils, "he will tell them that he will give this perfection of wisdom to those who come to where he is, but not to those who do not." (AP 168) Even for those who come gladly, many struggles will follow, since nothing can be verbally delivered.

When Subhuti, after being catechized, comes to instruct others, his pupils, the gods, murmur. "The gods: 'What Subhuti has just taught, uttered, demonstrated, expounded about the perfection of wisdom, that we do not understand.' Subhuti: 'And why? For not in the letters is the perfection of wisdom, and therefore it is not something that can be cognized or heard or demonstrated.' The gods: 'May the holy Subhuti enlarge on the perfection of wisdom! For what he demonstrates is deeper than the deep, subtler than the subtle.' Subhuti: 'The enlightenment of the Tathagata cannot be talked about, it is incommunicable. Nothing is thereby demonstrated by anyone, nor heard, nor discerned.' " (MP 209f,a) If that means more than Augustine wishes to affirm, as it does, it means at least this with which he is sympathetic: that the teacher can transmit no discursive understanding to a pupil except with that pupil's secret detection of a felt truth that subtly warrants all meaningfulness. Otherwise, teaching is empty.

That is the haunting thesis of *The Teacher*. Like the words they use, teachers only point; and, if learning results from teaching, it is by what is properly an "education," as the realities themselves "draw out" (*educo*) the student. We here contact again what we earlier called the catalytic power of conception, which is positive for Augustine as it is not for Nagarjuna; but we must accompany that with how conception is reduced to emptiness in the absence of perceptual authority. The teacher helps us see, but talk is never seeing, neither in the physical nor the spiritual senses. Only knowledge may be conveyed by talk, which is merely parabolic to wisdom.

"The maximum import I can attribute to words is this. They suggest we look for things, but they do not so exhibit these to us that we may know them. He alone teaches me anything who sets before my eyes, or one of my other bodily senses, or my mind, the things which I desire to know. From words we can only learn words.... With the knowledge of things there is completed the knowledge of words, but when mere words are learned, not even those are learned.... In all things which we understand, we consult not the speaker who says words, but the truth within presiding over the mind itself, though we may have been prompted by words to do so." (Mg 36, 38) The words of a teacher have no power to make us know even physical realities unless the pupil by them is provoked to empirical experience. Still less can religious words make us know intelligible realities unless the mind of the student manages with the words to evoke some sacred experience.

The mullah can handle the husks of religion, knowing that there is a pith within. When the disciple is handed these husks, he himself must break them open to savor that pith. Even the *Qur'an*, Ghazali reminds us, rather surprisingly for a Muslim, does not directly teach, but calls us to reflect on "signs" (*āyāt*), or what Ghazali calls "leads" (*dalīl*). "We shall show them Our signs in the horizon and in themselves, till it is clear to them that it is the truth." (S 41.53*a*) The *Qur'an* regularly uses the word "perchance"—"perhaps you may..."—which presents the indications of knowledge and then waits for the awakening of point.[8] Among Ghazali's chief marvels of the heart is that religion is inner (*bāṭin*), not superficial (*ẓāhir*), private, not public. Hence the "I bear witness" of the *shahādah*, since the teacher is only a witness, both licensed and limited only to point, and the rest is between the listener and God. To the guru one should listen, continues Sankara, and then reflect. But teaching does not take place finally in any guru's argument or any student's cogitation, but by an intimate discovery by the self of the Self. The *bodhisattva* preaches relative, never absolute truths; only an ignorant professor of religion expects to come by a thesis upon which he or she can rest a final tutorial efficacy.

"Can one learn this knowledge?" asks Wittgenstein. "Yes; some can. Not, however by taking a course in it, but through '*experience*'.—Can someone else be a man's teacher in this? Certainly. From time to time he gives him the right *tip*.—This is what 'learning' and 'teaching' are like here.—What one acquires here is not a technique; one learns correct judgments. There are also rules, but they do not form a system, and only experienced people can apply them right. Unlike calculating rules. What is most difficult here is to put this indefiniteness, correctly and unfalsified, into words."[9] The teacher only coaches. Like loves and skills, religion can and cannot be taught; it can only be taught about. All teaching of religion is in this sense a teaching of the phenomenology of religion, for the noumenal realm cannot be taught. To gain communion with that realm so paradoxically is, and is not, to be able to converse about it.

Where now is the often-heard lament that catechizing hands over ready-made answers from a dominant teacher to a passive, subordinate learner? The transmission of theses from master to

---

[8] See Othman, *Concept of Man in Islam*, p. 120ff.

[9] L. Wittgenstein, *Philosophical Investigations*, 3rd ed. (New York: Macmillan, 1968), p. 227.

pupil is precisely what should not be confused with the teaching of religion. Our classic catechists all insist on a direct engagement of the pupil with the thing to be known. Catechetical "input" in what we might call a *strong* sense is impossible, and were it possible, it would not be desirable. Sometimes, there may be the illusion of inquiry through special pleading, but this power of pleading, or rhetoric, Augustine tried and passionately rejected. To think that learning is transmitted so is to rest on the empty theses scorned by Nagarjuna, on the vain "authoritative instruction" which Ghazali abandoned.

The teacher's authority is always provisional, soon to pass to objective self-certification of the truth. The saintly catechist effaces both self and tutorial system. If first indispensable, these are soon dispensable, and the catechumen is plunged on toward making his or her own confessional witness. Is such a catechetical instruction somehow not free? The teacher must, but can only advocate. The master must, but can only be a good spiritual friend, and Ghazali spent his life opposing mere taqlīd, authority, and urging ma'rifa, experience. Each of our saints wants education to be thoroughly critical, the student to take nothing from the professor. That is more, not less than an academic freedom, because it is an existential one. A Socratic process characterizes the *Upanishads*, the *Mahā-Prajñā-Pāramitā Sūtra*, and the Augustinian dialogues and catechisms, because the teacher is always a midwife through whom faith seeks understanding, one who helps another give birth to truth, never an authoritarian professor.[10]

IV. The Confessional: Studying Religiously

The searching soul moves finally to the *confessional* level of the *Soliloquies* and the *Confessions*, to the silence of *prajñā*, to the intimate unitary consciousness of Brahman, to Ghazali's level of private intercourse with God, deeper even than the saints may converse about. In the catechetical study we have just considered,

---

[10] This ideal, though, is often compromised by our saints in trying to deal with the massive illiteracy of the common folk of their day.

we have, *horizontally*, a human mentor. But now, at the confessional level, *vertically*, we reach an internal, divine teacher, and have come into direct encounter with what we know. Here knowledge is by acknowledgment. My education cannot be another's, but must be my own. It must be confessional, and religion is, in Whitehead's phrase, what I do with my aloneness. The focus is not theology but God, not *dharma* but Brahman or *śūnyatā*, not the relative but the absolute. "Religion" is not the object of study but it has become an operative adverb; we study the ultimate reality "religiously." Here, where education lies in union, there is a coalescence of teacher and taught, of subject and object, and all real education is private education.

1. The ultimate teacher

The saint always eventually detects being taught by the subject of his devotion. This is most readily seen in theism, but not really altered when the sacred object is more diffused or inarticulate. The highest consultation, Augustine tells us, is with the eternal teacher, the *magister interior*, an immanent *Logos*. "Our actual teacher is the Christ listened to within, dwelling in the inner man, as the unchangeable power and eternal wisdom of God. This wisdom every rational soul does in fact consult, but to each is disclosed only so much as he is capable of receiving." (Mg 38; Sm 210) God is the impregnating cause of learning; human teachers are but midwives. Learning is inward but not autonomous, not our own discovery but rather our participant reflection of the wisdom of our Author. "The Spirit of God will guide you into all truth." (Jn. 16.13)

"Now if we ourselves were the authors of our nature, then we would generate our own wisdom and would not need to get an education from our teachers. If we were the source and only goal of our love, we would be self-sufficient and would need enjoyment of no outside good to make us blessed. But, rather, God is the author of our nature and therefore he must be our teacher, if ever we are to be wise." (CG 11-25) Final educational power rests not in the student or professor, nor in organized religion or human rationality, but in the Spirit before whom we bow as the only adequate explanation of the presence of truth in the human mind, a mind which but borrows that intelligible spirituality. Augustine's concept of divine illumination involves this tuition by God, for God is the source of all enlightenment.

Allah is *Al-Hadī*, the Guide. "*Al-Hadī* is the One who guides his elect servants to the knowledge (*ma'rifa*) of his essence. He measures, and guides aright. The guiding ones among men are the prophets and the theologians who direct men to happiness in the hereafter and guide them to the straight path of God. But in reality it is God who guides through the tongues of these leaders, and they are only instruments." (NN 124f,a) That is why religious knowledge must rest on revelation, why teaching comes through the *Qur'an*, where God says of such a prophet, "We taught him knowledge from ourself." And unless through the *Qur'an* there is in the reader in turn an "inspiration" nothing is learned from it. "All knowledge is attained and known in the substance of the primal universal soul, the Universal Mind." (Ri 364ff,m; S. 18.65) Ghazali's *Niche for Lights* is a long commentary on a single Qur'anic verse, the light verse, about how "Allah guides to his light." From this Ghazali concludes, "The man for whom God does not cause light, no light at all has he." (Ni 44; S. 24.35) These ideas gather in the *hadīth*, the tradition of the "guides," that "God is the only guide to God."

"I am the teacher, the knower of Vedanta.... It is I who cause the teaching of the Vedanta to be handed down in regular succession." That is Ishvara speaking through Krishna. (BhG 15-15m) The highest Lord is ever our teacher, and the guru mediates between us and God. (Hy 6, 27) India's propensity to regard all its *āchāryas*, Sankara included, as less or more the incarnation of God, proportionately to their wisdom, reveals once again this vesting of ultimate teaching in the divine behind the human master. As deeper insight comes, in successful education we are yoked to Brahman in *jñāna yoga*, and the Ishvara-teacher is then depersonified to *nirguṇa* Brahman. All teachers, including the avatars, are sublated and relativized in the Absolute, because they are found to be channels of the one monistic educating force. In learning too, *jñāna* is never by our action but springs up from the receptive contemplation of Brahman, when we are conformed to it. All spiritually formative power rests with Brahman, the light of lights, by which all truth is perceived. (VS 1-3-22)

"The perfect Buddha, the foremost of all teachers, I salute." So Nagarjuna prefaces the *Kārikās* (Stcherbatsky, 69,72). At the first level that is a tribute to Gautama, but at a deeper level it is a prostration before the perfect wisdom which is incarnate in him. Gautama has passed to *parinirvāṇa*, beyond teaching, but the *dharma-kāya*, the Buddha essence, which moved him still moves in the *tathāgatas*. Not even a Buddha has personal authority; he has only the tactfulness to help us toward a self-authenticating "thus-ness." And, though barred by silence from professing any Real, Madhyamika clings almost to the end to a lingering personification of *prajñā*. "For this very perfection of wisdom should in this context be regarded as the 'teacher,' nor is the teacher one thing and the perfection of wisdom another, but just the perfection of wisdom is the teacher and just the teacher is the perfection of wisdom." (MP 257) "The perfection of wisdom gives light, O Lord. She is worthy of homage. She removes the darkness from everyone in the triple world. She does her utmost to bring about the forsak-ing of the blinding darkness caused by the defilements and by false views. She makes us seek the safety of all the dharmas which act as wings to enlightenment.... The perfection of wisdom is the mother of the Bodhisattvas." (MP 283)

So, despite their differences, our saints concur that our final educational freedom is to be drawn (*educo*) to and by the divine source of all intelligibility and wisdom.

2. The ultimate disciple

But if, from the divine side, the disciple learns from an ultimate teacher, we may then say, from the human side, relative to all teachers, that the ultimate disciple is self-taught, that is, privately taught. The actual locus of learning is along a self-Real axis to which any teacher is quite peripheral. If the *bodhisattva* is to be "trained in all-knowledge" and "trained in all dharmas," he must be "self-trained." (cf AP 88) "What you seek to understand," confides Augustine to his pupils, "is something which can be seen only by the most pure, and you are too poorly trained for such vision. In all these laborious arguments we have been trying to exercise your own powers to make you capable of seeing this yourself." (S1 2-34) This "self-teaching" must be deciphered, stretched, and finally exploded. The intimacy involved will be cherished, while any autonomy of self is banished. No catechist can teach me now; my education is my responsibility. Yet that is a *response*-ability as I become sensitive to the divine by a retraining of my self, by a restraining of my self.

What the *bodhisattva* has to teach the self is that there is no self, no ego personally articulated from the nonduality by which he or she is instructed. What the impure, proud pupil has to uncover is the self-humbling that sees God, because it is convivial with what God teaches us in Christ about the inner divine being. What Ghazali taught himself was "self-mortification" as the "key to illumination." The Advaitan training is, quite precisely and yet so puzzlingly, that the self is to be taught by the Self. At this reach, to be self-educated is to be self-prosecuting, for the truth comes by self-rectification. Information is by reformation, when the self is led out, educated, expanded, emptied into the divine. We are disinterested in ourselves and thus rightly interested in the real. This final educational freedom through giving up self is the correspondent truthfulness with which we began, taken now in the end at a confessional pitch.

Augustine contends that this tutorial act is "intellectual" in the highest sense, merging the conceptual and the perceptual elements. We are past the academic, and even the rational, so far as this means what can be calculated and discussed, what can be "taught." Education is the discovery of such intelligibility in things that they gather into the divine unity, sacredly into a universe. This occurs when the disciple is forcefully and simultaneously brought into that unity. Here love and righteousness do not come *with* but *are* this intelligibility. A just charity is the essence of that purposefulness which makes sense of the whole. The supremely intellectual act, *intellection*, is thus coincident with the supremely spiritual act, *loving*.

As we move eastward, we stumble increasingly over this intellectuality, for the *Logos* is replaced by an inarticulate Absolute, a silent void. Activity of mind becomes extinct. What remains, to the nonparticipant, is indeterminate; but, to the participant, this is an enlightenment beyond intellection. But somehow there too, if not intellectually at least perceptually, the supremely educational act is coincident with the supremely spiritual state, *jñāna* and perfect wisdom. Vedanta is the end of wisdom (*vāda*), and Buddhism is the freeing of the mind (*buddhi*).

Teaching becomes unanimous with worship. Study is piety. Intellectual honesty is in religious commitment, since spiritual conformation is identical with mental confirmation. To behold this truth is to be brought to one's knees, as this real's being true demands our being true. As we found that catechetical instruction, rightly understood, encouraged critical inquiry, so here the confessional context, rightly understood, is educational because of, and not in spite of, the fact that all the evocative elements in religious life operate. Teaching is by meditation and prayer, by hymn and sacrament, by alms and service, by communal or monastic life, by art, liturgy, and devotion, as these support conviction. They reteach the self its legitimate location of worth. The root of worship is sacred worth; and, when education comes to the address of worth, our homage to it becomes the conclusion of learning. We may earlier be learners, but now we must be more. We must become "disciples," past being mere learners; we have a spiritual vocation as well as a cognitive one.

Most of us live short of such ultimacy all of the time, and all of us live short of it some of the time. Perhaps indeed all fall short of it all of the time. The mystic returns from his ecstasies; the beatific vision never lasts. The *jīvan-mukti* and the *arahat* have residual *karma* to expend; *agapē* is mixed with *erōs*. The *bodhisattva* has not yet passed finally to *nirvāṇa* ; the saint is still a sinner. There is always duality between the ego and the real, the ego and the world; and confusion troubles our universe. We see through a glass darkly, the *imago Dei* is broken, we are "perpetually convalescent." (Augustine) We cannot assume that these educational goals are, in this life, ever reached. But neither can we assume that they are never sought, nor approached. Unless their religion was wholly in error, these four doctors were actually schooled by some reality-value which elevated them. Their spirituality significantly detached their selves from, or in, or for, the world by participation in an eternal truth. Perhaps they did not succeed in becoming ultimate and consummate disciples, but they tried to be. Whether such pilgrims ever arrive, they do travel hopefully, and they seek an ultimate education.

Whoever wishes to understand religion has a heavy assignment. The reader has perhaps puzzled that our long course has not sufficiently distinguished between whether we are making a religious inquiry or asking about it, between whether this study is participatory or academic, theological or philosophical. But we are refusing to make such distinctions, since understanding religious persons is not separable from being or becoming religious persons. To inquire "about" religion is to go on a religious inquiry. We have been inquiring of those who have found their thirsts quenched by living waters, and to come without being religious is to find that the well is deep and that we have nothing to draw with.

V. The Educational: All Education as Religious

"Fall deeply in love with understanding." (Ep 120-1) Augustine speaks for all our masters when he finds that the converse of evil as straying from education is that all education is the search for the *summum bonum*, and, as such, is the only ultimate good. Augustine holds that learning is finally only by religious intellection, by a comprehensive apprehension of God. Mere training is not religious, of course, for technical skills belong to sciences that stop short of wisdom. There is no education until there is a turning to goals, presumptions, and faiths. Then one leaves the sciences for the humanities, where later if not sooner, the inquiry will be about humanity's emplacement in the universal whole, and the question will become religious. "Those who are well educated in the liberal arts...are not content until they behold the full face of spiritual truth, whose splendor already in part glows in these liberal arts." (Sl 2-35) What is meant by liberal education is truth that makes us free. In this light savagery is ignorance and culture is liberating wisdom, and this freedom in truth is the ultimate academic freedom. Here there is *vidyā*, vision, and *bodhi-buddha*, enlightenment of the mind; here there is *mokṣa*, release. True philosophers, insisted Plato, are ever seeking "to release the soul."[11] Truth is finally saving, though it may intermediately trouble us, and saints know better than philosophers that there must be a releasing *from* as well as a releasing *of* the self.

Understanding puts things into wholes, and we are led out, educated, from self-centricity into the significant organization of the self and the world as an intelligible community. We understand each other and the world particulars not in their separated "own-being," for as such they are "empty," but in God. We thus reach the only proper sense in which theology ever bids to be queen of the sciences, not in claiming any oversight of them, but in the religious significance of true education. The seeming arrogance in the Madhyamika boast of "perfect wisdom" lies not in any theses which are levied on us, but in an insistence that no wisdom is perfected until relative theses cohere in a highest truth. All persons are not religious, but all persons who in this Augustinian sense "understand" are, since by their understanding they place themselves and that which they study sympathetically in a valuational gestalt. They add wisdom to knowledge, and in this sense van der Leeuw writes, "All comprehension, irrespective of whatever object it refers to, is ultimately religious: all significance sooner or later leads to ultimate significance."[12]

This may offend any persons who think of themselves as being educated and also not religious, and so we grant that our saints have by no means presented all the religious options, nor need one be classically religious with them in the finding of some supernal realm which superintends the secular. There are naturalistic, socialistic, and positivistic faiths. But Augustine's insistence, against the Academics, was that we recognize the fiduciary or religious content of every life-orienting view. So far as these give us a truth-focus, so far as we are catechized in them, as we believe in them in order to understand them and to understand with them,

---

[11] Plato, *Phaedo*, 67d.

[12] Gerardus van der Leeuw, *Religion in Essence and Manifestation* (London: George Allen and Unwin, 1938, 1964), p. 684.

they become religious. Further on, with deepening trust in them, we confess them and relocate the self about them.

If it is ever conclusive, all education is a putting of trust somewhere, and if that something be secular, as it may, then the secular is soon removed to locations before denoted sacred. It assumes ultimacy. Further, similarly to the way in which philosophy may be the love of wisdom with reticent modesty about the finding of it, an education may provoke religious searching which remains uncentered and uncommitted. But such inquiry remains religious, even when it is not conclusive. The point remains if we say, less provocatively, that all education is axiological, involving us in a locating of values. But worth, we were saying, is the root of worship. Education is about and of one's loves, a drawing of the self out toward universal value; and that makes it a passionate question, sooner or later tributary to religion.

Education is a matter of "getting things together," always by some rubric which becomes increasingly religious with its success. Having amply allowed that the mind is constitutive of the whole person, we may call education the rise of the mind to intelligible reality, the seeing of an eternal sense in things. Or, for those more Eastern, it is the perfect wisdom, the unitive cognition by which all things go into Brahman or śūnyatā. This discovery, with the discoverer's own incorporation into it, lifts us past secular pluralisms into the sacred unity. These gestalts by which we get things together, and get together with them, never lie on the surfaces of things, nor can they be calculated by the conceptual yet nonperceptual mind, nor by the egotistic and nonmoral self.

To the protest that we need no God, Brahman, or śūnyatā, nor any supernal vision, to illuminate things, our doctors invite us to consider how unity is not found until believed in. Even in the empirical order, to say nothing of any level with deeper import, unity never lies baldly with the phenomena, but must be detected by the penetrant mind, with its laws, models, theories, paradigms, symbols, and faiths that see and perceive more than meets the senses. Phenomena, including religious phenomena, are never self-interpreting; they are "empty," "illusory," "mutable and perishing." Lacking "own-being," they must be sent into an integral, intelligible framework, one of seeing the invisible. "Know" what we may, we do not "understand" until we pass away into *tawḥīd*, unity. Otherwise, alas, an education has so far failed us, and we stay lost in the pluralities of phenomena, subjects midst too many objects, in a chaos not a cosmos. Those who never get, or who give up, religion or its surrogates typically find the world impenetrable and absurd, or they remain agnostic, literally "without understanding," make what sense they may of their local environments for their everyday courses. There is never any bare, empirical education.

The seeming ambiguity in the word "religious," by which it means alternately "perceiving a supernal realm transcending the phenomenal" and "having a life-orienting and soteriological world view," permits us to say that all education is religious in the second but not the first sense. But we do not equivocate, for these senses are allied in that no universal view of worth by which we are oriented lies simply with the phenomena, but exceeds this by a penetration inward, by trusting, by a presiding gestalt which oversees the seen. Education, literally a "drawing out," is a drawing out of persons so as to enable them to draw out from the phenomena the unity which is behind, within, and under all. If that is not done with God, Brahman, or *śūnyatā*, it will be, if at all, with some crypto-religious Tao, some cosmic way, perhaps with Mother Earth or Evolution, perhaps with Society, Nation, or History, perhaps with Science, Law, or Culture. By some unifying value, meaning and order are overlaid on or found despite the otherwise perishing fluxes. To find something less or more nonsublatable about the surroundings which we rise from and live through, to rejoice and be saved in this finding, is to have a religious understanding.

"In God being is not one thing and living another—as though he could be and not be living. Nor in God is it one thing to live and another to understand—as though he could live without understanding. Nor in him is it one thing to know and another to be blessed. For in God, to live, to know, and to be blessed is one and the same thing as to be." (CG 8-6) Something like this unity in Augustine's God must be also contained in that single Brahmanic essence, "being, consciousness, and bliss." For us who image God, to get things together in him is to find that being, living, understanding, and blessedness are one and the same. It is to reach the three Augustinian apodictic certainties that I am, I live, and I love to understand. Stones are, but do not live; animals live but do not understand; humans live and love to understand. Their understanding is one with their life and being. (Lb 2-7) Thus they are the more God-like as they are the more educated, the peculiar and wise genus of *Homo sapiens*. So any of us stray from education who do not go on religious inquiry.

We thus lament the university with no place for a participant "faith," and if this be the modern university, so much the worse for it. The faithless cannot succeed in their education. Very often those disciplines to which the university "educated" reduce religion— whether psychology, history, philosophy, sociology, or ethics—are by the same stroke elevated into religion, with much trusting in them. The university should be a place of multiple faiths, if it is an ecumenical university. Or it may elect to catechize in some specific faith, while giving fair witness to all, if it is centered in some one faith. It can even be secular, if it admits its life-orienting secularity to be a variant faith, and if it grants that no strict secularity by itself, without an evaluative overlay and interpretation, is educational in our unifying sense.

The university cannot demand of its scholars an education without faith; it ought rather to ask that its scholars specify those owned faiths by which they understand. The disorder which affects much contemporary education is as old as Augustine's quarrel with the "academics" who thought to understand without faith, or Ghazali's quarrel with the philosophers who thought that the nonreligious intellect could find the meaningful coherences in the world. It is as old as Sankara's insistence that logic is always an auxiliary of intuitive insight, or Nagarjuna's conviction that relative theses, propositionalized conceptions, do not of themselves yield perfect wisdom.

No university which intends to foster ultimate truth ought by institutional control to prevent the empirical, ecumenical, catechetical, and confessional freedoms of inquiry which we have recognized in this chapter. But a secular university will as soon, if not sooner, be tempted to do this as will a Catholic one. A "university" is where one is free to "find a universe," with its centered turning. That finding is always by inquiry integrated with some religious view, some vision. The mark of a university is whether it could have welcomed teachers such as Augustine, Nagarjuna, Sankara, and Ghazali for their educational provocation, even if that encounter led to counterstandings and variant advocacies, a welcoming which the secular university would find as difficult as would any religious one.

Here is Augustine in dialogue with a pupil about education. "Augustine: 'Do you think that understanding can only be good?' Euodius: 'Yes, so good that I cannot see how any human possession could be more excellent, and I could not possibly say that it is ever bad to understand anything.' Augustine: 'Then if all understanding is good and there is no learning without it, everyone who learns is doing good. So do not look to find an evil teacher of any kind. For if he is evil, he is not a teacher; if a teacher, he is not evil.'" (Lb 1-3a) That is, in a way, only a semantic point, by which "good" has been built into the meaning of "understanding" and "doing good" of "teacher." Like Augustine's remark that an unjust law is no law at all, the intended truth is analytic.

But that is, in a way, very much more, it is an insight into the genius of understanding and the moral character of those whose profession is education. The dismissal of the unjust law as no law at all rests, more deeply, on the detection of a permanent rightness in things. Likewise, understanding as nonnegotiably good rises from the faith that things are intelligible and that the finding of this intelligibility frees and blesses us by leading to the divine. Under that perception, if any indeed teach they do good, and if they successfully teach religion, and not merely about it, if they unite us with what ultimately is, they do the supreme good.

Bibliography

The principal sources are cataloged, with abbreviations noted at the left. Selected secondary references are included but no comprehensive bibliography is attempted. Where these diverse sources have been editorially modified for conformity and English fluency (by respelling, repunctuation, parenthetical adjustment, etc.), quotations are concluded with an "m". In a few cases there are abridgments, marked with an "a".

Augustine

The Augustinian library is readily accessible in the Latin in Jacques Paul Migne, ed., *Patrologia Latina* (Paris, 1844-66), the sixteen volumes 32-47. Quotations are translations by the author from the Latin, though we have made ample use of the standard translations. The principal English editions are:

A Select Library of the Nicene and Post-Nicene Fathers of the Christian Church, First Series, ed. Philip Schaff, 8 volumes. New York: Scribner's, 1886-1889.

Fathers of the Church: A New Translation, ed. Ludwig Schopp et al., 20 volumes, *Writings of St. Augustine*. New York: C.I.M.A. Publishing Company and Fathers of the Church, Inc., 1948ff.

The Library of Christian Classics, ed. John Baillie, John T. McNeill and Henry P. Van Dusen, volumes 6-8. Philadelphia: The Westminster Press, 1953.

Basic Writings of St. Augustine, ed. Whitney J. Oates, 2 volumes. New York: Random House, 1948.

Augustine's major works follow, as they appear in the *Latin Patrology*. We cite by book (if there is more than one), chapter, and section, though in many shorter works chapter references are superfluous, as the sections are consecutive, and in such cases *we omit the chapter reference.*

Rt	*The Retractions (Retractationum)*
Co	*The Confessions (Confessionum)*
Sl	*The Soliloquies (Soliloquiorum)*
Ac	*Answer to Skeptics (Contra Academicos)*
BV	*The Happy Life (De beata vita)*
Or	*Divine Order (De ordine)*
Im	*The Immortality of the Soul (De immortalitate animae)*
Qu	*The Greatness of the Soul (De quantitate animae)*
Mg	*The Teacher (De magistro)*
Lb	*Free Will (De libero arbitrio)*
CM	*The Catholic and Manichean Ways of Life (De moribus Ecclesiae Catholicae et de moribus Manichaeorum)*
Ep	*Letters (Epistolae)*
CD	*Christian Education (De doctrina christiana)*
VR	*True Religion (De vera religione)*
LG	*Literal Commentary on Genesis (De Genesi ad litteram)*
HG	*Harmony of the Gospels (De concensu Evangelistarum)*
GJ	*Lectures on the Gospel of John (In Joannis Evangelium tractatus)*

LJ	*Lectures on the Letters of John (In Epistolam Joannis tractatus)*
NP	*Narrations on the Psalms (Enarrationes in psalmos)*
Sm	*Sermons (Sermones)*
DQ	*Various Questions (De diversis quaestionibus)*
QS	*Various Questions to Simplician (De diversis quaestionibus ad Simplicianum)*
FR	*Faith in Things which Are Unseen (De fide rerum quae non videntur)*
FC	*Faith and the Creed (De fide et symbolo)*
En	*Enchiridion (Enchiridion)*
CI	*Catechizing the Uninstructed (De catechizandis rudibus)*
AC	*The Christian Struggle (De agone Christiano)*
CG	*The City of God (De civitate Dei)*
Cr	*The Usefulness of Believing (De utilitate credendi)*
Tr	*The Trinity (De Trinitate)*
SL	*The Spirit and the Letter (De spiritu et littera)*
NG	*Nature and Grace (De natura et gratia)*
PJ	*The Perfectly Righteous Man (De perfectione iustitiae hominis)*
Pg	*The Proceedings of Pelagius (De gestis Pelagii)*
GC	*The Grace of Christ and Original Sin (De gratia Christi et de peccato originali)*
GL	*Grace and Free Will (De gratia et libero arbitrio)*
PS	*The Predestination of Saints (De praedestinatione sanctorum)*

Bible citations are ordinarily from the Revised Standard Version with standard abbreviations; in a few cases Augustine's translations or my own translations from the Greek are used.

Vernon J. Bourke, *Augustine's View of Reality*. Villanova, Pa.: Villanova Press, 1964.

Mary T. Clark, *Augustine, Philosopher of Freedom*. New York: Desclée, 1958.

Bernard J. Cooke, "The Mutability-Immutability Principle in St. Augustine's Metaphysics." *Modern Schoolman* 23(1946):175-193; 24(1946):37-49.

Robert E. Cushman, "Faith and Reason." In R.W. Battenhouse, *A Companion to the Study of St. Augustine*, pp. 287-314. New York; Oxford University Press, 1955.

Robert C. Gassert, "The Meaning of *Cogitatio* in St. Augustine." *Modern Schoolman* 25(1948):238-245.

Étienne Gilson, *The Christian Philosophy of Saint Augustine*. New York: Random House, 1960. Contains an excellent bibliography.

George Howie, *Educational Theory and Practice in St. Augustine*. London: Routledge and Kegan Paul. 1969.

Jacques Maritain, "Concerning Augustinian Wisdom." In *The Degrees of Knowledge*, pp. 358-381. New York: Scribner's 1938.

Henri I. Marrou, *Saint Augustine and his Influence through the Ages*. New York: Harper's, 1957.

Ronald H. Nash, *The Light of the Mind: St. Augustine's Theory of Knowledge*. Lexington: University Press of Kentucky, 1969.

Anton C. Pegis, "The Mind of St. Augustine." *Mediaeval Studies* 6(1944):1-61.

Peter J. Riga, "The Act of Faith in Augustine and Aquinas." *Thomist* 35(1971):143-174.

Eugene TeSelle, *Augustine the Theologian*. New York: Herder. 1970.

Ghazali

Here and below, diacritical marks are those used in the titles cited.

Ih   *The Revivification of the Sciences of Religion (Iḥyā' 'Ulūm al-Dīn)*. In Arabic, this work appears in several modern editions, including that published by the Uth-māniyyah Press at Cairo, 1933, in 4 volumes, but there is no definitive Arabic edition. There is no comprehensive English or other European translation of the four quarters in forty books, only translations of selected books. We cite by quarter, book, and page number in the English or other translation or synopsis. There is in Arabic a ten volume commentary by Sayyid Murtadha, the introduction to which contains much of the sources of the life of Ghazali.

I, 1   *The Book of Knowledge*, trans. Nabih Amin Faris. Lahore: Muhammad Ashraf, 1962.

I, 2   *The Foundations of the Articles of Faith*, trans. Nabih Amin Faris. Lahore: Muhammad Ashraf, 1963. Section 3 of this book is known as "The Jerusalem Tract," and has also been translated by A.L. Tibawi, "Al-Ghazāli's Tract on Dogmatic Theology," *The Islamic Quarterly* 9(1965):65-122.

I, 3   *The Mysteries of Purity*, trans. Nabih Amin Faris. Lahore: Muhammad Ashraf, 1966.

I, 4   *Worship in Islam (The Book on Worship)*, trans. Edwin Elliott Calverley. London: Luzac, 1925, 1957. This book is condensed in Edwin E. Calverley, "Vitalizing of the Religious Sciences," *The Muslim World* 14(1924):10-22.

I, 5   *The Mysteries of Almsgiving*, trans. Nabih Amin Faris. Beirut: The American University of Beirut, 1966.

I, 6   *The Mysteries of Fasting*, trans. Nabih Amin Faris. Lahore: Muhammad Ashraf, 1968.

I, 9   *Ghazali on Prayer* (*The Book on Prayer*), trans. Kojiro Nakamura. Tokyo: The University of Tokyo, 1973.

II, 8   *Emotional Religion in Islām as affected by Music and Singing* (*The Book on Music and Ecstasy*), trans. Duncan B. Macdonald. In *Journal of the Royal Asiatic Society*, 1901, pages 195-252, 705-748, and 1902, pages 1-28.

II, 10   *Book XX of Al-Ghazālī's Ihyā' 'Ulūm al-Dīn* (*The Book on Prophetship*), trans. L. Zolondek. Leiden: E.J. Brill, 1963.

III, 1   *Die Wunder des Herzens* (*Book of the Marvels of the Heart*), trans. into German by Karl Eckmann (Mainz, 1960). This book is also extensively outlined and cited in Duncan Black Macdonald, *The Religious Attitude and Life in Islam*. Chicago: University of Chicago Press, 1909.

IV, 3   *Al-Ghazali's Book of Fear and Hope*, trans. William McKane. Leiden: E.J. Brill, 1962.

IV, 5   *Al-Ġazzālī's Buch Vom Gottvertrauen* (*The Book on the Unity of God and Trusting in God*), trans. into German by Hans Wehr. Halle: Max Niemeyer, 1940.

IV, 6   *The Book on Love and Longing for God*. This is synopsized in an article by Duncan Black Macdonald, "Blessedness (Muhammadan)" in James Hastings, ed., *Encyclopedia of Religion and Ethics*, 5:677-680. New York: Scribner's, 1955.

IV, 7   *Über Intention, Reine Absicht und Wahrhaftigkeit*

(*The Book on Resolve, Truthfulness, and Sincerity*), trans. into German by Hans Bauer. Halle: Max Niemeyer, 1916.

Several other books (II, 1: on good usage in eating; II, 2: on marriage; II, 4: on lawful and unlawful things; II, 9: on good counseling) are available in French or German but incidental to this study.

B   *Ih'ya 'Ouloûm ed-Dîn ou Vivification des Sciences de la Foi*, edited by G.H. Bousquet (Paris: Max Besson, 1955), is a useful and extensive French synopsis of all of the *Ihyâ'*, book by book, which we cite with a B preceding the page number.

D1   *The Deliverance from Error (al-Munqidh min aḍ-Ḍalāl)*, trans. W. Montgomery Watt, in *The Faith and Practice of Al-Ghazālī*. London: Allen and Unwin, 1953, 1970. The "Confessions" of Ghazali. Cited by page.

BG   *The Beginning of Guidance (Bidāyat al-Hidāyah)*, trans. Watt, *ibid.* Cited by page.

NN   *The Ninety-Nine Names of God in Islam (Al-Maqṣad al-Asnā)*, trans. Robert Charles Stade. Ibadan, Nigeria: Daystar Press, 1970. Cited by page.

Ay   *Al-Ghazali's Ayyuha'l-Walad (O Disciple)*, trans. George Henry Scherer. Beirut: American Press, 1933. Cited by page. Reprinted, slightly revised, as *O Disciple*. Beirut: Catholic Press, 1951.

A1   *The Alchemy of Happiness (Kimiya'e Saadat)*, trans. Claud Field. London: John Murray, 1910. A Persian abridgment of the *Ihyā'*. Cited by page.

DP   *Al-Ghazali on Divine Predicates (Al-Iqtiṣād Fil-i'tiqād)*,

trans. 'Abdu-r-Raḥmān Abū Zayd. Lahore: Muhammad
Ashraf, 1970. Cited by page.

In   *Al-Ghazali's Tahāfut al-Falāsifah (The Incoherence of
the Philosophers)*, trans. Sabih Ahmad Kamali.
Lahore: Pakistan Philosophical Congress, 1958. Cited by page.

Ri   *Al-Risālat Al-Laduniyya (On Knowledge Gained Immediately from Allah)*, trans. Margaret Smith. In *Journal of the Royal Asiatic Society*, 1938, pages 177-200,
353-374. Cited by page.

Ni   *Al-Ghazzālī's Mishkāt al-Anwār (The Niche for Lights)*,
trans. W.H.T. Gairdner. London: Royal Asiatic Society,
1924. Cited by page.

RD   *Réfutation excellente de la divinité de Jésus-Christ
d'après les Évangiles (Courteous Refutation of the Divinity of Jesus Christ According to the Gospels) (Ar-
Radd ul-Jamīl li Ilāhiyat 'Īsā bi ṣarīḥ il-Injīl)*, trans. to
French by R. Chidiac. Paris: Leroux, 1939. See also
Franz-Elmar Wilms, *Al-Ghazālīs Schrift Wider die Gott-
heit Jesus*. Leiden: E.J. Brill, 1966.

S   *The Qur'an*, cited by sura and verse. Unless otherwise
indicated, the citation is from Ghazali, *ad loc. cit.* Citations from *The Koran Interpreted* by A.J. Arberry
a   (New York: Macmillan, 1955) are concluded by an "a".
Those from *The Meaning of the Glorious Koran* by
Mohammed Marmaduke Pickthall (New York: Mentor,
p   1953) are concluded by a "p".

Mohammed Arkoun, "Révélation, vérité et histoire d'après l'oeu-
vre de Gazâlî." *Studia Islamica* 31(1970):53-69.

Frederick J. Barny, "The Moslem Idea of 'Ilm (Knowledge), Illustrated by Al-Ghazali's Experience." *The Muslim World* 9(1919): 159-168.

Simon van den Bergh, "Ghazali on 'Gratitude Towards God' and its Greek Sources." *Studia Islamica* 7(1957) 77-98.

Simon van den Bergh, "The 'Love of God' in Ghazali's *Vivification of Theology.*" *Journal of Semitic Studies* 1(1965):305-321.

N.A. Faris, "Al-Ghazzali's Epistle of the Birds: A Translation of the Risālat al-Ṭayr. *The Muslim World* 34(1944):46-53.

Heinrich Frick, *Ghazālī's Selbstbiographie: ein Vergleich mit Augustins Konfessionem.* Leipzig: J.C. Hinrichs, 1919.

W.H.T. Gairdner, "Al-Ghazālī's Mishkāt al-Anwār and the Ghazālī-Problem." *Der Islam* 5(1914):121-153.

W.R.W. Gardner, *Al-Ghazali.* Madras: Christian Literature Society for India, 1919.

W.R.W. Gardner, "Al-Ghazali as Sufi." *The Muslim World* 7(1917): 131-143.

Farid Jabre, *La Notion de Certitude selon Ghazali.* Paris: Librairie Philosophique J. Vrin, 1958.

Farid Jabre, *La Notion de la Ma'rifa chez Ghazali.* Beirut: Lettres Orientales, 1958.

Duncan Black Macdonald, *The Development of Muslim Theology, Jurisprudence, and Constitutional Theory.* New York: Russell & Russell, 1903, 1965. One chapter (pp. 215-242) is devoted to Ghazali.

Duncan Black Macdonald, "The Life of al-Ghazzālī." *Journal of the American Oriental Society* 20(1899):71-132.

Michael E. Marmura, "Ghazali and Demonstrative Science." *Journal of the History of Philosophy* 3(1965):183-204.

Sami M. Najm, "The Place and Function of Doubt in the Philosophies of Descartes and Al-Ghazālī." *Philosophy East and West* 16(1966):133-141.

Ali Issa Othman, *The Concept of Man in Islam, in the Writings of Al-Ghazali*. Cairo: Dar al-Maaref, 1960.

M.A. Quraishi, "Al-Ghazzali's Philosophy of Education." *Journal of the Maharaja Sayajirao University of Baroda* (India) 13(1964): 63-69.

Arvind Sharma, "The Spiritual Biography of Al-Ghazālī." *Studies in Islam* 9(1972):65-85.

Fadlou Shehadi, *Ghazali's Unique Unknowable God*. Leiden: E.J. Brill, 1964.

Mohammed Ahmed Sherif, *Ghazali's Theory of Virtue*. Albany: State University of New York Press, 1975.

Margaret Smith, "Al-Ghazālī on the Practice of the Presence of God." *The Muslim World* 23(1933)16-23.

Margaret Smith, *Al-Ghazālī the Mystic*. London: Luzac & Co., 1944.

Claudia Reed Upper, "Al-Ghazālī's Thought concerning the Nature of Man and Union with God." *Muslim World* 42(1952):23-32.

W. Montgomery Watt, *Muslim Intellectual: A Study of Al-Ghazali*. Edinburgh: University Press, 1963.

W. Montgomery Watt, "The Study of Al-Ġazālī." *Oriens: Journal of the International Society for Oriental Research* 13/14(1960-61):121-131.

A.J. Wensick, *La Pensée de Ghazzālī*. Paris: Adrien-Maisonneuve, 1940.

S.M. Zwemer, "Jesus Christ in the Ihya of Al-Ghazali." *The Muslim World* 7(1917):144-158.

Samuel M. Zwemer, *A Moslem Seeker after God*. London: F.H. Revell, 1920.

Nagarjuna

Ka   *Mūla-madhyamaka-kārikās*, trans. from Sanskrit as *Fundamentals of the Middle Way* by Frederick J. Streng in *Emptiness* (see below), pp. 183-220. We refer to this as the *Kārikās* and cite by chapter and verse.

i   Another translation, noted by an *i* when used, is Kenneth K. Inada, *Nāgārjuna: A Translation of his Mūla-madhyamakakārikā*. Tokyo: The Hokuseido Press, 1970.

     Stcherbatsky (see below) translates chapters 1 and 25,
s   noted by an *s*, together with an early commentary by
Ca   Candrakirti, cited by page from Stcherbatsky.

MP   *The Large Sutra on Perfect Wisdom (Mahā-Prajñā-Para-mitā-Sūtra)*, trans. from Sanskrit by Edward Conze. Berkeley: University of California Press, 1975. Set as a discourse on Vulture Peak between Buddha and his disciples, notably Sariputra and Subhuti, we refer to this as the *Sūtra*, or *Great Sūtra*, and in this recension cite by page in Conze. The *Sūtra* exists in Sanskrit and other languages in four main recensions, named as versions in 8,000, 18,000, 25,000, and 100,000 lines, respectively the *Aṣṭasāhasrikā*, *Aṣṭādaśasāhasrikā*, *Pañcaviṃśatisāhasrikā*, and *Satasāhasrikā*. This edition is largely the version in 25,000 lines, the one on which Nagarjuna comments. Especially in the longer versions, the *Sūtra* is quite repetitive, to say nothing of Nagarjuna's even longer commentary.

AP   *The Perfection of Wisdom in Eight Thousand Lines and Its Verse Summary (Astasāhasrikā Prajñāpāramitā)*, trans. from Sanskrit by Edward Conze. Bolinas, CA: Four Seasons Foundation, 1973. The earliest recension of the *Sūtra* is often for our purposes conveniently compact. We cite by page in Conze.

MPC   *Commentary on the Large Sutra on Perfect Wisdom. (Mahā-Prajñā-Pāramitā-Śāstra)*. Ascribed to Nagarjuna, this work is found completely in a modern edition only in the Chinese as volume 25 of the *Taishô Issaikyô*, ed. J. Takakusu and K. Watanabe (Tokyo, 1924-1929), pages 57a-756c, in 3-columned pages, 100 chapters. We refer to this as the *Śāstra*, and cite it only from one of the editions below.

MPC1   *Le Traité de la Grande Vertu de Sagesse de Nāgārjuna*, trans. Étienne Lamotte. Louvain: Institut Orientaliste, 1949, 1967, 1970, 1976. Four volumes with successive pagination. This translates some one-half of the *Śāstra* (48 chapters), *Taishô* pages 57a-296b, and is comment mainly upon the opening pages of the *Sūtra*, where lists of the characteristics and skills of the *bodhisattvas* gathered to hear Buddha provide Nagarjuna with an opportunity to say much in elaborate prolegomena. Quotations from this work are my own translations from the French, and reference is to page in Lamotte's translation.

MPCv   Krishniah Venkata Ramanan, *Nāgārjuna's Philosophy as Presented in the Mahā-Prajñāpāramitā-Śāstra*. Rutland, Vermont: Charles E. Tuttle, Co., 1966; reprinted Delhi, India: Motilal Banarsidass, 1975, 1978. This work

VR	is intended largely as a synopsis of the *Sāstra* and is replete with extracts. We use it for citations from the remainder of the *Sāstra* (*Taishô* pages 296c-756c), and cite by page in Venkata Ramanan. The *Taishô* reference may be had from either of the above editions. We cite Venkata Ramanan's own text as VR.
MPCc	Conze, in the *Large Sūtra* above, sometimes includes Nagarjuna's commentary, and we have used this for occasional citation, by page number in Conze.
SP	*Selected Sayings from the Perfection of Wisdom*, trans. Edward Conze. London: The Buddhist Society, 1955. The sayings are drawn from various *Prajñā-Pāramitā* works, especially from the several versions of the *Great Sūtra*. We cite by page in Conze, from which original sources may be had. A few citations are from Conze's introduction.
VV	*Vigraha-vyavartanī: Averting the Arguments*, trans. from Sanskrit by Streng in *Emptiness* (see below), pages 221-227, cited by verse.
Rv	*The Ratnāvalī of Nāgārjuna*, trans. from Sanskrit by Giuseppe Tucci. In *Journal of the Royal Asiatic Society*, 1934, pages 307-325, 1936, pages 237-252, 423-435. An address to a king, which we cite by chapter and verse. See also Nagarjuna and the Seventh Dalai Lama, *The Precious Garland and The Song of the Four Mindfulnesses*, trans. Jeffrey Hopkins and Lati Rimpoche. London: George Allen and Unwin, 1975.
CS	"Two Hymns of the *Catuḥ-stava* of Nāgārjuna," trans. from Sanskrit by Giuseppe Tucci. In *Journal of the Royal Asiatic Society*, 1932, pages 309-325. Two devotional hymns from an earlier set of four, cited by hymn and verse.

Ek   *The Ekashloka Shastra* (*Commentary on the One Verse*), ascribed to Nagarjuna, trans. from Chinese by Joseph Edkins, in Chinese *Buddhism: A Volume of Sketches*, pp. 302-317. London: Trübner and Co., 1880.

SL   *Suh-ki-li-lih-kiu.* The *Suhṛil-lekha or "Friendly Letter,"* ascribed to Nagarjuna, trans. from Chinese by Samuel Beal. London: Luzac, 1892. Another work addressed to a king, which we cite by stanza. Another translation, with a nineteenth century commentary by Lama Mipham, appears as *Golden Zephyr*, trans. Leslie Kawamura. Emeryville, Calif.: Dharma Publishing, 1975.

PD   *She-rab Dong-bu* or *Prajnya Danda* (*The Tree of Wisdom*), ascribed to Nagarjuna, trans. from Tibetan by W.L. Campbell. Calcutta: Baptist Mission Press and Calcutta University, 1919. We cite by stanza. The last three works are of uncertain origin, and we make minor use of them. "Nāgārjuna's *Mahāyāna-viṁśaka*," trans. from Tibetan and Chinese by Susumu Yamaguchi, *Eastern Buddhist* 4(1926-1928): 56-60, 169-176, is not used here and not thought authentic.

Edward Conze, Buddhist Thought in India, pp. 195-249. London: George Allen and Unwin, 1962.

Edward Conze, "The Ontology of the Prajñāpāramitā." *Philosophy East and West* 3(1953):117-129.

Edward Conze, *The Prajñāpāramita Literature*. The Hague: Mouton, 1960.

Vicente Fatone, *The Philosophy of Nāgārjuna*. Delhi: Motilal Banarsidass, 1981. A translation of *El Budismo Nihilista*, University of Buenos Aires, 1962.

Winston L. King, "Śūnyatā as a Master-Symbol." *Numen* 17(1970): 95-104.

Shōsen Miyamoto, *Study of Nāgārjuna*. Unpublished dissertation at Oxford University, 1928.

T.R.V. Murti, *The Central Philosophy of Buddhism*. London: George Allen and Unwin, 1955, 1970. A study of the Madhyamika system.

Harsh Narain, "Śūnyavāda: A Reinterpretation." *Philosophy East and West* 13(1964):311-338.

R.C. Pandeya, "The Mādhyamika Philosophy: A New Approach." *Philosophy East and West* 14(1964):3-24.

Raymond Panikkar, "The 'Crisis' of Mādhyamika and Indian Philosophy Today." *Philosophy East and West* 16(1966):117-131.

Richard H. Robinson, "Did Nagarjuna Really Refute All Philosophical Views?" *Philosophy East and West* 22(1972):325-331.

Richard H. Robinson, *Early Mādhyamika in India and China*. Madison: University of Wisconsin Press, 1967.

Bratindra Kumar Sengupta, "A Study of Nāgārjuna." *Indian Historical Quarterly* 31(1955):257-262.

Th. Stcherbatsky, *The Conception of Buddhist Nirvāṇa*. The Hague: Mouton, 1965. Includes chapters 1 and 25 of the *Kārikās*, and Candrakirti's commentary (see above).

Frederick J. Streng, *Emptiness: A Study in Religious Meaning*. Nashville: Abingdon Press, 1967. A depth study of Nagarjuna, with a long bibliography.

M. Walleser, "The Life of Nāgārjuna from Tibetan and Chinese

Sources," in Bruno Schindler, ed., *Hirth Anniversary Volume*, pp. 421-455. London: Probsthain and Co., 1923.

Sankara

VS   *The Vedānta Sūtras of Bādarāyana, with the Commentary by Śankara*, trans. from Sanskrit by George Thibaut, 2 vols. New York: Dover Publications, 1962. Originally published in 1890 and 1896 in the series *The Sacred Books of the East*. Sankara's systematic commentary on the aphorisms of Badarayana, cited by part, chapter, and section. Another translation is *Brahma-Sūtra-Shānkara-Bhāshya*, trans. V.M. Apte. Bombay: G.R. Bhatkal, 1960.

Eight Upaniṣads, with the Commentary of Śankarācārya, trans. from Sanskrit by Swāmī Gambhīrānanda, 2 vols. Calcutta: Advaita Ashrama, 1958, 1972. Commentaries on the following *Upanishads*, cited by part (if appropriate), chapter, and verse.

IsU   *Īśā Upaniṣad*

KeU   *Kena Upaniṣad*

KaU   *Katha Upaniṣad*

TaU   *Taittirīya Upaniṣad*

AiU   *Aitareya Upaniṣad*

MuU   *Muṇḍaka Upaniṣad*

MaU   *Māṇḍūkya Upaniṣad*

GaK   *Gauḍapāda's Kārikā on the Māṇḍūkya Upaniṣad*

PrU   *Praśna Upaniṣad*

ChU *The Chhándogya Upanishad with extracts from the Commentary of Śankara Ácharya*, trans. from Sanskrit by Rájendralála Mitra. Calcutta: Baptist Mission Press, 1862. Cited by chapter, section, and verse.

BrU *The Bṛhadāraṇyaka Upaniṣad, with the Commentary of Śaṅkarācārya*, trans. from Sanskrit by Swāmī Mādhavānanda. Calcutta: Advaita Ashrama, 1934, 1965. A long commmentary on a major *Upanishad* cited by part, chapter, and verse.

BhG *The Bhagavad-Gîtâ, with the Commentary of Śrî Sankarachâryâ*, trans. from Sanskrit by A. Mahâdeva Śâstri. Madras: V.R. Sastrulu & Sons, 1897, 1972.

    Upanishad and *Gita* quotations are from the above editions, with the abbreviations then italicized. Other translations used are: *The Upanishads*, trans. Swami Prabhavananda and Frederick Manchester (New York: Mentor, 1957), and *The Song of God: Bhagavad-Gita*, trans. Swami Prabhavananda and Christopher Isherwood (New York: Mentor, 1951), cited using the above

p abbreviations italicized and with a terminal "p", and *The Upanishads*, trans. Swami Nikhilananda, 4 vols.

n (London: Phoenix House, 1951-9), using a terminal "n".

Hy *The Hymns of Śaṅkara*, trans. T.M.P. Mahadevan. Madras, India: Ganesh & Co., 1970. Cited by page.

VC *Shankara's Crest Jewel of Discrimination (Viveka Chudamani)*, trans. Swami Prabhavananda and Christopher Isherwood. New York: Mentor, 1970. Cited by page.

    Prapancasāra Tantra of Śaṅkarācārya, edited by Arthur Avalon and Aṭalānanda Sarasvatī. *Delhi: Motilal Banarsidass, 1981. Reprint of a 1935 edition of a text ascribed to Sankara in Sanskrit with English summary.*

A.R. Bhattacharya, "Brahman of Śankara and Śūnyatā of Mādhyamikas." *Indian Historical Quarterly* 32(1956):270-285.

Paul Deussen, *The System of the Vedanta*, trans. Charles Johnston. New York: Dover, 1973. First published in German in 1883.

N.K. Devaraja, *An Introduction to Śankara's Theory of Knowledge*, rev. ed. Delhi: Motilal Banarsi Dass, 1962.

V.S. Ghate, "Śankarāchārya" in James Hastings, ed., *Encyclopedia of Religion and Ethics*, 11:185-189. New York: Scribner's, 1955.

Paul Hacker, "Śankara's Conception of Man." *Studia Missionalia* 19(1970):123-131.

Paul Hacker, "Śraddha" (Faith), *Wiener Zeitschrift für die Kunde Süd-und Ostasiens* 7(1963):151-189.

Daniel H.H. Ingalls, "Śamkara on the Question: Whose is Avidyā?" *Philosophy East and West* 3(1953):69-72.

Daniel H.H. Ingalls, "Śamkara's Arguments Against the Buddhists." *Philosophy East and West* 3(1953):291-306.

C.N. Krishnas (w)ami Aiyar and Sitanath Tattvabhusan, *Sri Sankaracharya: I. His Life and Times.II His Philosophy*. Madras: G.A. Natesan, 1903, 192?

T.M.P. Mahadevan, "The Metaphysics of Śamkara." *Philosophy East and West* 3(1953):359-363.

K. Satchidananda Murty, *Revelation and Reason in Advaita Vedanta*. New York: Columbia University Press, 1959.

L. Thomas O'Neil, *Māyā in Śankara: Measuring the Immeasurable*. Delhi: Motilal Banarsidass, 1980. An effort to give a positive account of *māyā*.

Sarvepalli Radhakrishnan, *Indian Philosophy*, 2 vols. New York: Macmillan, 1958.

P.T. Raju, "Intuition as a Philosophical Method in India," *Philosophy East and West* 2(1952):187-207.

S.N.L. Shrivastava, "Śaṁkara on God, Religion, and Morality." *Philosophy East and West* 7(1957-8):91-106.

R.P. Singh, *The Vedānta of Śaṅkara, a Metaphysics of Value.* Jaipur: Bharat Publishing House, 1949.

Walter T. Stace, "Oriental Conceptions of Detachment and Enlightenment." *Philosophy East and West* 2(1952) :20-30.

M.K. Venkatarama Iyer, *Advaita Vedanta According to Samkara.* New York: Asia Publishing House, 1964.

Index

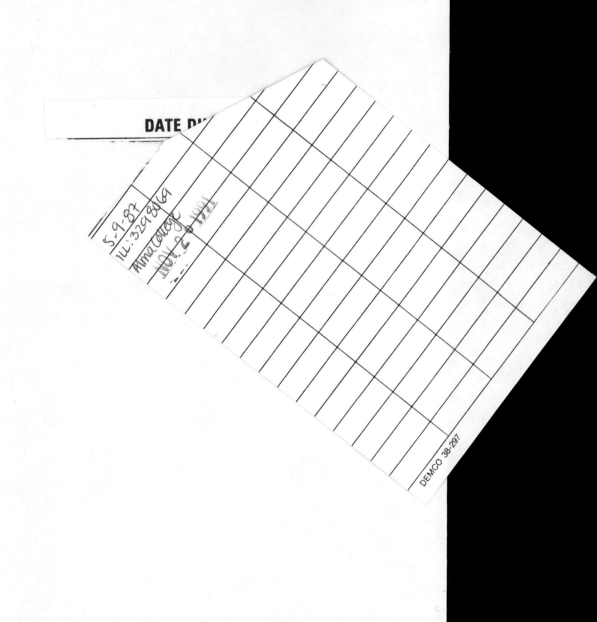